blue planet V2

Original Creation

Jeffrey Barber

Line Developer

Greg Benage

Writing

Jeffrey Barber
Greg Benage
Gareth Hanrahan
Gobion Rowlands
William Timmins

Cover Artwork

Scott Schomburg

Interior Artwork

Mitch Cotie
Ben Prenevost
Scott Schomburg
Kieran Yanner

Graphic Design

Brian Schomburg

Editing

Greg Benage

Layout

Greg Benage

Publisher

Christian T. Petersen

Printing

Quebecor Printing, Inc.
Printed in Canada.

FANTASY FLIGHT GAMES
2021 W. County Rd. C
Roseville, MN 55113
651.639.1905
www.rpg.net/ffg

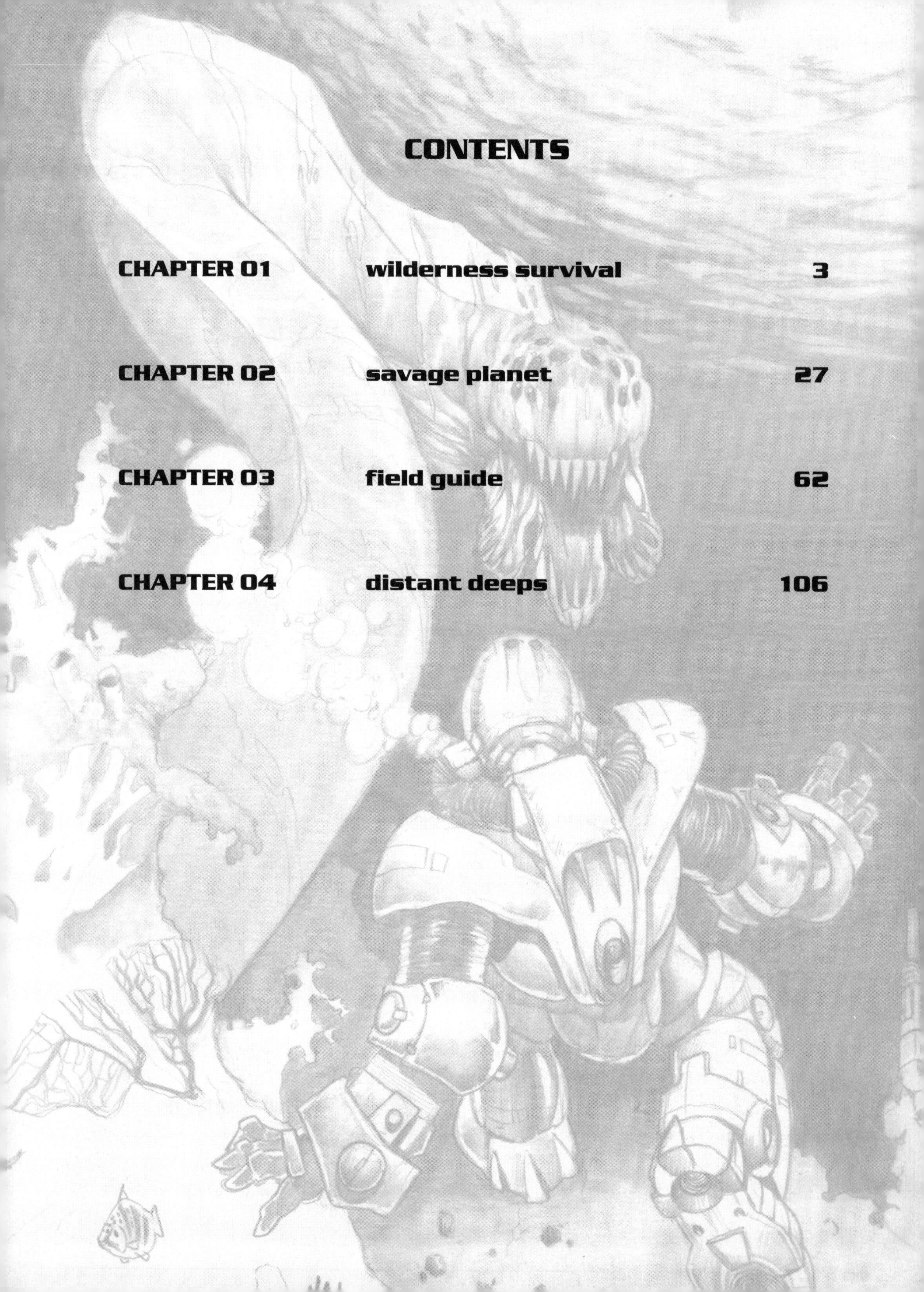

CONTENTS

WILDERNESS SURVIVAL

CHAPTER

01

SURVIVAL GUIDE

PREPARATION

Staying alive in a hostile environment requires some degree of mental, physical, and material preparation. Fitness, the right attitude, and proper equipment are essential for survival.

Physical conditioning is sometimes all that separates a survivor from a victim. A person who spends his days in a stationary environment will not likely fare as well lost in an unfriendly jungle as an athlete who trains regularly. Agility and endurance are needed to thrive beyond the borders of civilization.

Survival training is available in many areas and is advised for anyone planning to venture far from settled areas. Instruction ranges from informal one-on-one sessions with a native elder to formal workshops taught by professional survival experts and frontiersmen. The best teachers are, of course, those who have fully experienced Poseidon's outback firsthand, and the local natives are an excellent resource for information regarding what to expect and how to best plan for it.

Mental preparation is important, too. One should stay aware of what is happening around him at all times. This reduces the chances of getting lost, being caught in inclement weather, or taken by surprise. It is very easy to become discouraged, frightened, or confused when things seem to be going wrong, and a positive attitude is sometimes all that keeps one focused. Trust in one's abilities should be balanced with realistic expectations, however.

Knowing what items are essential—and how to use them—can make a normally deadly situation survivable. Proper outfitting requires consideration of the environment and needs of the individual. Know what to expect from the area in terms of wildlife, food and water availability, weather conditions, and terrain to plan what gear is needed.

Choosing items to include in a kit involves weight considerations, as the heavier a pack is, the more energy it requires to carry. By selecting multipurpose gear, such as a rain poncho that doubles as an emergency shelter, the weight and bulk of the kit is reduced. Water repellence, portability, durability, functionality, and comfort are key features of any

item in a good survival kit. Every item should be practical and necessary. A pillow is a nice comfort, but a waterproof jacket will work and can serve as a small tarp or even a sail, in a pinch.

Most survival kits come with the essentials: a water purifier, desalination tablets, fire paste (PG 138), basic tools, a knife, survival plastic (PG 140), a locator beacon, and a standard medkit (PG 133). Other items worth consideration—depending on weight, availability, price, and capacity restrictions—include spare power cells, extra medical supplies, a map box (PG 138), survival grenades, a survival guide, pest spikes (FM 38), rescue dye, a tube or two of chew goo, and emergency bottles. Many frontiersmen subscribe to the somewhat-reliable GEO Poseidon Biological Survey to help identify fauna and flora encountered during their travels.

Before traveling to any area, one should check the weather and conditions. Storms are seasonal and only the foolhardy do not anticipate them. Other factors to identify and allow for are wildlife threats, terrain, and food and water availability. Pack accordingly to insure comfort and safety.

IMPROVISED TOOLS

One of the things that sets a true survivor apart from others is his ability to improvise. Being able to create tools—and weapons—from available materials is a skill that requires creativity and common sense.

Lashing materials are extremely handy for toolmaking as well as other survival activities. If nothing in one's supplies can be used for tying, certain natural materials can be used. Animal tendons (sinews) are very strong and reliable if one has time to prepare them. They must be dried completely, and then crushed to aid in pulling the fibers apart. Soak the fibers until soft, then twist or braid them into a continuous strand. Use the strand while damp: The lashing will dry hard.

Lashing materials can also be made from rawhide. Remove the skin of the animal and scrape the meat and fat from it. Allow it to dry flat in the sun, then cut it into long strips. Soaking the strips for a few hours will make them flexible enough for weaving or tying. Rawhide also dries hard.

Some types of tree bark can be stripped and braided together if pressed for time or no appropriate game is available. Test the strength of the roping before relying on it; some barks dry too brittle to make good cording.

Clubs can be made from natural materials. A basic club is merely a length of wood short enough to handle—about a meter long—yet thick enough to pound on something without splitting. Straight-grained hardwoods are strongest. Soft woods tend to break easily and should be avoided if possible.

A weighted club may simply be a basic club with a knot at the business end or can be created by splitting the wood and lashing a rock between the splits. The rock should be shaped appropriately—round rocks are harder to fasten than flat ones; very flat rocks don't make good pounding tools. Choose the stone according to the purpose of the tool.

Once a suitable stone has been found, find or make a forked branch by wrapping some lashing 15 to 20 cm from the end of the club and then splitting the wood down to the lashing. Wrapping the crotch securely will help prevent further splitting. Insert the rock between the forks, and lash above, across, and below the stone to hold it securely.

A sling makes a decent weapon when modern weapons are unavailable. A sling is another form of weighted club, with a 1.5 to 2.5-kilogram stone tied to a length of lashing eight to 10cm from the end of a club. Allowing the stone to swing free and using a shorter (35 to 45cm) club allows the user to maintain control while creating more damage than a basic club.

A knife can be fashioned from hardwood or bone. If using wood, choose a straight piece two to three centimeters in diameter and 30cm long. Shave about 15cm into a blade. Dry the wood to make it harder and then sharpen the blade using a rough rock.

Bone knives are made by shattering a large bone on a hard surface to create splinters from which a suitable knife can be fashioned. Choose a pointed splinter and lash a wooden handle to it. Sharpen the blade with rough stone.

FIREBUILDING

Fire is essential for cooking, heat, and even signaling for help. One should know how to build a fire when the fire paste runs out.

Choose a location protected from the wind and rain. Be sure that the smoke is not going to blow directly into the shelter. Clear flammable brush from a one-meter area to prevent spreading the fire.

Build a fire pit by digging a shallow impression in the ground or forming a circle of rocks. This will help keep embers and sparks from escaping. A fire-base can be used in snowy areas. Lay enough green logs side-by-side on the ground to form a foundation. Put another layer across the first one to complete the base. This will keep the melting snow from putting out the fire.

Fires require tinder, kindling, and fuel. Tinder consists of very small, dry, flammable materials that will ignite with just a spark. Material can be shredded or shaved to make tinder, from dead palm fronds to pocket lint to scraps of paper. Kindling is larger and is used to raise the temperature of the fire. Wax-soaked pinecone analogs, small scraps of wood, and dry twigs make good kindling. Once the kindling is burning well, add a fuel source such as a dry log or chunk of dried peat. As long as the fire has fuel and oxygen it will continue to burn.

Lay the fire. The cone shape is a popular method because it works with damp wood and requires little maintenance. The tinder and kindling is arranged in a cone shape with the larger logs tented up around them. This allows the fire to self-feed. As the fire burns, logs fall from the cone into the fire.

A cross-ditch lets air circulate below the fire to help keep it burning. Dig an X about 30cm x 30cm and eight centimeters deep. Put tinder in the center of the X and build a pyramid of kindling above it. Add fuel as needed.

The lean-to method is a good way to build a fire in a windy location. Drive a green stick into the ground at about 30°. Create a tent by standing kindling sticks against the green stick. Put the tinder inside and light it. Add fuel as needed.

If matches or a lighter are not available, the fire can be started using a variety of other techniques. Use a convex lens to direct sunlight onto tinder. Strike a flint with a piece of hard metal, such as a knife blade. Rapidly rub a groove into a piece of soft wood with a stick of harder wood. This builds up heat and ignites the wood fibers that are scraped loose. In critical situations, a power cell can create

enough of a spark by fastening a wire to each terminal and then touching the wires together near the tinder.

FINDING WATER

Dan Cencer has been exploring remote areas on the southern end of Isla Verde. Two days ago, stick monkeys swarmed into his small camp, attacking him and destroying most of his equipment, including his bodycomp. His ride back to Santa Elena is not due for another week and he has no way to alert anyone of his predicament.

Dan suffered several deep scratches and a few bruised ribs, but he escaped serious harm. He was able to recover enough antibiotics and rations to last the week, but his solar still was demolished, leaving him with just two liters of drinkable water. He has been able to rig the still so that it remains afloat in the small inlet he chose for his camp, but he fears if he leaves it unattended the monkeys he hears screaming in the jungle will come back and damage it.

The average human requires two to three liters of water per day to avoid dehydration. If he is active

or the temperature is high, he needs even more than that. The environment offers many ways to collect that precious fluid. Rainwater is generally safe and easy to come by on Poseidon. Simply leaving a cup or bowl out in a storm can yield as much as a liter an hour. High-mountain regions and the arctic areas have snow in abundance, which can be melted. One should never eat snow or ice; they reduce body temperature, which is dangerous to someone who is already dehydrated. Gray or opaque ice most likely has a high salt content and should be treated by melting and desalinating it.

Nature offers a variety of ways in which to collect water. Fruits are a good source. Digging in low areas, in dry river beds, in damp sand, and near green vegetation often yields ground water, which can be claimed by allowing the water to seep into the hole and then scooping it out or soaking it up with a cloth. Condensation can be collected from ceramic or metal objects left outside overnight. Watch for natural collection places such as depressions in stone or hollow stumps.

Salt water can be boiled and the steam collected on a cloth, which can be wrung out into a cup.

Certain vines, such as the Poseidon climber, contain a sweet, lemony liquid that is excellent not only for rehydration, but also for treating sunburn. These vines are generally about the diameter of a man's thumb and grow in tropical areas. Slice a notch high up on the vine. Cut the vine open at a lower point and collect the fluid that runs out. If it is clear or white and not salty or bitter, it is safe to drink. Yellow liquid, which comes from the ant vine, is mildly toxic. The brown liquid from the ubiquitous changa vine is fairly revolting, though it is perfectly harmless to drink.

Purify pond, lake, spring, and stream water by boiling it for one minute plus one minute for every 1,000 feet above sea level. Bad-tasting or -smelling water can be made less unpleasant by filtering it though several layers of cloth, or adding a few small pieces of charcoal and letting it stand for about an hour.

FINDING FOOD

Once a water source is located, food is the next essential need for a survivor. A general rule to follow is: If it grows in the ground, crawls, walks, or swims, it can be eaten.

Insect analogs, nuts, and seeds are high in protein and can be used to supplement a meat-poor diet. Fruits provide much-needed energy in the form of sugars, and many roots are high in carbohydrates, which are also used for producing energy. Organ meat is rich in vitamins.

Birds and fish can be caught in nets, small mammals may be trapped as they follow trails and runways, and larger game generally requires patience and tracking abilities. As Earthlike as Poseidon is, recognizing edible plants is tricky. Terrestrial cherries, for instance, are edible and considered quite good. Poseidon cherries are sweet too, but toxic.

To reduce the chances of eating spoiled food, collect and eat it fresh from the source. Thoroughly dry anything to be saved for later use. Remember that the sap from the Poseidon lemon and orange trees is a natural preservative that can be put on dried vegetables, fruit, or meat.

Do not eat seeds, fruit, or leaves that have fallen from the plant. They may have begun to rot or may have microscopic fungus growing on them. This fungus can be deadly. Avoid foods that are bitter or leave a burning sensation on the skin or in the mouth—that is nature's way of warning animals not to eat those plants. Boil meat and insects, if possible, to kill parasites. Do not eat anything that smells odd, tastes peppery or metallic, or has an odd color.

Try only one part of a plant—the roots, for instance—at a time. The basic edible components of plants are the leaves, roots, stems, buds, flowers, and fruit. Rub plant components on the inside of the elbow or wrist to test for contact poisons. If there is no reaction within 15 minutes, the plant should be safe.

Test the edibility of a food before eating it. The test should be done on an empty stomach. Chew a small piece without swallowing. Hold the chewed matter in the mouth for at least 10 minutes, noting any reactions such as burning, numbness, or itching. If no reaction occurs, swallow the food. Do not ingest any other food for five hours. If nausea or any other symptoms of poisoning occur, induce vomiting and drink plenty of water. If no ill effects are noted, prepare small portions at a time.

Be sure to wash food in clean water. Do not eat too much plant matter at one time, particularly on an empty stomach. Cramping, bloating, and diarrhea are typical effects.

Test each part of a plant before eating. Some plants have edible and inedible parts. Avoid mushroom-like fungi, shellfish not covered by water at high tide, plants that resemble Terrestrial onions or carrots, or have sap that turns black. Fish should have pink or red gills, not gray or blue. Do not puncture an animal's bladder, which can contaminate the meat.

SHELTER

Exposure to extreme conditions can be fatal. Cold causes the body to start shutting down. Heat causes rapid dehydration. Shelter is as necessary as food and water for survival.

Begin seeking shelter at least two hours before sunset. This allows enough time to discover any problems with the location, build or improvise needed structures, and collect supplies. A good shelter should not only protect a person from the elements, but also provide concealment from predators.

Make sure the area is not prone to flooding, is above the high-tide mark, and is free of insects and other pests. Fuel and water sources should be nearby and the location should afford protection from the wind.

A lean-to can be constructed between two trees with three stakes or heavy rocks, a length of rope, and a poncho. This simple structure is good for keeping the wind and rain off of a person. Tie two corners of the same side of the poncho to two trees, about waist high. Pull the poncho snug and peg it to the ground with the stakes. The open side should be away from the wind. Spread a thick layer of leaves or other insulating material on the ground to prevent loss of body heat while sleeping.

A large poncho or tarp can also be made into a tent by tying a rope between two trees about thigh high and draping the poncho over the rope. Secure the tent sides with stakes. A trench can be dug around the perimeter of the tent to prevent rainwater from running in. A variation of this tent is made by lashing a long, sturdy pole to a tree about waist high and draping the poncho over it. Additional poles can be rolled in the excess material to hold the sides down, if stakes will puncture the fabric.

A more permanent lean-to can be built by lashing several poles in a crisscross pattern to form a roof structure. Lean the roof against two trees and secure it with rope. Cover the roof with canvas, grass, leaves, or brush.

Build a tree-pit shelter in deep snow by selecting an evergreen with wide, low branches that will provide good cover. Dig a pit in the snow around the tree trunk, packing snow along the pit sides for support. Lay evergreen branches across the open areas above the snowline to keep wind and snow out of the pit.

A beach shelter can be made fairly easily with materials found on location. Dig a trench above the high-water mark. Heap the soil along the sides of the trench, building what looks like a valley between two mountains. Make the trench large enough to lie in comfortably. The mounds along the sides should be high enough to allow sufficient space in the shelter for movement. Lay branches or driftwood support beams across the mounds over the trench. Cover the supports with brush and leaves to form a roof. Additional soil can be packed over the roof if the wind is hard enough to blow the leaves and brush away.

WATER CROSSINGS

Water obstacles such as marshes, bogs, rivers, and streams are potentially dangerous hazards. Know the proper way to navigate them.

Crossing swift-moving water can be deadly if not done with proper care. The first step one must take in any water crossing is to locate a safe place to cross. On a river or stream, this requires finding a level area where a river breaks into several channels, sandbars, or places where the water is relatively calm. Look for signs of strong undercurrents by watching for swirls on an otherwise serene surface.

Especially rocky areas are dangerously slippery and pose a serious danger if one falls on them. Do not attempt to cross at waterfalls or deep channels. Plot a trajectory of 45°, not straight across. Move with the current. Consider removing clothing that can cause extra drag and keep gear stowed in a quick-release pack that can be jettisoned in case of a fall.

Crossing in a group is best accomplished using a solid pole, held on the same side by each person.

Face upstream and cross carrying the pole parallel to the current while moving across. By putting the heaviest person on the downstream end of the pole and the lightest person upstream, the current is broken by the smallest person, creating the least drag for the others. Should one person slip or lose grip, do not attempt to grab him. Sudden movements can shift the balance of every person and cause more than one to be lost.

When caught in shallow rapids, float face-up and ride the rapids feet first. Deeper rapids are more easily maneuvered face-down and head first. Swim towards the opposite shore, but do not struggle against the current.

Quicksand is made up of water and sand. It is found on level shores, in silty, shifty rivers, and near river mouths. It tends to look like sand but acts like water. Quicksand, marshes, and bogs should not be crossed simply by walking through. The bottoms of these types of areas are soft and offer very little support. In fact, mud may trap one's feet, making movement impossible and sinking likely. Cross using bridging materials such as logs or branches, or swim across. The water is likely murkier and worse smelling than an average pond, but is not much more difficult to swim. If additional flotation is needed, a pair of pants can be tied at the ankles and waist after inflating them. Wear the pants like a life jacket.

Gear can be floated on a makeshift raft formed by lashing logs together and stretching a tarp across the top. Solar blankets float, and can handle most standard travel gear. Large groups may wish to put all of their equipment into a rescue ball and tow or push it across. Bioplastic in most forms floats and can be used to float gear or people, depending on the object's size and shape.

MARINE SURVIVAL

Ninety-seven percent of Poseidon's surface is covered by water, and most every colonist will be required to travel frequently over open ocean. The odds that a colonist will eventually find himself in a survival situation in a marine environment are therefore extremely high.

PREPARATION

Other than the hard vacuum of space, the open ocean provides the fewest survival resources of any environment the typical colonist is likely to face. The only readily accessible resource on the open ocean is saltwater, which is undrinkable for humans without the salt tolerance biomod. Even in the most inhospitable desert, it is much easier to find food, potable water, and shelter from the elements.

As a result, survival on the open ocean usually depends on the resources the individual brings into the water with him. Because most such survival situations are the result of travel accidents, these resources typically consist of emergency equipment and salvageable debris from a crashed, capsized, or otherwise inoperable vehicle or vessel. It is therefore of paramount importance to familiarize oneself with the available resources when one first boards the ship or aircraft. Passengers should learn what survival equipment is carried onboard and where it is stored. For personal vehicles, travelers should insure that the vehicle is well stocked with emergency supplies and equipment, including evac pods or rescue balls.

INITIAL ACTIONS

Survivors of an aircraft crash or sinking vessel must first get clear of the vehicle. A sinking object as large as a ship or aircraft can suck a survivor in the water under the surface. When moving away from the vehicle, survivors should attempt to position themselves upwind, for two reasons. First, high winds or sudden gusts may otherwise blow dangerous wreckage and debris onto the survivor. Second, the wind may carry toxic fumes or other chemical hazards.

Once clear of the vehicle, survivors should attempt to find a raft, rescue ball, or evac pod, if they are not already in one. If no such emergency device is available, the survivor should attempt to locate and cling to a large, buoyant piece of debris. Conservation of energy should be one of the survivor's primary short- and long-term goals. If no flotation at all is available, humans can nevertheless float in water with very little expenditure of energy. The key is to relax—the body's natural buoyancy will keep the top of the head above the surface; only minimal movement is then necessary to keep the face above water. The most energy-efficient technique is for the survivor to float on his back with his arms at his side, finning the hands back and forth to maintain maximum buoyancy.

The survivor's next immediate action should be to locate other survivors. Groups are always more likely to survive than individuals. Groups allow sharing of resources, mutual protection from potential predator attacks, teamwork, and mitigation of survival stress.

SURVIVAL CHECKLIST

Once the immediate danger is past, a group of survivors on the open ocean should attempt to accomplish each of the tasks on the following checklist:

• Assess the condition and structural integrity of the emergency craft. If leaks are found, patch them with whatever materials are on hand. All commercial emergency craft come equipped with adhesive patches, but if they are not available, use chewing gum, seaweed dipped in machine oil, lubricated condoms, animal fat, or anything else that will keep the craft inflated.

• Assess the physical condition of everyone onboard, administering first aid as necessary.

• If there are other groups of survivors, lash rafts, rescue balls, or evac pods together, leaving eight to 10 meters between them. The more expansive the formation, the easier it will be for rescue craft to spot the survivors.

• Attempt to salvage all floating equipment and resources from the crash site. If it looks like it may have a potential use, regardless of how unlikely, take it. Store perishable items on the emergency craft, taking care not to exceed its weight limit. If possible, lash and tow other buoyant equipment. Only expert swimmers or those equipped with underwater gear should attempt to dive for sunken salvage.

• Find the locator beacon, emergency radio, or GPS unit and insure that it is functioning properly. Deploy disposable emergency beacons, such as flares or rescue dye, if rescue craft are suspected of being in the area. Otherwise, save them until there is someone in the area to see them.

• If the emergency craft lacks station-keeping propulsion or an anchor, jury-rig a drag using rope or clothing and any available non-buoyant object. Remaining near the crash site will maximize the chances of a quick rescue.

• Work as a team. Assign every capable survivor specific tasks, such as lookout, radio operator, food gatherer, water collector, and bailer. This will organize the survivors' efforts and mitigate survival stress, both of which will increase their chances of survival.

• In stormy weather, wave action and rain can fill a raft or other open emergency craft with water. Deploy or rig a canopy to keep the inside of the craft as dry as possible.

• In a cold climate, survivors should huddle together to keep warm. In an open craft, make sure the canopy protects the interior as much as possible from wind and water.

• In a hot climate, leave space in the canopy of an open craft for ventilation and take appropriate measures (sunscreen, protective clothing) to protect skin from excessive exposure to the sun.

FOOD AND WATER

Fish are the most abundant food sources on the open ocean. If fishing gear is unavailable, improvise line from shoelaces, parachute suspension cords, clothing thread, or unwound rope. Make hooks out of needles, wire, nails, wood, or bioplastic fragments. Small fish will often seek shelter in the shadow of the emergency raft—catch them and use them as bait for larger fish. At night, shine a light on the surface to attract fish.

When near land, survivors may also be able find edible birds, especially if firearms are available. Likewise, seaweed and other marine plants floating on the surface may be harvested for food. Unprepared seaweed, however, tends to cause diarrhea and can therefore cause dehydration, especially when soaked in saltwater. If freshwater is available, clean it thoroughly before eating. Otherwise, eat seaweed only in small portions.

Harvesting local food sources in marine survival situations shares the same hazards as most every other environment on Poseidon. Follow established procedures for determining toxicity (see page 7) before eating unknown plants and animals.

If the emergency craft contains a still or other device for producing potable water, get it operational immediately. Likewise, utilize available desalting kits and water purifiers. If no such resources are available, rig a water trap to collect rainwater and dew. At night, simply stretch a tarpaulin or other available fabric out flat and turn the edges up so it can collect dew.

Never drink saltwater on Poseidon, as it actually worsens dehydration.

PREDATORS

There are many predators in Poseidon's oceans, and survivors must take precautions to protect themselves from animal attacks.

• Maintain constant lookouts
• Do not throw waste overboard
• Do not clean fish in the water
• Keep arms and legs out of the water and remain as quiet as possible
• Dispose of corpses immediately

Some survival guides suggest various deterrents in the event of a predator attack, such as slapping the surface or yelling underwater. Research has shown, however, that while any given tactic may work on some predators, it may actually incite, enrage, or otherwise attract others. Therefore, if a predator cannot be identified, the best course of action is to avoid attracting the predator's attention. Otherwise, the only consistently effective way to survive a predator attack at sea is to inflict enough damage on the animal to incapacitate it or drive it off. If possible, strike the predator's head with blunt objects—this is usually effective, and it typically does not result in significant bleeding, which can attract other predators.

TROPICAL SURVIVAL

Other than the ocean, tropical environments are most often encountered in survival situations on Poseidon. The jungles offer a number of unique challenges and obstacles to the would-be survivor.

TRAVEL

Efficient travel is often crucial to survival in Poseidon's jungles. The chances of rescue deep in a tropical rainforest are extremely remote—it is usually necessary for the survivor to travel to a suitable rescue point.

Jungle travel can be both rigorous and dangerous. Important equipment includes:

• A machete for clearing vegetation, obtaining food, and rigging improvised equipment, such as shelters and rafts

• A GPS unit or compass for direction finding

• Broad-spectrum antibiotics for treating infection

• Rugged and comfortable clothing, including footwear

• A hammock to avoid sleeping on the ground

• Insect netting

If at all possible, travel through the jungle only during the day. Under a thick canopy, it is often completely dark at night, and vegetation and other obstacles can be hazardous. Also, most large tropical predators are nocturnal.

Maximize the efficiency of travel. Move slowly and carefully through dense vegetation, stopping frequently to get bearings and check orientation. Choose a direction and stick with it, but do not necessarily travel in a straight line. Move around obstacles where possible, and adjust pace and stride to the terrain. Cut through vegetation only when necessary; an upward slash is less noisy than a downward cut.

Develop "jungle eyes." Ignore vegetation in the foreground and focus directly beyond it. Do not look at the jungle; look *through* it. At regular intervals, drop to the ground and sight along the jungle floor. This will aid in traveling efficiently, and also in avoiding abrasions, lacerations, and loss of direction.

Always seek the safest and easiest route out of a jungle. The path of least resistance is usually a river or large stream. A waterway will always lead to a larger body of water that offers a clearing in the jungle canopy, and often to habitations. Travel downstream to the ocean or a lake, set up camp, and deploy signaling devices.

Traveling along a river requires water crossings, frequent detours, and the clearing of often-dense vegetation. However, it provides a definite and easily followed direction, a ready source of food and water, and the possibility of traveling by watercraft.

In mountainous regions, travel along ridges rather than through valleys. The ridge offers less dense underbrush and fewer marshy areas, as well as a clear direction and vantage point.

Many animals in the jungle use clear game trails, which often lead to clearings or bodies of freshwater. When following game trails, stay alert for

predators and check bearings frequently to maintain the desired direction of travel.

Schedule each day so there is sufficient time and energy to establish a secure campsite in the evening. The sun sets quickly in the tropics, usually in less than 30 minutes, so set camp well before sunset. Do not camp too close to waterways, as heavy rainfall can cause flashfloods. Rivers and streams are also common hunting grounds for nocturnal predators. Likewise, do not camp on obvious game trails. Clear the campsite of underbrush to allow easy movement and adequate ventilation for a fire. Always be sure to get sufficient sleep before resuming travel.

FOOD

Foraging in a rainforest is often surprisingly difficult, as edible fruits and nuts are usually too high in the trees to reach easily. Accessible edible plants will often be found along waterways, in clearings, and at the edge of the jungle. Many jungle animals can be safely eaten. Fish are available in rivers and streams. Follow the general guidelines for capturing and preparing game (see page 7).

HAZARDS

Despite popular images of large, voracious jungle predators, the most serious danger of tropical environments is from insectoids. Insect bites are often poisonous, and can also transmit disease and cause infection. Take the following precautions to minimize the danger of insect bites and stings:

• If possible, avoid areas where they are especially populous. Unfortunately, this will often rule out waterways as a desirable route out of the jungle.

• Use pest spikes, or apply chemical insect repellent to exposed skin and openings in the clothing. Always remain fully clothed, especially at night when insects are most abundant. If insect repellents are unavailable, smear mud on exposed skin.

• Close openings in clothing whenever possible. Keep sleeves rolled down and buttoned, tuck pant legs into boots, and keep shirts buttoned at the collar. Wear gloves and insect netting if possible.

• Maintain hygiene, bathing daily if possible. Keep clothing clean, especially footwear. Never walk barefoot in the jungle.

TROPICAL WATERS

Reefs can be abundant sources of food, but also very dangerous. Never walk barefoot on coral reefs: The coral will lacerate the skin, infectious contaminants such as lime or silica can become lodged under the skin, and accidental contact with poisonous sea life is a constant threat. Incoming tides sweeping over a reef make both walking and swimming hazardous.

If traveling through surf, do so during the lull between large waves. Always head into the waves. Do not get caught under large breaking waves in shallow water. Dive and grab hold of a rock until the wave breaks and passes.

When walking over muddy or sandy bottoms of rivers and coastal shallows, slide or shuffle along the bottom to avoid stepping on potentially poisonous or spined animals, such as sand archers.

DESERT SURVIVAL

While popular images of Poseidon are dominated by open ocean, volcanic islands, and dense jungles, the colony world has several arid environments that pose serious challenges in a survival situation. These include:

• Scarce water
• Intense heat
• Dramatic temperature changes
• Sparse vegetation
• High surface mineral content (salt flats)
• Sandstorms
• Mirages

The scarcity of water is usually the most immediate challenge to survival in an arid region. Some deserts, such as Hell's Basin on Westcape, receive only a few centimeters of annual rainfall, and this usually comes in brief torrents that are quickly absorbed.

Understanding the relationship between physical activity, air temperature, and water consumption is crucial to survival in a desert environment. The amount of water the human body needs is dependent on the individual's level of activity and the temperature. The following table shows the minimum safe daily water requirement for an average human in relation to temperature level, assuming the individual is resting in the shade. Extended physical activity exposed to heat and sunlight can double this requirement.

Temperature (C)	Liters of Water
25	4.5
30	5.6
35	7.5
40	8.8
45	12.3
50	14.2

The human body sheds excess heat by sweating. The warmer the body becomes, the more the person sweats. Sweating results in lost moisture. If a person stops sweating during periods of physical activity exposed to intense heat, the body will overheat and the person will suffer from heat stroke or exhaustion. To avoid this potentially life-threatening condition, survivors in desert environments should:

- Find shade
- Limit physical activity during the daytime
- Always try to sit or lie on some kind of ground cover when resting
- Conserve sweat by remaining fully clothed, with a head cover and a scarf or neck wrap
- Keep the mouth clothed and breathe through the nose
- If adequate water is unavailable, do not eat, as digestion requires water

HEAT CONDITIONS

Illness due to overheating and dehydration is often unavoidable in a survival situation in a desert environment. There are three main types of heat condition: heat cramps, heat exhaustion, and heat stroke.

Heat cramps are usually caused by the loss of salt that results from excessive sweating. This condition causes moderate to severe muscle cramps in the extremities and abdomen. At the first sign of discomfort, the victim should immediately cease physical activity, seek shade, and drink water in slow sips, if it is available.

Heat exhaustion is caused by significant loss of body water and salt. The condition causes headaches, disorientation, irritability, excessive sweating, physical weakness, dizziness, severe muscle cramps, and clammy skin. The victim should lie down in the shade, preferably elevated at least 50 centimeters from the ground. Fan and sprinkle water on the victim, and allow him to drink small sips of water approximately every three minutes. The victim should rest and continue treatment until symptoms are gone and strength returns.

Heat stroke is simply a severe case of heat exhaustion. Loss of water and salt is extreme, and the body is unable to cool itself. Symptoms include no sweating, hot, dry skin, headaches, dizziness, racing pulse, nausea and vomiting, disorientation, and possibly unconsciousness. Follow the same treatments as listed for heat exhaustion, but pour water on the victim more liberally and massage the extremities. Death is a real threat if the victim is not cooled immediately.

HAZARDS

As in tropical environments, insects, poisonous animals, and thorned or barbed flora are potential dangers in most deserts. Take standard precautions to avoid these hazards. Regularly inspect clothing and sleeping materials for potentially dangerous animal life, and carefully inspect resting areas before sitting or lying down.

Standing water in arid environments is frequently contaminated. Assume that it is and use water purifiers wherever possible. Drinking contaminated water can cause severe gastrointestinal problems that exacerbate dehydration.

Sunburn, as all but the most sheltered tourists know, is caused by overexposure of the skin to sunlight. It is just as much of a danger with a cloud cover as on a clear day. Remain fully clothed, use available sunscreens, and limit activity during the daytime to minimize the risk of sunburn. If severe sunburn does occur, treat it like any other burn. Take care to keep blistered areas clean, as infection will cause further complications. The damage caused by sunburn can be exacerbated by chapping due to wind and sand. Again, full clothing to limit exposed areas is the best protection.

The glare caused by intense sunlight on the sand can cause severe eyestrain, and potentially even blindness. Windblown sand can further damage the eyes. If eye protection is unavailable, try to shield the eyes with headwear and wraps.

The temperature can drop rapidly after sunset, and arid environments dry out the nasal passages, increasing the risk of head and chest colds. Always wear warm clothing at night. If physical activity and travel is restricted to the nighttime hours, this will also help to keep the body warm.

Due to the extreme physiological stresses placed on the body in desert survival situations, adequate rest is absolutely crucial. The average human requires 20 minutes of rest for each hour of physical activity in the heat, and at least seven to eight hours of sleep each 30-hour day.

Because infections and gastrointestinal disorders can lead to excessive loss of moisture, good hygiene is also crucial. Waste should be buried so as not to attract disease-carrying insect analogs. The hands should be washed regularly, in clean sand if water is unavailable, as should cooking and eating utensils.

ARCTIC SURVIVAL

While tropical and subtropical climates prevail throughout most of the settled Pacifica Archipelago, arctic conditions are common in the polar regions and are also encountered in high-mountain regions, such as the central peaks of Prime Meridian. Arctic environments can be uniquely deadly in survival situations.

The cold is a deadly adversary for humans. While the extreme heat of Poseidon's deserts can kill in hours, extreme cold can kill in minutes. Dangerously cold air temperatures are often exacerbated by even moderate winds— the phenomenon known as windchill.

In a cold environment, every major survival task— travel, and obtaining food, water, and shelter—is more difficult than in a warm environment. And even if these needs are provided for, the would-be survivor must still keep his body warm or he will die in a very short time.

When healthy, a human's body temperature is almost constant at 37°C. Since the extremities do not have as much insulating body tissue, their temperature tends to vary a lot more and will often not reach this core body temperature.

The human body has a climate-control system that it uses to maintain its temperature. This control system has three main components: heat production, heat loss, and evaporation.

Heat production is determined by the difference between body temperature and the surrounding temperature. In general, the body is a lot more efficient at shedding heat than at producing it.

The muscle activity involved in shivering produces heat, and is one of the body's involuntary responses to cold. However, it also causes fatigue eventually, which in turn results in dropping body temperature.

- At windchills between -28° and -56°C, exposed flesh may freeze within one minute
- At windchills below -56°C, exposed flesh may freeze within 30 seconds

Hypothermia occurs when body temperature drops to between 35°C and 25°C. This extremely dangerous condition can even occur when air temperatures are above freezing. Symptoms of this condition include sluggish movement, deteriorating coordination, and mental impairment. A victim of hypothermia whose core body temperature drops below 25°C is almost certain to die.

The only way to effectively treat hypothermia is to rewarm the body. One of the best methods, if the means are available, is to immerse the victim's torso in warm water. Immersing the entire body all at once can induce shock and cardiac arrest. Warm-water enemas are the quickest way to increase the core body temperature.

If warm water is unavailable, the victim should be wrapped in a warm cover, such as an insulated sleeping bag, with another warm person. Both should be naked to allow for maximum heat transfer. A conscious victim should be given hot, sweetened fluids.

Frostbite is a condition caused by frozen tissue. Light frostbite only affects the skin, giving it a dull white coloration. Deep frostbite extends to the tissue below the skin, and the tissues become solid and immobile. The extremities are especially vulnerable to frostbite.

Check for frostbite regularly. Groups should check each other to maximize the chances of detection. Treat areas affected by light frostbite by rewarming, and take extra care to prevent the affected areas from refreezing. Do not attempt to rewarm areas affected by deep frostbite—if the area becomes refrozen again, it will cause extremely severe damage.

OTHER HAZARDS

Snow blindness is caused by the reflection of bright sunlight off of a snow covering. The condition causes a sensation of grit in the eyes, pain that increases with eye movement, watery and red eyes, and headaches that intensify with continued exposure to light. Prolonged exposure can result in permanent damage and blindness. The condition must be treated by completely covering the eyes until the symptoms disappear.

If protective eyewear is not available, cut narrow slits in a thin piece of wood, bioplastic, or other material. Attach a cord, string, or wire to the improvised glasses and fasten securely behind the head. This will dramatically decrease the amount of light that reaches the eyes.

STAYING WARM

The only way to stay warm for an indefinite period in an extreme-cold environment is to wear proper clothing and wear them properly. Follow these three guidelines:

- Wear clothing loose and in layers. This will allow ample circulation, and air trapped between the layers will increase insulation.

- Keep clothing dry. Wear waterproofed clothing, if possible. Be careful to avoid overheating, as inner clothing will absorb sweat. If clothing does become wet, dry it near a fire or heat source; if none is available, use body heat to dry it while camped.

- Keep clothing clean. Dirt and contaminants can cause clothing to lose much of their insulating properties.

WATER

Water is typically more abundant and sanitary in arctic environments than in others due to prevailing conditions. However, if possible, always purify water before drinking it. Ice and snow can be melted for water, but make sure it is freshwater before drinking it. Always melt ice or snow to produce water for drinking; melting it in the mouth uses body heat and may cause injury. Limit water consumption before going to sleep - heeding the call of nature in the middle of the night will result in further exposure to cold.

FOOD

While edible flora is frequently scarce in arctic regions, game is often abundant. Always skin and butcher game while it is still warm. Cut the meat into individual pieces and freeze them separately, so they can be thawed and cooked as needed. As always, never eat anything unless you know it is edible. Unknown flora and fauna is much more common than known on Poseidon, so always use the Universal Edibility Test when in doubt.

TRAVEL

Travel through arctic environments can be both rigorous and treacherous. Follow these guidelines where possible:

- Never travel during blizzards. Seek shelter and warmth.

- When crossing ice-covered waterways, be alert for thin ice. Distribute body weight by lying flat and crawling.

- Freeze and thaw cycles may cause the level of waterways to vary dramatically at any time of day, depending on distance to source, temperature, and terrain. Always cross waterways when the water level is at its lowest point.

- When camping, allow plenty of time to build adequate shelter before sunset.

- Because they are typically clear of obstacles and terrain hazards, both frozen and unfrozen rivers make good travel routes.

- Use snowshoes when traveling through heavy snow. If necessary, jury-rig them using available materials. Anything that broadens the footprint and prevents sinking into the snow will suffice. Traveling through deep snow without snowshoes or skis is extremely rigorous.

WILDLIFE ENCOUNTERS

The plants and animals presented in Blue Planet are meant to serve a number of functions in the game. They are intended to enrich the setting, helping to foster the sense of an alien world, cultivating a deeper, more realistic background. They are intended to serve as plot devices, challenging and

motivating characters in any number of ways. They are also meant to threaten player characters, to create a sense of danger for adventures at sea or in the outback. They are intended to provide lethal opponents for characters to outsmart, overcome, or battle.

These intentions are best realized through encounters with these creatures, and game moderators are encouraged to use the biota of **Blue Planet** in ways that add realism, depth, mystery, danger, and action to their adventures. The following wildlife encounters are intended to help moderators use the flora and fauna of the game effectively. These set-piece encounters can be used as written or they can be mined for cool ideas and customized to fit a specific campaign. They should also be used to inspire moderators to create similar encounters of their own, encounters that go beyond simply killing monsters, instead using those monsters to add substance, variety, and a sense of originality to the game.

Because a sense of the unknown is so important to wilderness encounters in **Blue Planet**, these entries

should be considered **Access Denied**, for the game moderator's eyes only.

ATTACK OF INCONVENIENCE

A research outpost in the Anderson Reef has been plagued by a problem in the past few days. Any human or cetacean approaching a certain rift is assaulted by tiny eduropods. While not overtly dangerous, the animals soon become so numerous that they cloud the water, and the individual is soon covered with numerous tiny bites. While in the area, the trespasser soon becomes covered in a thick mass of squirming eduropods. Bites on exposed skin are painful, but the biggest danger is that the creatures will clog artificial gills, MHD intakes, and other equipment. The research outpost is interested in operations around this reef, and is desperate for a resolution of the problem that does not damage the ecosystem.

The eduropods have migrated from many kilometers in all directions, gathering in crevasses throughout the reef in preparation for mating. Currently, the males are competing for prime territory. Any large animal wandering into the area will be overwhelmed. The problem will become worse before it gets better, as ever-increasing numbers gather. Eventually, the water around the reef will be teaming with the eduropods and the predators feeding on them.

There are three solutions to the problem. The first is simply to wait. There is clear evidence that the eduropods' numbers are massively inflated and that this is almost certainly a temporary matter. Educated analysis of the situation will reveal that the population bloom is unlikely to last more than one or two weeks. Simply making observations and minimizing activities until the cycle completes will have the least impact, along with gathering valuable information about the reef ecosystem. This will have a negative impact on some studies, but with care the problems should be minimal.

A second solution is to use some form of chemical agent to protect individuals. With a little analysis and testing, even amateur chemists could develop an effective repellent. The eduropods will still gather, but will be unable to get near a protected individual or piece of equipment. This gel, however, will damage all eduropods it contacts, causing unknown disruption of their life cycle.

The third solution is to kill the eduropods outright, or knock them out while researchers pass through and take samples. This solution is most likely to cause major damage to the ecosystem and skew research data.

The research outpost could be a Hanover operation, from nearby Lebensraum. It could also be a Haven Institute of Science and Technology outpost. Game moderators can adjust this as appropriate, or may set it in another reef system altogether.

BAD WATER

Residents of Poseidon know to be cautious of water, particularly freshwater supplies. Most would prefer to drink desalinated seawater than trust most sources of freshwater. Still, explorers in the rainforests are sometimes pressed for supplies. Wide-spectrum antibiotics and filtration systems are usually very effective.

Colonial organisms that can infest human skin live in many regions of the rainforests, however. Traveling through standing water and marshy areas is often sufficient exposure to cause infection. The parasite works its way into the pores, and a painful rash soon develops on the skin. If left untreated, the skin cells slowly dissolve over a period of weeks, an extremely painful process similar to the effects of some lethal animal toxins. The infection also releases toxic byproducts, and these can produce a number of complications. Though there is no known inoculation, the organism is thankfully easy to treat with a specific, topical treatment of antibiotics. The infection then clears up within a few days, leaving a faint discoloration the natives call "wash."

Travelers in rainforests and coastal marshes are encouraged to treat rashes as they appear with a variety of medications. Wash is only one of many organisms that find the human body a wonderful source of nutrients.

BLIMPBOMBS

Desmond Johnson has been working for the Haven Institute of Science and Technology for three years in their xenobiology department. Known for a brilliant imagination and attention to detail, his papers have been well received and he is expected to complete his doctorate within the next year.

The characters receive disturbing news, either from within HIST or from intercepted communications.

It seems that Desmond has uncovered some information about the biology of blimps, and is working with GenDiver on covert research. Two people involved in his work are dead, perhaps killed to safeguard secrets. Whether sent by a rival Incorporate, investigated by the GEO, or an internal Haven team, the players must uncover the truth.

The truth is that Desmond has snapped. He is convinced that blimps can be used as covert weapons, rigged with control devices and small charges, and is trying to get an Incorporate to give him money to develop the idea. The problems are many and insurmountable, of course, but this hasn't stopped Desmond. GenDiver, after studying his requests briefly, is no longer returning his calls. Though two researchers did die working with Desmond, the cover story is the real story; they died from a surprise stone snake attack.

BREEDIN' JOES

The remains of many large animals—including humans—have been discovered in an isolated mangrove forest. The remains are grouped in several locations and are relatively fresh. Examination indicates that the deaths occurred between one and two weeks ago, and the bones show distinct rasp marks.

The mangrove has become the mating grounds for several dozen Hangin' Joes. These dangerous organisms have congregated, and after a feeding frenzy, are beginning their courting rituals. In a few days the activity will be complete, the Joes will separate to lay eggs, and they will slowly disperse.

The party members could be explorers who inadvertently discover this evidence. They could also be alerted by other explorers, or be investigating missing persons. The biggest danger to the party will be right after the eggs are laid. The Hangin' Joes will be at their most mobile, rather densely grouped, and will not have eaten in a week. Approaching during mating is also dangerous, as the timing is inexact and there will be hungry Hangin' Joes surrounding the main group.

An enterprising group of characters can make some money from the situation. A high quality recording of the mating is worth 2,000 scrip from the Haven Institute of Science and Technology, or from interested Incorporate states. Recordings of egg laying can fetch 1,000 scrip, and a simple recording of a lone Hangin' Joe is worth 500 scrip.

Actual eggs are worth 500 scrip for a small sample, or up to 4,000 for a larger sample—all the eggs from one laying or a number of samples. This assumes the eggs are delivered intact and well preserved.

BUBBLE TROUBLE

When land is submerged, aquifers are often trapped within. This creates massive amounts of freshwater under the ocean along continental shelves. When sealed in limestone, the limestone slowly erodes away, eventually causing a sudden and massive upsurge of freshwater. Given freshwater's relatively low density, the flow can be quite strong. These freshwater sinkholes are dangerous to ships, which can fall into the less dense freshwater and then suffer from turbulence. The odds of encountering one, however, are quite small on Earth.

On Poseidon, these water bubbles are more rare. The fact that the planet has any lends some credence to the idea that more of its landmass was exposed in the recent past, although just how much more is debated. A few rather radical theories as to how freshwater reservoirs can form without dry land have been proposed. In any case, these water bubbles pose a distinct danger, particularly given undersea prospecting.

Operations on the sea bottom have a chance of disrupting these bubbles. Detailed penetrative sonar surveys should reveal them, but these are generally done late in a mining operation. Obvious sink formations and variations in water composition can reveal reservoirs that are close to collapse. More stable formations, however, only become a problem in short periods of time due to mining activities.

If the bubble opens, it will flood the surrounding area with freshwater. This will cause cetaceans great discomfort and system stress. It will also cause turbulence and a current flowing into the reservoir, from seawater replacing escaping freshwater. This will suck a poor prospector or pieces of equipment into the chamber. The sides of the chamber and falling rock can cause damage.

A bubble will rarely burst all at once. This depends on how easily freshwater can flow out of the reservoir. There may be repeated releases and corresponding currents. Chambers may also be laid out in a sprawling series.

CIRCUS CARCASS

In this encounter the players are residents or visitors in a native village, or maybe they are members of a small colony, or staff at a field research station. The morning after a violent storm they wake to find the carcass of a very large, very dead animal has washed ashore on their beach. Maybe it is a big greater white (MG 171) or even a corpse of the rare leviathan (see page 83). The body weighs 90 tons at least and the storm surge has stranded the beast high on the shore. The creature is immense, and has obviously been dead for some time as it is half decayed. Smaller scavengers, like seaghouls (see page 94), gather quickly and there are legitimate fears that larger, more threatening animals may soon be drawn to the mountain of carrion. The stink is overwhelming, and every resource in the town is soon bent to clearing the corpse away.

No local boat is powerful enough to drag the huge thing off the shore, even if there was enough cable available, and a way to secure it to the animal. There is absolutely no way to bury it, and the scavengers certainly are not going to eat it all before something dangerous shows up or the smell drives the residents away. Someone suggests chopping it into smaller pieces and trying to drag those off. This is tried, but after hours of chopping, cutting, and digging the gore-covered workers realize the huge creature is just too big to hack through with hand tools. Then someone suggests explosives, and in their fatigue and frustration the work crews give that a try. The bloody rain that results leaves the beach and village a gooey mess, with gobbets of rotting flesh hanging from tree branches, rooftops, and laundry lines. Pools of coagulated goo cover the streets and villagers stalk angrily through town looking for the smartass who suggested turning the pile of rotten meat into a bomb.

This encounter can remain a lighthearted comedy, or it can get serious when guards must be posted to keep niños muertos and pseudo eels at bay while the mess is cleaned up and hauled away. If enough large scavengers show up, this encounter could become deadly indeed.

CUDDLESLOTH

Found only in the southernmost Endeavor Islands, the cuddlesloth is a mild-mannered animal that resembles a Terrestrial sloth. It is a draconodont with six clawed limbs, about a meter tall. Like sloths of Earth, it is arboreal and slow moving. It does not have fur, but has a tight mass of epiphytes and moss that grow over its body. The head is owl-like, with soulful eyes, set on a long neck.

When held by a human, the cuddlesloth has a tendency to wrap its arms around the person, ducking its head under an arm. Owners report that the cuddlesloths are comforted by the warmth of a human and prefer human perches to trees, unless they are hungry. Unfortunately, cuddlesloths need their plant symbiotes, and die within days if the vegetation is cleaned off. They also fare poorly when moved to other regions. Still, they thrive as pets in their home regions, seem to emotionally bond with their owners, and have become quite popular.

Several disappearances of cuddlesloth owners have caused worry. Owners become isolated, shunning friends and family. Some move to more isolated homes or camps in the rainforest, and eventually cannot be found. On two occasions, family members trying to track their relatives report seeing brief glimpses of mossy people near where the relatives vanished.

There are a number of theories, any of which could be correct. There could be an unknown physiological effect of the cuddlesloths or the plants living on them, and these could cause antisocial behavior. Simple accidents or predation could also account for the vanishings.

Another theory is that it is purely psychological. Psychological disorders sometimes appear in societies and regions for a time, and then vanish. The isolation of the region and attachment to an alien organism could form some part of an unknown psychological pathology.

Wilder theories include the actions of aborigines and the infection of humans by the cuddlesloth symbiotes.

DATA ENTRY

The unfortunate player character subject to this encounter is staying in the home of a native family. One morning, as he is getting dressed or is otherwise distracted, he notices the family pet: A large basilisk (see page 66) has come into the room and is clawing through his gear. As he shoos the creature away he notices the end of a dataspike sticking out of the animal's mouth. The lizard swallows it, hisses at the character's attempts to fend it off, and then nonchalantly drags itself out the door. The data spike might be valueless, or it might contain the key to the whole adventure. If the latter, the character is going to have to exercise more than delicate diplomacy to recover his property.

DESERTIFICATION

It may seem odd in a world of water, but deserts can pose a problem even for prepared characters. There are a number of reasons why characters may brave the deserts. Smugglers and other criminals may operate out of desert regions, counting on minimal traffic to provide some protection. Researchers are interested in ecosystems throughout Poseidon, and deserts are known for the interesting chemicals developed by endemic flora and fauna. Deserts are also frequently the sites of prospecting efforts.

Water is the first noticeable difficulty characters may face. A malfunction in a refiltration unit or damage to water supplies can make the situation very dire. Characters may also become lost, particularly if they are working covertly and had to leave GPS units behind. Heat stroke can creep up on characters quickly, rendering every decision difficult and putting considerable stress on the body. Veteran explorers will be alert enough to minimize these problems. Other characters may let their guard down, used to thinking of danger only in terms of jungles or sea.

DIGGING IN THE DIRT

This encounter has the player characters spending the night on an empty beach. They might be sleeping on the sand, in tents, or even in a jumpcraft. As they sleep, a colony of digger crabs (MG 167) expands their underground warren so that it now extends beneath the unsuspecting characters. As they roll over in their sleep, or get up in the morning, the warren suddenly collapses. One or more of the characters instantly find themselves lying at the bottom of a deep hole, half-filled with cold seawater, a dozen digger crabs eying them with bad intent. Maybe they are wrapped helplessly in their now soggy tent, or perhaps their jumpcraft is now hopelessly sunk, half upended, in the muddy hole. Whether presented as comic relief or with a more serious tone, this encounter offers an unexpected twist.

FISH OF A DIFFERENT COLOR

There have been stories, lately, of a lone schooler that has been attacking and killing cetaceans and humans. There is considerable interest in this matter. Speculation runs from there being rogues among the schoolers, to there being a distinct but different species that exhibits more aggressive behavior.

The stories can be tracked to a five-year-old native girl whose parents were eaten, as far as she can tell, by an evil schooler, and from sonar recordings from an outpost whose crew all disappeared. These facts, as well as some other tentative disappearances and fragmented stories, may lead a party to the south of Islas Bonitas.

The truth is that it is not a schooler at all, but several young greater whites, each between three and five meters long. Uncovering the truth will bring modest rewards to the party, particularly if they manage to capture one of the greater whites. The difficulty is that efforts to track or hunt the young greater whites are likely to attract the attention of larger adults in deeper waters.

GHOST IN THE NIGHT

This encounter does not need to be a dangerous one, and in fact is probably best used in one of those special roleplaying moments when a moderator wants to press home the alien feel of life on Poseidon. Of course, if danger is called for, this encounter can easily be dressed up a bit. The encounter must be set up carefully, and the moderator needs to be ready by having set the right tone and having plenty of eerie description ready.

The players are traveling by watercraft at night, or better yet, they are asleep at anchor on some remote reef. Dimly flickering electric lights aboard the vessel wake them, and when they come out on deck to investigate they discover their boat has been surrounded by a drifting ghoster (MG 170). The colonial creature stretches for hundreds of meters in every direction and its electrical discharge is creating sympathetic glow in the boat's fluorescent lighting. Describe the scene as surreal and emotionally moving. The gently undulating glow of the water-rocked creature would be inspiring and hypnotic, like staring into a campfire. The twinkling trails left behind as small creatures collide with the ghoster make the mass look like a slowly drifting galaxy and prove to the characters in no uncertain terms that they are very far from Earth.

To add an element of danger to this encounter, the moderator should describe a moving patch of brighter, sparking light where the ghoster is being disturbed by something larger moving just below the surface. The glow begins to circle the boat moving closer and closer with each pass. A greater (MG 171) or lesser white (see page 85), a pseudo eel (see page 95) or a stone snake (MG 188) could be on the prowl, and the players might soon be thrown into a desperate fight for survival.

KNOCK KNOCK

In this encounter the player characters are getting ready to exit a submarine or an underwater facility. They are about to enter an airlock or a moon pool, and maybe some of them are half into their diving gear or organizing equipment and weapons. However it is set up, the encounter should be a total surprise. When the inner lock is opened, or the players head for the pool, a pseudo eel (see page 95) erupts out onto the deck. Maybe it was waiting for prey to come out of the "cave," or maybe it was simply using the lock as a refuge. Either way, when the creature suddenly finds itself out of the water, it will panic and thrash about. It will not try to attack, but it will bite at anything in range, knock over equipment, and trash controls and fixtures. Dealing with the creature might include driving it back into the lock, or attacking it with spears or improvised weapons, as gunfire within the facility might prove more dangerous than the eel.

LAND WAR

In the dark, wet jungle of some remote island the player characters have stumbled upon the half eaten carcass of a niño muerto (see page 86). The ground has been torn up in some sort of struggle, and any native or frontiersmen characters might notice signs of a land lizard (MG 175) attack. Maybe the players even witnessed the kill, and are now watching the large amphibian consume its prey from the safety of the undergrowth. Just as those characters with experience in the outback realize what is about to happen, the moderator should have the remainder of the dead niño's troop show up, enraged by the smell of their bloody packmate. The players suddenly find themselves caught between two of the deadliest terrestrial predators on the planet—one angered in defense of its food, and the other an encircling pack of arboreal killers defending their territory. This encounter is about as deadly as they get and a moderator should make sure his player's characters are well armed (or expendable) if he decides to throw this one at them. Alternatively, perhaps the niños and lizard are so intent on each other that they can

spare only a cursory attack or two for the characters.

LOVE IS IN THE AIR

Alex's ribbonsquid is a newly observed species, from six to eight meters in length. The ribbonsquid exhibits long migration patterns, and researchers are eager for samples. Natives are known to prepare a variety of medicines from the occasional ribbonsquid catch, so several Incorporates have prepared teams to investigate.

The species is sexually dimorphic. The female has very short arms, tucked in two flat structures on the posterior end. Unfortunately, with her tentacles retracted, the female resembles a dolphin, in shape, color, and other cues.

Characters are most likely to encounter Alex's ribbonsquid during mating season, when the animals move through continental shallows. Dolphins investigating a ribbonsquid migration are likely to be the unhappy recipients of courtship and contact with gangs of eager cephalopods. Territorial males will attack other characters.

Enterprising and brave dolphins may endure the indignity and risk possible harm for the opportunity to take samples and observe ribbonsquid behavior close up.

ONE SNOWY EVENING

Along the eastern edge of the Pacifica Archipelago, currents send nutrient-rich waters out into the deep ocean. Agriculture, prospecting, and research bring many people to the area. A common problem is generally referred to as "snowfall."

Snowfall originates within the seas around the major landmasses. Storms kick up massive amounts of nutrients and rip biota free from shallow waters. As these nutrients and detritus travel west, large numbers of other animals and plants grow in the rich waters, causing a bloom. This current is generally driven downward—by friction, winds, and freshwater—to spill off the eastern edge of the continental shelves. Once the waters drop below the photic layer, the environment shifts and cools rapidly. This bloom becomes an opaque mess, occluding waters throughout the area, becoming turbidity currents when they hit the abyssal plain.

Closer to the surface, this debris can be harmful to cetaceans, due to parasites and infection. The blooms also cause difficulty with sonar, though this is not due to the organic material. Snowfall is accompanied by light, less salinated warm water. Thermoclines can become layered and turbulent, creating noise. Sonar and communications can be disrupted by the effect.

Snowfall is considered beautiful by some, and provides vital nutrients to a large number of benthic animals. Some have considered the use of these blooms in agriculture, drawing nutrients and organic material from the water during the snowfalls. No economic method to harvest these blooms has yet been invented.

PHEROMONES

A rather large number of Hydrospan watercraft have disappeared in the southern waters of the Zion Islands, particularly between Boa Vista and Navajo. Other than frantic calls about being attacked by "clouds," there is no clear evidence of what is causing these disappearances. Part of one craft containing a transponder has been found, the craft having evidently suffered a major impact.

The biggest problem is that this region is a major traffic route. Many vessels travel westward along the southern edge of the Poseidon Antilles, moving through the gap between Boa Vista and Navajo, and then north-northeast to New Jamaica. It would cost Hydrospan a great deal to avoid the route.

Hydrospan is obviously concerned. Security personnel wonder whether the disappearances are the result of actions by rival Incorporate states, ecoterrorists, violent natives, or aborigines. Other vessels have moved through the danger zone with no problem—only Hydrospan watercraft have been targets. Security has put some observation drones in the area, but these have limited coverage. Hydrospan is unused to being targeted by such attacks and will pay handsomely for a resolution of the problem.

The culprit is actually a natural one. A migration and breeding season has begun for several species of fish, eduropods, sponges, and a type of airborne insect that dives for plankton in the waters near reefs. The Caribe Reef nearby is bristling with activity, with huge numbers of sponges covering the reef, eduropods gathering in great numbers,

fish gorging themselves on them, and stone snakes feeding on all the others.

The problem is that a new quick-drying paint, developed by Hydrospan and currently used on their newest line of vessels, contains a chemical that resembles a trigger for eduropod mating. As a Hydrospan vessel moves near the reef, it attracts a growing number of eduropods, followed by fish and stone snakes. The water is soon teaming, the air filled with insectoids feeding on eduropods, and birds swarming to feed on the insects. An ecosystem in miniature tightens around the watercraft. This is frightening and distracting, but the danger is in the greater whites that follow these concentrations. The greater whites emerge from the depths and swallow gaping mouthfuls of the abundant organisms, and they've been gulping down the watercraft as well.

POLYPLUG

This encounter could be dangerous depending how it plays out, so moderators should be prepared. The characters are about to weigh anchor after spending a couple days in a quiet bay or moored near a sheltered reef. When the helmsman goes to start the MHD drive (PG 158), warning indicators report a blockage in the vessel's drive tube. Reversing the flow does not eject the plug, and no other such maneuvering seems to clear the problem. When someone goes over the side to investigate, he comes face-to-face with an adult polypod (MG 180) that has taken refuge inside the drive tube. Apparently thinking the tube was a cave or a ready spot from which to stage an ambush, the creature now feels threatened and is likely to attack. Assuming the diver survives this first encounter, he and his shipmates should have an interesting time trying to figure out how to get rid of their aquatic stowaway without damaging their boat or themselves.

SEX GLUE

There are many reefs capped by pseudo-coral. They are not true corals, and are not eduropods. Although they are animals, they have unusual similarities to fungi. At a certain point of their breeding cycle, many of these species are stimulated by exposure to freshwater, generally in the form of rain. They respond to the freshwater by releasing huge numbers of gametes and a slimy substance that pours along the reef, fertilizing other pseudo-coral. This fluid can cause trouble for nearby animals, choking fish and other large chordates.

Frequently, other fish and animals are attracted when the fluid is released, waiting out of the deadly range. Plankton feed on the unused fluid, and the food chain receives a brief boost.

Characters working on or near reefs may be subjected to this unusual environmental encounter. During a rainstorm, the characters will notice the water becoming increasingly cloudy. The material will accrete to the surfaces of all submerged objects, and clog intakes. Flippers or arms will be coated, becoming gummy, and stick together. Gills will become choked. All physical actions in the water will suffer a -1 penalty per fifteen minutes, with a maximum penalty of -4. Gills will become inoperable, requiring aquaforms to immediately leave the water. The water more than 200 meters from the reef will be uncontaminated by the substance. The production only lasts 1-2 hours, after which the fluid disperses.

SLIME SHOWERS

This unpleasant phenomenon is particularly common to subtropical regions. Under certain condi-tions, sargassum islands gathered in thick numbers will pollinate in sequence. Massive amounts of pollen fill the air, and soon mix with water. Slick brownish green rain soon falls, coating ship decks, coastline, and unlucky people with the slippery substance.

STINGING IN THE RAIN

A blustery, nighttime storm has blown a group of blimps (MG 164) ashore where they have hung up on the surrounding terrain. Their tentacles are stuck in trees, tangled in vegetation, wedged between rocks, and draped thickly over the charac-ters' hut, tent, or jumpcraft. When they awake, they are confronted with a sticky barricade of proto-plasm and stinging cells that takes time and inge-nuity to get through. The tentacles are soft and gooey, and cutting them is akin to pushing on a rope. Even when detached from the main body, the severed bits still sting and are difficult to clear away. To add an additional element of confusion and surprise, combine this encounter with the events in "Digging in the Dirt" above, then sit back and watch the fun.

STORM CHILDREN

A rare species related to the ghoster lives in the Storm Belt on the open ocean. The organism forms large mats that float along the water and can sink to variable depths to avoid the worst storms. These organisms, known as storm children by local natives, have also evolved a unique method of feeding. During a storm, the organism forms a cone shape, dispersing in a wide ring and forming a deep concentration of filaments. These filaments create a potential that attracts lightning. When lightning strikes the center of the storm child, biological inductance taps and rapidly stores large amounts of energy. After the strike, the colony repairs whatev-er damage has been done and rapidly metabolizes the energy into useable forms.

Travelers trapped in a storm at sea may blunder into a storm children colony. To those few who are familiar with the creatures, the faintly glowing rings offer a warning that lightning will strike near-by. Researchers of storm children may face great danger during storms, and the safest approach is to submerge until the danger has passed.

SUNBURST ATTACK

Tourists and researchers near Westscape have reported distressing news. Small groups of sun-bursts have attacked children and isolated individ-uals, ganging up on them and dragging them into the depths. The sunbursts then batter their victims to death. The usual rumors abound, and officials in Dyfedd are concerned about the impact on tourism in the area.

It is mating season for the caneopoise, and small bands of juvenile sunbursts are in a hyperaggres-sive state. They are too young to attract mates, so they practice their dominance behavior on any small animals that get in their way. The solution is simply to identify the behavior and the timing, and issue proper advisories.

THE DOLPHIBAT AND BARNACLE MULE

One of the problems with classifying and identify-ing life on Poseidon is that most observers are untrained, undisciplined, and often untrustworthy. Particularly among the native community, there are a large number of animals described that most sci-entist suspect are pure invention. The problem is, of course, that truth is often stranger than fiction. Absurd animals have been found on Earth through-out history, the platypus being just one well-known example.

Sometimes scientists are the brunt of jokes. Two popular and probably invented life forms are the dolphibat and the barnacle mule.

The dolphibat is supposedly a fusiform animal with long batwings. Though some scientists have speculated that it could be a relative of the eel dragon, the lack of any physical or recorded evidence leads most biologists to assume it to be a native tall tale.

The barnacle mule is a large, rubber shrimp-like animal that dwells in the coastal marshes. Six legs radiate from the center, reaching out to pull up nearby underbrush. When the underbrush is stripped bare, it everts and lumbers to a new location, and then folds back up. Natives claim barnacle mules are used as pack animals. Though this sort of animal is plausible for Poseidon, there is no evidence that they exist. When pressed, natives claim that they do not use barnacle mules, but other natives in neighboring islands do.

The pursuit of cryptozoology is alive and well on Poseidon. With so many animals to identify and classify, sifting through stories and accounts becomes important. Part biology and part psychology, understanding perception and how stories evolve gives scientists important clues when using untrained but eager observers.

Player characters can expect rewards from a variety of interested parties for verified animals. Sifting through stories and accounts may be a bit tedious, but the fieldwork involved can keep players very busy.

THE POWER OF MANY

The articulated rook is a relative of the night crawler found only on some of the smaller islands of Poseidon. It is diurnal and bears some resemblance to a squat castle tower. Weighing in at 10 kilograms, the articulated rook is known to scientists as a solitary scavenger and opportunistic predator in reef and island shallows ecosystems. What is unknown, however, is that its behavior shifts dramatically during the migration of other amphibious and aquatic species.

During these periods, the rook is social and hunts the shores in packs. One or two will frighten or bully their prey. Animals that are more aggressive are baited. Whether pushing the animal or being chased, the rooks lead the animal to the shore, where up to 20 more of the animals lurk in ambush. The group attacks en masse. They are often successful and quickly carve up the prey, passing pieces of the carcass to the females. The females,

in turn, carry the pieces to above-water lairs and crevasses. Rooks will also attack animals in the water, but only in shallows. During migration, rooks can eat huge numbers of passing sunbursts, land lizards, and other surprisingly large animals.

When hunting humans, the lead rooks will first see if the humans are interested in chasing them. If not, they will wave their claws and nip at the humans, to frighten them toward the water. A human can try to avoid them, but must be alert and quick. The problem is that many of these islands are small, and there may be numerous hunting packs ringing the island. Cetaceans are less likely to be attacked, but may be ambushed by the entire group if their territory in the shallows is approached.

A number of explorers and researchers have vanished over the past few years. Though some remains and equipment have been discovered, the nature of the attacks is a mystery. There is a pattern to the disappearances that requires some research to understand. The location of the attacks and the timing of sunburst and other migrations might also give a hint. Discovering, and surviving, the social nature of the articulated rook may be worth some fame and money to researchers.

THE TROUBLE WITH TOWELS

The creeping towel is an organism unique to Port-Au-Prince, with a flat body up to 50cm long and only a few centimeters thick. It forms a velvety sheet, covered with small tendrils on the underside. Crawling through shaded forest undergrowth and marshy regions, its small feet pick up moisture and decaying organic material. It has yet to be classified, though it has tentatively been placed in Laxopeda.

Inhabitants of the region have discovered several amusing uses of the towel. As its name suggests, it can be used to dry off after a swim. Its feet will also consume hair and a thin layer of epidermis, so that it functions like a shaver and exfoliation device. The animals keep themselves particularly clean, if kept in proper conditions, and exude natural antibiotics. Natives have used these animals to debride wounds and collect the antibiotic exudations for medicines. Small populations of the towels have been exported to neighboring native settlements. Towels require a great deal of care but do fairly well in captivity. All attempts to transplant them to other regions have failed, however.

In the last year, rumors of severe allergic reactions and carnivorous towels have caused a scare, accompanied by several disappearances. Scientists have theorized that annual variations may have caused a shift in behavior or morphology. GEO and Incorporate states have restricted exports of the organisms and confiscated them from private owners. Natives have shunned inquiries.

The truth is that someone at Hanover Industries is interested in cultivating the organism. Several early reports from Hanover researchers indicated that portions of the creeping towel have amazing antibiotic and regenerative properties. Julia Pohl, a low-ranking Hanover executive, has intercepted these reports, and has concocted a plan to further her career. She has pulled in favors, creating an effort to secure the resource of creeping towels for further research. The stories about the dangers of these organisms are intended to discourage their trade and other potential researchers, though this method may backfire on her. Ms. Pohl plans on heading a team in Port-Au-Prince to do further research into the towels.

GenDiver will eventually learn of the scheme and seek to interfere or take the resource for themselves. Other groups may also become involved. The effect this will have on the characters depends on their affiliations.

Ultimately, the reports on the towels turn out to be without merit. The towels have a robust ability to regenerate their own tissue, but this has no useful application. The antiseptic properties of towels are relatively mild, compared to what Hanover has already developed.

TUG BOAT

The player characters are crew or passengers on a boat in this encounter. Maybe it is a research or commercial fishing vessel. Maybe the crew has a long anchor line, solar blanket (FM 39), fishing net, or perhaps an ROV (PG 141) in the water. The encounter begins when a large animal, maybe a lesser white (see page 85) or a leviathan (see page 83), gets entangled in the line or swallows the submerged equipment. The cable snaps taut, and the boat is dragged in circles as the creature tries to escape. Maybe the stern of the boat is pulled under a few times as the animal dives, water washing over the deck. If the cables are too strong, the crew must race to cut the equipment loose or risk sinking. Perhaps the entangled animal breaches the surface and threatens the boat, or maybe it stays below, a frightening, inexorable mystery that refuses to show itself. The encounter could end with the connecting lines snapping, the creature attacking in self-defense, or with the boat being pulled under. However it goes down, the encounter should be played as a frantic emergency that requires quick thinking and fast action on the part of the characters.

UNLIKELY THREATS

One of the most ignoble ways to lose an aircraft is to be taken down by a bird. A tradition dating to the beginning of flight, birds have always represented a deadly inconvenience to pilots. Though modern aircraft are durable, an avian traveling at sufficient speed can cause considerable damage to a windshield or, at the least, reduce visibility. More severe damage occurs to jet air intakes or turbofans.

This does not occur particularly often, but the situation is exacerbated by migration patterns. In regions with large seasonal shifts, insect populations often boom. In some places, the air can become opaque, thick with millions of small insects. The danger to pilots is in the huge numbers of birds that gather to feast on them. When these smoky shapes form, pilots are advised to steer well clear.

Aircraft are also occasionally forced to fly through migrating flocks. At the speed many aircraft travel, there is often little opportunity to detect the flock early enough to avoid it.

Low-flying aircraft often travel much more slowly. This gives the aircraft more opportunity to detect possible collisions, but also increases the number of potential targets. Eel dragons and blimps are both rather low-flying animals.

SAVAGE PLANET

CHAPTER

02

POSEIDON TAXONOMY

**Haven Institute of Science and Technology
Department of Xenobiology
Dr. Antonina Dyson, PhD, presiding chair**

In memoriam, Dr. Fredrick Glasser, Tomas Aguillar, Sharon Cade, Maria Aguillar, David Gold, and Paul Smith

My colleagues have honored me with the opportunity to open this year's Haven Institute of Science and Technology's *Journal of Poseidon Studies*. I am quite proud to be a part of the efforts of my peers and our wonderful students in making this a banner year. Each day that passes adds immeasurably to the store of our knowledge.

With the public interest shown in past journals, this year brings a new design. The main journal is presented here as prepared excerpts from the 34 articles. Interested parties can read the full entries as desired. In this way, the main journal can be perused quickly, and more technically versed readers can then refer to the full 548-page journal.

I open this year's work with an excerpt from my own paper, written with the invaluable help of my students Kenneth Ho and Rutger Harris.

POSEIDON TAXONOMY

Excerpts from *2199: Results of the 4th Annual HIST Xenobiological Taxonomy Committee*, by Dr. Antonina Dyson, PhD, with Kenneth Ho and Rutger Harris

The goal of creating a coherent taxonomic classification for Poseidon has always been hampered by several major obstacles. The first is a paucity of information about life on Poseidon. The second is an almost absolute lack of information about the paleohistory of Poseidon. On Earth, fossil finds are critical in connecting and understanding the development of classifications, and in understanding how classifications developed over Earth paleohistory. There is a lamentable absence of fossil evidence available for Poseidon.

These obstacles are somewhat understandable. Classification of life on Earth has, to a large extent, been founded on the work of large numbers of people over many centuries of sampling, examination, and exploration of Earth's ecosystems.

During the time of the initial colonists, the lack of luxury and very few numbers meant that observations were limited. Even the last 40 years of expanding population and technology have made modest inroads, compared to what has typically been available on Earth.

Some obstacles are less understandable. Gathering samples, information, and, in particular, fossils are very low priorities for most exploratory groups on Poseidon. Their focus is typically on the immediate potential use of geological or biological specimens. This is a shortsighted attitude.

The most sweeping understanding of life on Poseidon will only come by researching how the ecosystems of Poseidon came about and interact, as well as the structure and development of organisms within these systems. This understanding will do more to help civilization on Poseidon than any amount of blinkered inquiry.

There are other difficulties with developing a taxonomy for life on Poseidon. Common names have always been a problem. It is understandable for people to relate animals or plants to those they are familiar with, but such names are misleading. This is a relatively benign version of a more significant problem.

The problem endemic to taxonomy on Poseidon is that of similarity. The traditional attempt among biologists has been to classify organisms of Poseidon according to definitions established for life on Earth. This approach has grown mired in what now seem insurmountable difficulties. Life on Poseidon evolved in similar ways to that on Earth, due to similar conditions and forces. Ultimately, however, the nature of simple random chance must logically result in a distinct and unique path of development. Attempting to fit one categorization to another is doomed to fail, as is the pursuit of a common classification that fits both planets.

This is not to say that Earth taxonomy must be abandoned completely. Analogous structures and morphology can communicate a great deal about how life on Poseidon evolved and is grouped, based on the knowledge of how such forms evolved on Earth. Similar terms are used to denote

these parallels. It is our responsibility, as scientists, to avoid being misled by them.

Consider digger crabs. They bear many striking similarities to crustaceans on Earth. It is usually assumed that they are related to other crustacean-like Poseidon animals, and all of the same class.

There are a number of species that have been identified, tentatively, as pseudo-crinoid. These animals, most notably the scarlet Kauai frond crab, show characteristics of both crinoids and crustaceans. Genetic studies compellingly support the placement of pseudo-crinoids and crustaceans in the same phylum. This is a large difference from the taxonomy of Earth, where crinoids are more closely related to humans than to crabs.

The common reaction has been to argue that some part of these studies is flawed. One common argument claims that the frond crab is simply an arthropod with traits that happen to resemble crinoid traits, and that there is no crinoid-crustacea connection. The frond crab is not a crustacean, necessarily, but belongs to some group within Arthropoda that bears superficial similarities to crinoids.

This problem is mostly caused by comparative terms. The arthropods of Poseidon are fairly analogous to those of Earth, but there are consistent and characteristic differences. As with Earth biology, then, it becomes a delicate judgment of exactly where the lines and groupings should go.

Part of the mandate of the xenobiology department has been to make these determinations. There is considerable argument, of course, but great advances have been made at identifying useful and defensible groupings of Poseidon biota. There necessarily remain a great number of "island" classifications, where lack of information, fossil evidence, or related specimens cannot justify determination of groupings.

Some have argued that completely new terms should be generated to avoid confusion. Precedent and functional similarities have maintained the use of analogous terms. Many classifications, particularly in genus or species, retain *simila*. Other classifications have simply used the same terms. One development has been to append a subscript 'p' or 'e' to denote organisms from Poseidon or Earth,

particularly in papers relating organisms from both planets.

Taxonomic classifications of organisms on Earth are readily accessible through CommCore and may be used as a reference.

POSEIDON MACRO-TAXONOMY

Note that most connections and statements about the history of life on Poseidon are rather theoretical, and much empirical work needs to be done. Indications of uncertainty will be restricted to relationships that are particularly speculative.

EUKARYOTES

This classification encompasses all nucleated life. As with Earth, Poseidon Eukaryotes account for nearly all macroscopic life. It is assumed that Eukaryotes evolved in a similar way on Poseidon, though there is no supporting fossil evidence.

One macroscopic prokaryotic example is the tidal muds reefs. Composed of possibly several kingdoms resembling cyanobacteria, they form a visible reef structure throughout Poseidon. They likely represent a surviving vestige of ancestral bacterial mats.

KINGDOMS

Below this level, Poseidon life is divided much like that of Earth. Animals, fungi, several types of algae and plant microbes, plants, and a wide variety of protists form separate kingdoms. Earth fungi and animals are more closely related than other kingdoms, but it is not clear if this is also true on Poseidon.

Among possible other kingdoms may be a group containing the Howell's leech and another containing the harvester worm. The ghoster forms yet another kingdom, with a debated relationship to fungi. A crossover kingdom covering species bearing characteristics of both plants and animals has also been proposed.

PHYLA OF THE ANIMAL KINGDOM
Porifera

Porifera (or "pore bearing") include sponges of a wide variety. They show a greater diversity on Poseidon than on Earth. A number of encrusting sponges have complex relationships with reef production beyond their analogs on Earth. Several freestanding orders use water propulsion to migrate or disperse young.

Cnidaria

On Earth, this phylum consists of sea anemones, corals, jellyfish, sea pens, and hydra. Defined as having stinging cells (nemocytes), cnidarians consist of two cell layers (epidermis and endodermis) connected by the mesoglea, the "jelly" that serves as a glue for the vast bulk of the animal. Cnidarians are exclusively carnivorous, though the degree to which they actively hunt or passively ingest food varies.

On Poseidon, there is a well-defined phylum that resembles cnidarians to a large extent. Developmental changes are rather different, but most of the observed traits of Earth cnidarians apply to those on Poseidon. Most Earth orders have analogs on Poseidon.

Blimps are the most famous example of cnidarians on Poseidon. Corals are a ubiquitous and important part of Poseidon ecology.

Eduropoda (Arthropoda)

Arthropods cover a variety of invertebrate animals with a segmented body, jointed appendages, a frequently chitinous exoskeleton molted at intervals, and a dorsal anterior brain connected to a ventral chain of ganglia. On Earth, arthropods include such notable Classes as insects, arachnids, and crustaceans.

On Poseidon, the situation is a bit more complex and less clear. Arthropoda of Poseidon share several strong characteristics with Echinodermata of Earth. In addition, Eduropods seem to be more closely related to pseudo-chordates on Poseidon than the analogous phyla of Earth.

These differences have resulted in a renaming of the phylum as Eduropoda, to discourage confusion. Eduropoda have the following characteristics:

A water vascular system, similar to Echinodermata. There are gill structures and other advanced organs in many Eduropods, but it is thought that these evolved from pseudo-tubefeet in ancient forms. This water vascular system extends throughout Eduropods, and their digestive and respiratory systems are not as specialized or complex as arthropods of Earth. This is less true of Class

Insecta of Poseidon, which has more distinct respiratory and digestive systems.

The digestive system has a slight radial structure that does not strongly resemble either Arthropods or Echinodermata. Many details of this structure are still not completely understood.

Eduropoda skeletal structure is somewhat variable. Generally forming from "seeds" in a series of spiral scales, these usually grow into sheets that bind and harden or form segments. Most Eduropods form exterior chitinous scales, but the Cristatoids (pseudo-Crinoids) develop flesh over thick sheaves of scales, which share many of the same functions as an internal skeleton. Ligaments allow Eduropods to form variably rigid structures. In some, these ligaments form a major part of the rigid structure of the animal.

Eduropods are bilaterally symmetrical, with sometimes-considerable irregularity. Among the Cristatoids in particular, this symmetry is frequently missed, with limbs extending in many directions.

Eduropods have two sexes, and a frequently pronounced sexual dimorphism.

The Eduropod nervous system is rather like that of Arthropods, with ganglial structures and a brain.

Eduropoda consists of Insecta, Crustacea (including the notable Genera of Cancersimila, pseudo-crabs), and Cristatoids (pseudo-crinoids). A large number of animals have been included in this phylum, but Class divisions are still often unclear. Insects, in particular, seem to be divided into a number of distinct groups. The well-known Poseidon scorpion is part of a small group of quadrupedal insects. There is also an important group of insectoids with a pseudo-radial symmetry. The rubber shrimp has been categorized as Cristatoid.

Mollusca

Poseidon mollusca share a number of similarities with those of Earth. They are invertebrates, soft, and some have calcareous shells. On Earth, mollusks include clams (bivalvia), snails (gastropoda), and squid (cephalopods).

Analogs to these groups are also present on Poseidon, along with analogs of extinct trivalves.

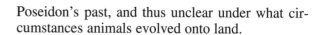

Most of the characteristics are parallel. Poseidon mollusks have two sexes, but frequently produce young by budding.

Reefworms are now thought to be Mollusca and have been placed in their own class, Gracilid.

Squirts are Mollusca. Initially grouped with polypods as Poseidon "pseudo-cephalopods" (now simply cephalopods), there is some evidence that they may be more closely related to reefworms and are thus categorized as Gracilid.

Chordata

Chordates (animals with backbones) seem to have developed similarly on Poseidon, although their relationships with other phyla are quite different. Earth chordates are closely related to echinoderms and arose from a variety of worms. It is believed that Poseidon chordates evolved from proto-arthropods. One sign of this is that chordates are all hexapedal in structure, a trait common to many eduropods. Jaws evolved early in the development of Poseidon chordates, much earlier than similar developments on Earth. The stone worm, one of the few representatives of an ancient phylum, is related to the roots of both Eduropods and Chordates.

Chordates on Poseidon developed as a radiation from an unknown Eduropod form. A centralized nervous system developed from the ganglial system, and the seed-scale system was fully internalized. Instead of chitin, ligaments and collagen provide most of the structural materials, with calcareous growth of bone. The vascular system has evolved into more specialized systems, and bilateral symmetry is a rigorous norm amongst most chordates.

The fish of Poseidon show a number of distinct traits that betray their Eduropod relationship. The skeleton shows a slight knobbiness, compared to Earth fish. This is caused by a seeding growth pattern of the skeleton. The surface scales, too, are chitinous in at least two observed species. The development of fishes on Poseidon is uncertain. Whether there was an age of bony fishes and parallel developments will depend on an adequate fossil record.

The development of land animals on Poseidon is a matter of considerable debate. It is unclear how much land was exposed at various periods in Poseidon's past, and thus unclear under what circumstances animals evolved onto land.

Most land chordates are amphibious to some degree, representing a wide variety of orders. Many of these forms have evolved land characteristics and shed them. The water rat, for example, shows signs of having evolved on land, having adapted for a purely aquatic life, and then evolved for a more purely land habitat. At one point some researches even placed water rats and schoolers into the same order, but recent evidence disputes this.

Chordates on Poseidon are of particular interest and have received more research than other phyla.

Notable Classes of Chordata

Piscisimilis (fish-like): This class comprises all of the known fish of Poseidon. There are a number of identified orders, including a rather young order that includes trident fish.

Caudata (tailed): Analogs of salamanders and newts. A variety of legged and legless amphibians are grouped as pseudo-salamanders, including the hellbender. The eel dragon has tentatively been placed in this Order. Evidence suggests that Poseidon caudates have adapted a great deal more than their analogs on Earth, and have more complex structures. They are closely related to Draconodonta.

Luteupods (muddy feet): This order is unique to Poseidon. It consists of thin-toed amphibians common to mangrove forests. This group is considered more ancestral than the caudates.

Arbutida (fruit-like): Another unique order, these amphibians have adopted an almost sessile existence, functioning much like oceanic passive feeders. Their mobility is often tied to diurnal or seasonal cycles. They inhabit a wide variety of ecosystems, from wet rainforest undergrowth to the shallows of lagoons. A few forms are known to spend most of their day-to-day existence in trees, coming to water only to breed.

Draconodonta (dragontoothed): These amphibians closely resemble reptiles of Earth. It is thought that this group represents the ancestors of Poseidon mammals. The discovery of the prow-beaked fisher near the Midway Islands late last year has caused some debate, it being a reptiloid with a fused, bony jaw. Some think the fisher should be placed with pseudo-avians. Others believe that they are part of a transitional order. In any case, draconodonts are close analogs of reptiles, though closely related to their caudate roots.

Chelonia: Analogs of turtles have rarely been observed. They are primarily represented by the loggerhead, and perhaps the weedeater (see page 101), though this is the subject of some debate.

Aves: Avians represent a small but robust class. Whether there was an age of reptiles remains unclear, but avian-like species dominate the air throughout Poseidon. Most are amphibious, at least to the extent of diving for food. Warm-blooded like mammals, avians typically retain claws on their wings, and many lay their eggs in marshy or damp environments. Like amphibians, they require a wet habitat to fertilize eggs, though many species have adapted a calcareous shell that develops after fertilization. Unusually, the structure of Poseidon avian feathers is constructed of a chitin-like substance.

Mammalia: The mammal analogs of Poseidon share important characteristics that identify them as such. Hairy and warm-blooded, Poseidon mammals are divided into many diverse groups, and are a very successful development.

Orders of Mammalia
Oviforma are egg bearing and include water rats.

Bimaxilla are marsupials and, rare amongst chordates, have two functioning mandibles. The side jaws are fused with the top jaw. Most also have an atrophied or absorbed pair of limbs. This order seems more consistently land-based and is not particularly numerous. It is likely that a larger percentage of Poseidon's land area was exposed at various times during the past, and that bimaxilla represents an order that was once common, specialized for land existence. As ocean levels began to rise, bimaxilla species were unable to adapt into sufficiently competitive forms.

Trianellida are also marsupials, but otherwise very similar to oviforma. They give birth to live young that crawl into a series of small pockets. One characteristic morphology of trianellidae is the heart's peculiar three-ringed structure. Hexa boar are members of this order.

Placentae are placental mammals, giving birth to live young. The mechanism is a bit different in many placentae, and some believe the order should be subdivided. In some placental mammals, such as the sunburst, eggs are fertilized internally. The egg expands, becoming more permeable, and then forms into a membrane much like a placenta.

Geminida are an unusual form of mammal, not closely analogous to those of Earth. They share some close features with the draconodonts, including both scales and fur. The mother forms an elaborate bank of internal cells, genetically identical to herself. These are absorbed and become part of the structure of the young, allowing short gestation times and live young. The offspring, for a few months, still has many cells that are genetic clones of the mother. As the young grows rapidly, the cells are absorbed and by the first year there is no trace of the original cellular material.

Catenida
This phylum includes stone worms. These animals are characterized by fully functional lungs, warm blood, and numerous individualized segments. Some researches believe that early forms of catenids developed from eduropods and then radiated into chordates.

Laxopoda
This is a strange group of animals found among coral reefs. There are some similarities to cnidarians and echinodermata.

A small, radial body connects many long, thin arms. The arms have a calcareous structure composed of loosely connected spines. With an open vascular structure, the arms function almost as separate animals, processing their own food and wastes. The structure of the flesh is very simple, composed of two layers like a cnidarian. The skeletal spines form as inclusions from nodules on the exterior into the connective layer. Channels resembling very primitive tubefeet often line the arms.

The arms are loose, and can become separated due to stress, predation, or possibly as part of reproduction. If the arm comes to rest in appropriate surroundings, one end will thicken and the arm will shrink, soon to be joined by new arms. Most laxopods are no more than a few centimeters long, and most observed genera form symbiotic relationships with bacteria or algae.

Arthrocepha

This phylum consists of common animals unique to Poseidon. Also known as "pseudo-corals," they caused much confusion until classified properly in 2197. Though they superficially resemble eduropods, their development is quite different. Very simple radial organisms, they seem to be an ancient group. They have several unusual characteristics that are reminiscent of fungi, such as indistinct cell boundaries.

From a casual inspection, however, they share many of the same niches as marine eduropods. The best observed is the pseudo-coral, which builds large calcareous reef structures. Though some reefs have both coral and pseudo-coral, there are no purely arthroceph reefs. There are indications of some free-swimming orders, and several types of mite-like animals found on both sargassum islands and rainforest are plausibly linked to this phylum.

These are distinct from the tidal muds reef organisms, which are a completely separate type of reef-building life.

PHYLA OF THE PLANT KINGDOM
Zygnematales

Very similar to the zygnematales of Earth, these include the most prolific green algae. The name comes from their reproduction, which is sexual and involves meiosis of a zygote. Unlike zygnematales of Earth, the gametes and sometimes the adult forms of these algae are flagellate (has a whip-tail).

Zygnematales includes Poseidon kelp and sargassum.

Prolifera

This order includes a wide variety of bushy seaplants with a simple, wort-like structure and long, thin fronds, frequently with a reddish-black coloration. Some have placed prolifera in their own kingdom.

Embryophytes

This is the core group of vascularized, photosynthetic plants. The name comes from the analogous phylum on Earth. These plants form embryo, and include seed-bearing plants (flowering and conifers), wort-like plants, and fern-like groups.

This group has gone through developments unique to Poseidon. Several orders are noted for carnivorous behavior and motility. Some genetic evidence suggests that the canyonlands, and the orders found there, form a major part of the development of embryophytes.

Water hemp and Poseidon mangrove are two examples of this phylum.

Xanthophytes

This is a distinct group of orange or yellow plants, noted for a bulbous or smooth appearance. These plants are unrelated to the xanthophytes of Earth. Two orders of xanthophytes have been discovered, Terelida and Limuphila. The Terelida is only represented by four known species. Each is a small land plant found on a few tropical islands, collectively known as ground lemons. Limuphila is more diverse, and is found in tidal muds reefs.

PHYLA OF THE GEMMAPHYTE KINGDOM

This is a small but significant kingdom. It is represented by a variety of algae, some of which strongly resemble diatoms. Many species have been found in symbiotic relationships with tidal muds reef organisms. Silicified shells or skeletons are common to many orders of Gemmaphyte. Some colonial varieties of these algae seem to use prisms of silicon as a component of their photosynthesis.

PHYLA OF THE FUNGAL KINGDOM

This kingdom remains rather enigmatic to mycologists. Phyla have not been dependably identified. One well-known fungus, the so-called "fast fungus," shows some similarity to slime molds in reproduction and structure. Fruiting bodies have been more difficult to identify among fungi of Poseidon, compared to those of Earth.

Fungi have been identified in mangrove forests and throughout Poseidon's island landmasses. The place of fungi in connecting plant species is harder to identify on Poseidon, as there are several widespread groups of colonial bacteria and protists that seem to serve as connective systems between plant species.

TAXONOMIC DIVERSITY

Organisms on Poseidon are roughly divided into two evolutionarily distant groups. This is similar to the division of life on Earth into Old World and New World varieties. On both planets, geographical isolation led to different evolutionary paths. The groups of Earth do not correspond to those of Poseidon, beyond this similar circumstance of isolation.

The Prime group, also known as Type I, covers the Pacifica Archipelago. The Darwin group, also known as Type II, covers Darwin's Archipelago, the Arc of Fire, and Endeavor Islands. The Tier-Humboldt line runs along 32° east longitude. Islands to the east are Type II and those to the west are Type I. The Camber line runs roughly along 80° west longitude, and divides the Type I region to the east from Type II islands to the west.

The Southern Hope Chain forms a distinct developmental region. Its connection to the others is still murky. Some have placed it within the Prime group, but this classification has been well disputed (Yi Anderson 2195, 2199, in preparation). There are Type I and Type II transplants in this region, but the origins of many are unclear, as is the direction of transmission.

Within these groups, particularly the Darwin group, there is a larger amount of regionalized taxonomy than found on Earth. The Challenger Deep,

Endeavor Islands, Darwin's Archipelago, and Arc of Fire each represent distinct groups of biota.

ANIMAL BEHAVIOR

Animal Behavior, Theory and Practice
by Mort B, graduate student of Evolutionary Behavior under Dr. Theodore Glassman

Animals have always posed a difficulty for humans. We share our world with them, and in ages past, depended on them for our survival. But we rarely understand them. Learning about the factors that affect and influence animals and animal development can help in understanding why they behave as they do.

There are reasons for animal behavior, and these are generally couched in evolutionary terms. Behaviors that endanger an animal's ability to reproduce are selected against, while helpful behaviors are selected for. These two forces form the bedrock of animal behavior. The great importance of passing on genes motivates elaborate mating ritual, dominance, and altruistic behavior.

Beyond these programmed strategies, animals exhibit a flexible and seemingly capricious individuality. Animals adapted to narrow niches and environments have a more limited reaction than those developed to forage in or adapt to many environments. Adaptable animals will change in response to variable environments, forming distinct personalities.

Evolution is the silent master. Strategies balance resources. Large animals move further and are more protected than small animals, but fewer can inhabit a given region. Elaborate sexual structures come at high metabolic cost, but can exert considerable pressure toward evolving more robust or successful forms.

Ultimately a certain level of unpredictability is inevitable, as organisms respond to a vast number of stimuli that cannot easily be identified. An animal's behavior may shift due to the time of day, year, odors, or many other factors.

However, there are some basic rules.

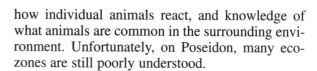

Animals protect themselves, protect their resources (territory), and protect their young. The order of importance varies between species and in response to variables. Some fish have nests where eggs are kept, and will vigorously defend these nests. Others spawn and then let the eggs fend for themselves. The shredded redfish, found in tidal temperate waters, drives out other fish from nesting areas but shows no particular inclination to attack crawling animals, even if they are clearly consuming the eggs.

More intelligent animals may sacrifice their young to save themselves, such as the verdant shrew of Martinique. There is no way to predict this prior to observation, as the delicate scales of evolution, which determine the cost of raising an animal compared to producing young, are invisible. Though it seems sensible that animals that raise a few young would be more protective, this is not always the case.

Simple animals have fairly predictive responses, based on their ability to sense and understand the environment around them. Sessile feeders will react to turbulence by withdrawing. Mobile feeders will hide or flee from large animals that behave, look, or smell like predators.

Herbivores and plankton feeders often exhibit hiding and fleeing tropes. Predators often use a variety of interesting hunting methods to improve their odds. Particularly intelligent predators will evaluate targets, engaging in hunting behavior similar to that of large predators on Earth.

Predation behavior is based on determining a proper target, then enacting the hunt. Quick hunters will often engage in a run and strike to disable the target. Among great cats, this comes in the form of a paw strike, a slash at the throat, or biting down on the throat or nose to suffocate the target. Cooperating hunters, such as niños muertos, frighten prey into tight groups and drive them toward other members. Opportunistic predators, including omnivores, tease and frighten their prey, waiting for a clear opening and only committing when a course is clear.

Danger is the inevitable result of simple statistics. Humans and cetaceans cross many ecozones. Even if 999 in 1,000 animals ignore them, that still leaves a large number of potential encounters. The number one protection is education: knowledge of

how individual animals react, and knowledge of what animals are common in the surrounding environment. Unfortunately, on Poseidon, many ecozones are still poorly understood.

Predators are necessarily rare, compared to omnivores and herbivores. Large lifeforms like humans and cetaceans are likely to be seen as a danger. Actions are likely to be interpreted, correctly or not, as threatening to the animals themselves, to their territory, or to their young. Perceived threats create reactions. Most animals flee or hide, which suits humans and cetaceans just fine. It is common to see fleeing fish or other animals withdrawing into rocky crevasses.

Many dangers are inadvertent. The squealer monkey throws rotting fruit and feces when an interloper invades its territory. The Poseidon scorpion stings only when threatened - such as when the sleeping human it has sought out for body warmth rolls over it in the night. These are perceived threats, and the only solution is for travelers to know the region, be alert, and avoid behaviors that will trigger dangerous responses.

Concealed animals pose the greatest danger. Although a cautious individual can avoid a spiny fish or needle shell, other animals hide from view. The only warning may be the attack itself. The solution is to be careful; avoid close proximity to likely hiding places and familiarize oneself with the animals common to the area one is visiting.

Small parasites are also a particular danger, whether on land or in the water. A number of insects and other animals are adapted to feed on Poseidon mammals, and a significant percentage will also target humans or cetaceans. Unfortunately, differences in biology often cause dangerous reactions.

The most dramatic danger comes from large predators, though these attacks are comparatively rare. There are only three possible responses to predation. If the predator is of similar size to the target, displays of aggression can sometimes cause the predator to back off, particularly if the predator is opportunistic. This is more likely to work if the individual has a size advantage or the advantage of numbers.

If this is not possible, the second best response is fleeing, particularly if the individual can fly and the predator cannot. This is extremely dangerous, as most predators are faster than humans and even common vehicles, and some marine predators are faster swimmers than cetaceans.

The last response, if the others are not viable, is to use deadly force. Note, however, that injuring a predator may only enrage it, and killing the predator may attract the unwelcome attention of other animals.

GAME ENCOUNTERS

Animal attacks can be divided into four types: territorialism, personal defense, parasitism, or predation.

Territorialism is common. Resources are vital to the survival of species, and many have evolved methods of protecting their territory. For sessile feeders and other animals, territory may be constrained enough so that territorialism and personal defense are essentially the same. Since territory is frequently under possible attack, most animals will not engage in deadly force. Territorial behavior usually consists of a series of displays designed to startle, confuse, frighten, or simply to inform.

Territorialism can be found among a large number of animals, particularly vertebrates. Many forms of invertebrates rely on chemical warnings. Though these warnings are more difficult for humans to identify, these animals usually pose little danger.

Characters are most likely to face attacks motivated by territorialism. Territories can cover large areas and are often impossible to identify. Characters must stay alert for warning displays. Even small animals may use poison or cause wounds that can become infected if untreated. There is no way to give such animals an avenue to escape, since the animal is not interested in flight. Characters may be pursued even beyond the normal boundaries of the territory as a way of ensuring that they will not return. Groups of animals may share territories and mob the character with displays or minor attacks. Stick monkeys offer a common example of this kind of behavior.

Personal defense is a common response from animals that feel threatened by a character. An animal may feel threatened by proximity, or only if cornered or touched. Personal defense can take the form of overt attack or startling displays. The best approach in these situations is usually to give the animal an avenue of retreat, to flee or hide. The perceptions of the animal may be limited, and some will not recognize an avenue of flight. Loud noises or forceful gestures may frighten a stubborn animal sufficiently to motivate it to flight.

Personal defense encounters are rather common. In all ecosystems, many animals will interpret large moving animals as threats. Sessile organisms will react with spines or poison, as will many animals that inhabit lairs or nests. Mobile animals are more likely to flee from approaching characters, and encounters motivated by personal defense are therefore less common.

Characters engaged in personal defense encounters can often escape simply by moving away from the threatened animal. Unfortunately, if there is a large group in the area, the character may blunder into more. Organisms that rely on poison for defense often use bright coloration as a warning. Animals that engage in warning displays are the safest, assuming the character perceives and understands the display.

Parasitism is distinct from predation. The character is identified as a food source for the animal or its young. Since parasites are typically much smaller than their hosts, the parasite interacts with the host more as an environment or resource than as prey. Many parasites have evolved adaptations targeted at specific hosts. Infection of characters is frequently an error, in which the parasite mistakes the human for its chosen host, or something close enough to provide for its specialized needs. An infection may then develop in ways characteristic of the parasite's biology.

Of course, an animal may not have the ability or necessary faculties to avoid such a counterproductive strategy. These situations are rather common among Terrestrial animals on Poseidon, since the indigenous parasites are not adapted to Earth biology. Parasites are common throughout the planet, in a wide variety of ecozones.

Characters traveling in regions of rich biodiversity, such as the mangrove forests and rainforests, are especially vulnerable to parasitic infection. Preventative medicine and antibiotics are the only reliable solutions, apart from fully sealed environment suits. Immunological symbiotes and anti-poison modifications may help deal with the effects of parasites, but actual medical treatment is almost always indicated.

Predation is not particularly common, at least among humans and cetaceans. Predators hunt animals that are typically no more than 3-4 times their mass, and most hunt prey that are smaller than themselves. Pack-hunting predators are apparently not as common on Poseidon as they are on Earth, but this strategy can dramatically increase the maximum size of potential prey. Because most predatory species on Poseidon are significantly smaller than humans, they are rarely perceived as appropriate prey.

Predators can be divided into two groups, full-time predators and opportunistic predators. This division is rough, as full-time predators will eat the kills of others and may supplement their diets with alternative food sources. The distinction is that full-time predators are highly evolved to hunt a specific range of animals, as this behavior provides them with the bulk of their diet. Opportunistic predators, often omnivorous, will hunt a variety of animals, and are more frequently scavengers and carrion eaters.

Predation requires the expenditure of a great deal of energy, and many hunts fail. Hunting is least taxing where large groups of undifferentiated prey animals are available to the predator. A marine predator will typically favor a large school of small fish to a single large prey animal. When hunting a large school, the predator can attack many times in quick succession with less expenditure of energy. Greater whites will consume a significant portion of the organic content in a mangrove in a single feeding frenzy. Some social predators use cooperative strategies to herd prey into tight groups before attacking and consuming them.

Larger—and often more solitary—prey animals are more exhausting and chancy, and predators that depend on them typically require specific adaptations to survive. These may include unusual speed or particularly lethal natural weapons. Many predators of large animals are adapted for pursuit. They are capable of brief bursts of amazing speed, but often lack the endurance for a prolonged chase. They often exhibit an eerie stillness punctuated by sudden flurries of motion. The great cat who crouches in the grass before suddenly pouncing is a ready example.

Opportunistic predators, as the term suggests, typically supplement their normal diet through predation when a promising opportunity presents itself. Opportunistic predators will often attack wounded animals, steal the kills of small predators, assault nests in search of eggs or young, or prey on animals who have become immobilized or incapacitated—animals trapped in mud flats or tar pits, for example. The hunting behavior of opportunistic predators is often different as well. They will frequently appear more cautious and tentative, testing the prey to determine whether it is vulnerable or dangerous. Opportunistic predators may launch quick, probing attacks, hoping to wound and weaken the prey, then withdraw to stalk and observe before darting in for another attack.

Because of their more tentative nature, opportunistic predators are typically easier for humans to frighten off. Any signal the animal will interpret as potentially dangerous can be an effective deterrent.

BIOMES AND ECOZONES

TERRESTRIAL BIOMES
RAINFOREST

Rainforests on Earth are the most complex biomes, both in terms of species diversity and the structure of the forest itself. Growing amidst abundant precipitation and year round warmth, rainforests have no strong seasonal rhythm.

Variations in precipitation can lead to periodic change of the forest itself, particularly where the variations are acute. Rainforests have adapted to recycling and containing large amounts of moisture. Often rainfall has a consistent daily cycle, due to strong links between sunlight and weather patterns.

Rainforests of Poseidon have a wider range than those of Earth, and are found within 30° of the equator. They occur at elevations below 1,000 meters. Seasonal variations in rain have an impact on the ecosystem, but water is never in short supply.

The rainforests of Poseidon are unique from those of Earth in that all are relatively close to the sea. The lack of large landmasses renders the development of deep, inland rainforest impossible. It has been suggested that the predominantly coastal nature of these forests encouraged the evolution of mangrove islands. The precursors of Poseidon mangrove adapted to seek light by growing out into the water, rather than up through the canopy.

STRUCTURE OF THE RAINFOREST

Plants within the rainforest are divided into five rough zones, corresponding to height, and therefore access to sunlight. The dominant competition in the forest is over access to light, leading to adaptations to reach sunlight or tolerate shade. Poseidon rainforests are much like Earth rainforests, though they are generally taller by on order of three or more.

The **emergent zone** consists of widely spaced trees, 100 to 120 meters in height, with an umbrella-like canopy extending above the general canopy around them. They must bear drying winds, so most have tiny leaves. Emergents faced with seasonal dry spells are often deciduous, shedding leaves during these seasons. This is more common at subtropical latitudes.

The **bright canopy** is a closed canopy of 90 meter-tall trees. Full sunlight falls on this layer, but is then blocked from lower levels. Trees of this and lower layers often have drip tips, extensions of the branches that encourage transpiration by exerting a drawing force.

The **dark canopy** is another closed canopy of 66 meter-tall trees. Air currents are sluggish in this layer, causing a great deal of humidity. Trees of this layer often have very large leaves to capture what light they can, and a tall, conical crown.

The **shrub/sapling layer** is marked by very little light. Less than three percent of the light from the top of the forest canopy reaches this layer. Saplings are common, stunted and doomed unless a hole appears in the canopy. If this opportunity arises, the sapling will then grow rapidly to fill the available niche.

Saplings often exhibit many of a layer's specific strategies as they grow within that layer. For example, an emergent tree at the dark canopy layer will often have broad leaves and drip tips.

The **ground layer** has very few plants. Only one percent or less of the light from the top of the for-

est reaches the floor. The ground layer is also less humid, with only two-thirds of precipitation reaching the ground. The rest is absorbed at higher layers.

FLORA

Plants on Poseidon have evolved in many parallel ways, given the strong similarities in environmental conditions.

Epiphytes, air plants, grow on the upper branches of trees. They use the limbs as a platform, extracting moisture from the air, and trapping constant leaf-fall and airborne dust. They are adapted for little water, with some forms evolved for desert and other dry ecosystems. Pineapples and orchids are well-known examples from Earth. The coffee button and the lead cactus are common to Poseidon. Epiphytes on Poseidon are often found in elaborate symbiotic relationships with algae and bacteria.

Lianas are woody vines, growing rapidly up tree trunks during temporary gaps in the canopy. They flower and form fruit in the emergent and bright canopy layers. Many are deciduous. A large number of Poseidon lianas are carniflora, though most only attack tiny animals, such as insects.

Climbers are green-stemmed plants that remain below the canopies. Many store nutrients in large roots and tubers.

Stranglers begin as epiphytes in the canopy and send roots to the forest floor. These are rarely observed in Poseidon rainforests.

Heterotrophs are non-photosynthetic plants that live on the forest floor. On Poseidon, particularly in shoreline rainforests, a number of carniflora species have lost any ability to photosynthesize and rely on prey.

Parasites draw nutrition from the roots or stems of photosynthetic plants. Some Poseidon species have quite exotic shapes, such as the iridescent apple and the mandrill spire.

Saprophytes draw nutrition from decaying organic matter. Many other species, particularly stranglers, utilize symbiosis with fungi and bacteria to take advantage of this strategy.

OTHER CHARACTERISTICS

The trees often have very thin, smooth bark, flowers and fruit grown directly from the trunk, and the trees use fleshy fruits to disperse seeds through animals.

The poor soils prevalent in old substrates of Earth are rare on Poseidon. Volcanic regions have rich and fertile soils, and even the older landmasses are fairly rich in nutrients. Rainforests on Poseidon are more robust and durable, a trait encouraged by the frequent storms.

There is considerable variety in rainforests. Species of fauna are often adapted to narrow conditions of temperature and humidity. Storm severity forms another variable to species development, along with distance from the shore and soil.

The clearest shifts in rainforest composition are between eastern and western sides of landmasses. High variations in storm severity and precipitation occur along this dimension. Another clear shift is between wet, tropical rainforests, drier subtropical rainforests, and subtropical or near-temperate rainforests exposed to frost.

DIVISIONS

Rainforests are roughly divided into two overall diversity types: Type I and II. **Type I** is common to the Pacifica Archipelago. **Type II** is found throughout the Darwin Archipelago, Arc of Fire, and Endeavor Islands.

Poseidon rainforests are further divided into main systems, inland systems, and coastal systems.

The **main system** is most common, and is most similar to the island rainforests of Earth. They are found along islands as well as in deep inland concentrations. The majority of both Type I and II biozones are main rainforest systems.

Inland systems are particular to Poseidon, found in a few large inland regions with large concentrations of freshwater. The growth stalls at a lower elevation and the ecosystem is marked by formation of marshes and bogs. This system has only been observed in Type I regions and is rather rare. Most inland regions are covered by conventional main systems.

Coastal systems are found at the mouths of rivers and at the coastal borders of main rainforest. Trees grow out into the water, consisting of a variety of species adapted to move laterally instead of vertically. They are also marked by competitive tree-killer symbiotic relationships, where plants host organisms that kill and fell other trees, giving the plant an opportunity to take advantage of the opening. These systems are only found in Type II regions, and may have influenced the evolution of Poseidon mangroves.

Type I trees are dominated by fretted palms - which resemble palm trees of Earth - and wing-leaf conifers. Type II trees are dominated by segmented palms, distantly related to fretted palms, a variety of flowering broad-leafed chandrids, and several orders of conifers.

FAUNA

Animals in rainforests are quite diverse. Many adapt an arboreal existence, develop bright colors and distinct patterns, use loud vocalizations to communicate over long distances, and rely on a diet of fruit. On Poseidon, many tropical species, particularly avians, are migratory due to the storm season. The vast majority simply migrates from one hemisphere to the other, avoiding the worst of the weather.

Many amphibious forms of life have evolved to take advantage of rainforests. These include land crabs, salmon mussels, tree hydrae, strand polypods, and others. These organisms take advantage of the dense vegetation and high humidity.

VARIATIONS

Where rainforest is rapidly cleared and the substrate becomes waterlogged, tropical grassland and palm savannas may develop. Particularly large reefs can sometimes evolve into islands covered in rainforest.

In regions marked by high seasonal variation in precipitation, monsoon forests form. These are marked by a more open canopy and dense understory. Trees are more frequently deciduous, responding to seasonal cycles of rain.

POSEIDON CREEPER FOREST

Creeper forests are an adaptation to the frequent and violent storms of the Poseidon tropics. In regions characterized by rapid shifts in weather and sealevel, rainforests give way to creeper forests.

FLORA

Creeper forests form under most of the same conditions as rainforest and are frequently found on the east sides of landmasses in the tropics. These edges face the brunt of storms traveling around the Storm Belt.

Many plant species are shared between rainforests and creeper forests, but there are significant differences. Creeper forests may look like the margins of rainforest to the untrained eye, but the differences are considerable.

Creeper trees are no more than 24 meters high, and many are shorter. The canopy is generally loose, supporting a midgrowth layer of two to 10 meter plants of wide variety. Midgrowth plants include hardy deciduous shrubs, creepers, and dwarf trees. Ground cover is quite dense, with saprophytes and ground-creepers forming a tight mesh. A good deal of light hits the ground, and the soil is kept protected from storm by this thick layer of plant material. Though lacking epiphytes and having few parasitic plants, creeper forests are nearly half as diverse as rainforests.

Creeper trees are closely related to carniflora, with a banded or viney appearance. Their bark is tougher and thicker than those found in rainforest.

Creeper trees have two major adaptations to storms. They are semi-deciduous, relying on two forms for different seasons. During the storm season, spring to mid-autumn, they grow short, palm-like leaves. These are built to take a lot of punishment. During the relatively dry season, branches grow horizontally, creating a more solid canopy. The palm-leaves die and are replaced with numerous small, rapidly growing leaves. When spring approaches again, the leaves are shed and the branches become limp. Shedding bark, the branches fall slowly and attach through creepers to the main trunk. New palm-leaves grow from the branch tips, and the cycle begins again.

Creeper trees also have long arm-vines growing throughout the underbrush, and have a peculiar root system. They are designed so that during fierce storms the trees will fall, with some flexibility, to the ground. Lax roots and arm-vines will take up some of the force of the fall. Once the storm is over, the tree will pull itself back up over the course of a few days.

FAUNA

Animals of the creeper forest have developed a number of ways to handle storms. Common adaptations include balling up (for animals with hard shells), attaching to undergrowth, burrows, or rapid breeding. Many species, particularly avians, rely on migratory patterns to avoid the worst of the storms. Some migrate no further than to the other side of the landmass they are on, a behavior well recorded on Prime Meridian.

VARIATIONS

Creeper forests, though highly developed, seem to be an older ecosystem than rainforest. Most are found in the islands of the Arc of Fire and Darwin's Archipelago. In the Pacifica Archipelago, there are signs that rainforests are slowly replacing these biomes. There are two prevailing theories concerning this. The first is that creeper forests and rainforests are in ecological competition, and the greater diversity within rainforests is giving them an edge. The second theory is that creeper forests form a beachhead biome, transitioning to rainforest over time. Studies of island ecosystems are underway, and researchers seek to determine the truth of

the relationship between rainforests and creeper forests.

TROPICAL ELEVATED REGIONS

On Earth, the mountains in tropical regions are marked by regions resembling temperate or arctic climes. Instead of an annual cycle of cold and warmth, the cycle is diurnal. Throughout the year, nighttime brings frost.

On Poseidon, tropical elevated regions are relatively common. Prime Meridian and the Zion Islands are marked with robust tropical elevated growth. Westscape has a simpler, less robust tropical elevated region, either due to its overall youth or volcanic action.

These ecosystems are rather isolated, developing from surrounding organisms in many parallel directions. There is considerable diversity between examples of this biome, even between isolated elevated regions on the same landmass.

Tropical elevated regions can be divided into two broad levels, the montane level and the dry level.

The **montane level** suffers variable temperatures unfamiliar to most tropical species and is often marked by dry conditions. The montane level exists from around 1,200 meters to approximately 4,200 meters, and often has several component levels of its own, corresponding to distinct conditions. Seasonal variations in rainfall become more acute at this level, leading to bands of deciduous or other hardy trees.

The **dry level** resembles dry, bare tundra, forming above 4,200 meters and continuing to the snowline. Along the tropics, the snowline is usually around 5,500 meters. Woody plants, shrubs, and ground plants dominate the landscape. Dry layers are particularly vulnerable to ecological damage.

POSEIDON DECIDUOUS FOREST

Deciduous forests are quite diverse on Earth. With a number of distinct groups that inhabit temperate regions and colder regions (taiga), these forests have an important place in the ecozones of Earth.

Poseidon is markedly different. Seasonal variations in temperature are more extreme, but the vast majority of landmass on Poseidon lies within the tropics. Most deciduous forest has evolved as a response to seasonal shifts in precipitation and storms.

There are three distinct groups of Poseidon deciduous forest. Temperate forests are found mainly in the southern hemisphere, on Westscape, the Southern Hope Chain, and the southern regions of the Arc of Fire. Dry tropical forest is typically formed in tropical regions marked by long dry seasons or lack of rainfall, and is common throughout the tropics. Montane forest develops at high elevations in the tropics.

TEMPERATE FOREST

This biome is marked by seasonal variations in temperature, light, and precipitation. These patterns are less clear-cut than in temperate forests of Earth, with forests entering winter phases in a somewhat irregular manner. The highs and lows of forest activity are not as pronounced as on Earth, though they approach typical Earth patterns at about 50° latitude and higher.

Flora

The structure of the forest consists of 18 to 300-meter trees, a small tree or sapling layer, a shrub layer, a seasonal layer of quick growing plants, and a ground layer of lichen and mosses. Lichen and mosses also grow in the thick bark of temperate trees. Lianas (climbing plants) of various kinds are common, seeking to flower and fruit high in the canopy.

Temperate forests spread through successive waves of transitional biomes. Grassland gives way to scrubland. Stands of fast growing, small trees form. The stands interlock into light forest, then slower growing, large trees form. Eventually, the final ecosystem develops. Fires, grazing, and other events help cycle these biomes.

The soil of temperate forests is unlike its analog on Earth. Poseidon temperate forests bind a great deal of nutrients in their root systems. Runners and interconnected root systems are used to provide stability and durability in the face of rapid weather shifts. In regions with thin or poor soil, trees have evolved a variety of ways to break up or "cook" the soil into something more fertile. These traits are found among their analogs on Earth, but are more highly developed on Poseidon.

In regions marked by volcanism, the soil is already rather rich. Temperate trees in these regions often develop fixing roots, designed to fix as many nutrients as possible. The undergrowth in these regions is also noted for large numbers of mosses.

Fauna

Herbivores and omnivores are most numerous among the animal populations of temperate forests. Nuts provide sustenance, but leaves are poor in nutrients, even more so than on Earth. Mammals and avians dominate these regions. Carnivores are generally ranging, as these regions are not quite as rich as in other ecosystems.

DRY TROPICAL FOREST

This biome has strong similarities to both temperate forest and rainforest. Like rainforests, there are minimal seasonal shifts in sunlight. Precipitation is generally low, though many patterns of rainfall are possible. Soil is usually fertile.

Flora

Dry tropical forest has close evolutionary ties to the rainforest. Many of the trees are related to vines, and have a winding look to them. Other trees are hardy, deciduous relatives of rainforest species.

Trees in this region release a lot of nutrients in their leaves, unlike in temperate forests. Nutrients are recycled quickly through the ecosystem.

The overall structure of dry tropical forests is much like temperate forests. Parasitic and saprophytic plants are common, except for the few examples of dry tropical forest in poor soil.

Fauna

Land lizards are especially common in dry tropical forests. Species flow between rainforests and dry tropical forest is very common.

MONTANE FOREST

This biome develops in the montane regions of tropical elevated environments. Marked by daily swings in temperature and low precipitation, these ecosystems more strongly resemble Earth temperate forests. Leaves are shed during particularly low seasons of precipitation, forming a protective layer of humus. Tree species are dominated by tall, hardy varieties. At higher elevations, the largest trees give way to smaller varieties, and then shrubs.

Montane forests have strong similarities to both rainforest and deciduous forest. In the tropics, most of the deciduous varieties evolved from rainforest flora. Toward the subtropics, where milder climate may have once held, surviving relatives of deciduous forests may be found.

TROPICAL SAVANNA

Tropical grasslands are transitional or flux biomes. The ecological climax of these regions is either rainforest or tropical deciduous forest. When some factor prevents the growth or spread of trees, hardy grasses have evolved to take advantage of the opportunity.

FLORA

Savannas are characterized by a primary cover of perennial grasses, often one to two meters tall. There are tree, park, shrub, and grass savannas. Tree savannas are also known as woodland savannas. Shrubs and trees, if present, are sparse. Woodland savannas are often identified by the dominant tree found, such as the acacia, palm, and pine savannas of Earth.

Savannas form when some element of the environment restricts the growth of trees. This may be due to extreme drought, damage due to browsing animals, frequent fires, toxic soil, or particularly thin soil. If the savanna is accompanied by scattered trees, the trees are species unusually resistant to the hazard. Grasses have evolved to thrive in regions where trees falter. These factors often change over time, causing dramatic shifts in the ecosystem.

FAUNA

It is thought that grassland is comparatively new to Poseidon. There are only a few mammals and draconodonts that have adapted to exclusive grass consumption. Most other herbivores are generalists: They either consume grass as part of their forest range or are poorly adapted to a grass diet. These few species still represent a large number of animals, and a variety of mammalian and draconodontid predators use the cover to stalk prey.

VARIATIONS

Cooler regions are usually characterized by shrubs and low-growing plants, not grasses. They form in similar ways to savanna, growing in areas somehow hostile to the growth of temperate deciduous forests. Chaparral is an example, forming in regions dominated by dry summers and wet win-

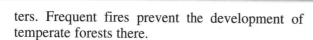

ters. Frequent fires prevent the development of temperate forests there.

DESERTS

Though less fertile than other regions, deserts support well-developed, diverse ecosystems. Life in the desert has evolved elaborate methods to tolerate or avoid the extremes of aridity and temperature.

Deserts form on Earth under four different conditions.

The simplest form of desert forms in the interior of a continent, far from available rainfall.

Another type of desert is formed on the tropics, around 30° latitude. High-pressure systems descend in these regions, causing rapid evaporation and arid conditions.

West coasts of continents between 20 and 30° latitude are often the sites of cold ocean currents and westerly winds. These create deserts, in which the primary source of precipitation is fog.

The last type of desert forms as the rain shadow of high mountain ranges. As a weather system travels up a mountain, it cools. Humidity is released as rain. Once it crests the mountain and comes back down the other side, the system warms, increasing its capacity for moisture. This results in dry winds. The overall effect is called a rain shadow.

Only two types of deserts form on Poseidon. The desert on Solstice, in the Endeavor Islands, is due to tropical-high pressure aridity. Vastly more common is the rain shadow desert, such as that found on Westscape.

Arid climates are defined as having less than 25cm of rainfall a year. Rainfall is often highly localized and unpredictable, though there are usually seasons in which precipitation is most likely. Annual variations in total precipitation are also great.

Temperatures are highly variable, exceeding 38°C on summer afternoons and then dipping to 20° at night. Deserts at high latitudes may experience periods of freezing temperatures. These conditions create very poor, sandy soils.

Aridity is the most significant factor in the creation of a desert.

FLORA

Plants have evolved strategies for reaching precious water. Poseidon desert plants show a great parallelism with those of Earth.

Phreatophytes have long taproots that may extend up to 10 meters to find supplies of groundwater. Underground streams or trapped sources of water may be available. The Westscape ziggurat tree is a common example.

Succulents store water accumulated during rains for use in the interim. Species vary in where they store their water, creating easily identified types. Both Earth and Poseidon species come in stem succulents, leaf succulents, root succulents, and fruit succulents.

Ephemerals live only during wet spells, with a two- to three-week life cycle. Ephemerals grow hardy seeds that can survive years of desiccation.

Cryptoperennials store nutrients and water in underground bulbs, remaining dormant most of the year.

Shrubs are the dominant plants in deserts. They may be evergreen or deciduous. Most have small leaves, spines, or thorns, and many produce aromatic oils. Root systems are broad but shallow to ensure that what little rainfall arrives reaches the plant. Desert shrubs form an open canopy, with bare ground between each plant.

FAUNA

Animals of the desert have their own strategies for handling the aridity and temperature variations.

Behavior is a relatively simple way of handling conditions. Many desert animals are active at night or twilight. Others burrow or stay in the shade during the day.

Morphological changes allow animals to survive desert conditions. Small body size and long limbs help radiate body heat from warm-blooded animals. Light coloration helps reflect sunlight and prevent absorption of background heat.

Physiological changes are relatively rare, but distinguish highly adapted species. Aestivation (dormancy during the summer), deposits of fat in tails or humps, lack of sweat glands, concentration of urine, and salt glands to secrete minerals without losing fluid all bestow survival benefits.

Draconodonts, like their reptile analogs on Earth, are well suited for desert conditions. Draconodonts are a bit closer to their amphibious roots, however. Poseidon groundbirds fill many niches in the deserts.

VOLCANIC ISLANDS

Volcanic islands are composed of a number of different types of rock. They range from light rock, full of silica and aluminum, to dense rock, rich in magnesium, iron, and titanium oxides. Poseidon is composed of a larger proportion of lighter materials, a difference reflected in the composition of these islands.

Dissolved gases may make rock light and "fluffy," like pumice. Thick, syrupy magma can cool into very dense rock. The light and porous rock erodes relatively quickly, and provides a lot of footholds and texture to trap sediments. These encourage the development of soils. Both types of rock are rich in minerals that plants thrive on.

FLORA

Volcanic islands often develop reef structures, whether tropical coralline reefs or temperate tidal muds reefs. They are quickly settled by a variety of life forms adapted to wide ranges, particularly palms and shoreline kelps. These are followed by a succession of plants, each thriving in successively richer soils. Lichens and mosses help break up stone and lay down organic material, and then epiphytes and other plants that can thrive on thin or sandy soil to establish themselves. Eventually, rainforests or deciduous forests appear.

Following the plants, highly mobile animals appear first. Even mainly land-dwelling animals can swim short distances, and can slowly fill chains of islands. Some lose their mobility over time.

VARIATIONS

Given the relatively large oceanic barriers, there is often highly regional development of species. Islands that are part of a chain will still show strong endemic variations, and chains separated by hundreds of kilometers of ocean will have quite distinct native forms.

POSEIDON TUNDRA

Tundra on Earth usually occurs at the northern edge of large continental landmasses in the northern hemisphere. They are characterized by a short growing season (seven to 11 weeks), long, cold winters, very little precipitation, and drying winds.

On Poseidon, these conditions are relatively rare and found predominantly in the southern latitudes, particularly in the Southern Hope Chain. While the Southern Hope Chain receives more moisture than is characteristic of tundra, the overall similarities are strong. Permafrost prevents the growth of true trees, as on Earth.

There are four types of Poseidon tundra.

Dry bare tundra is similar to that of Earth, dominated by low shrubs, lichen, and mosses. Leafy plants are often deciduous. Grasses like Earth's heath are common in some regions, particularly those at lower latitudes. This is one of the simplest ecosystems, in terms of species diversity and structure of food chains.

Wet scrub tundra is fairly similar to dry bare tundra, but it also resembles temperate scrubland. The shrubs are a bit taller and denser, forming a solid undergrowth for endemic animals, and the growth season is more spectacular. This is found in the northwest regions of the Southern Hope Chain, where weather systems from the Pacifica Archipelago deliver moisture during the early spring.

Sedge-kelp tundra is found along rocky coastline. Sedge-kelp is a particularly hardy form of kelp that has evolved to thrive on land. With long taproots reaching into the water, it has a complex vascular structure that allows it to derive moisture from seawater. These ecosystems can stretch for kilometers, though they only extend a dozen meters or so inland. Still, they provide a refuge for endemic species. They do not have as sharp a growing cycle as other plants, and are less frequented by migratory animals. Sedge-kelp is absent in more humid environments, where scrub dominates.

Tundra zones in the northern hemisphere are frequently sedge-kelp tundra.

Sedge intermediate is a variation of the sedge-kelp tundra. Coastlines close to soil are dominated by a symbiosis of sedge and other plants. In this

still very arid environment, sedge-kelp forms cooperative root structures with mosses and shrubs. The forest is only 70 to 80 centimeters tall, but extends almost 100 meters inland. Sedge intermediate tundra resembles scrubland in many respects.

FAUNA

There are few migratory land animals in this biome, given an absence of land routes to other climes. Those that do migrate are constrained to moving to moderately more tolerable climes when the seasons shift.

More mobile migratory animals reside for most of the year in the temperate forests of the Arc of Fire. Some dwell in Westscape or warmer regions of the Pacifica Archipelago, and a few are known to summer in the Endeavor Islands, particularly avian species. Migratory animals are almost exclusively carnivores, and many are insectivorous. They migrate to the tundra during the short growing season, timing their arrival to mid spring, when insect and herbivore populations are highest.

Aquatic migrations are common, with caneopoise and schooler pods making their way to the waters of Albion yearly.

With the prevalence of food, migratory animals take advantage of the abundance for mating. Some particularly fertile species may have two or more cycles of young during the short growth period.

There are a number of typical adaptations among endemic populations. Adaptations include cyclical variations in population size, hibernation, diurnal activity, burrowing behavior, large, compact bodies to conserve heat, a thick insulating layer of feathers or fur, and coloration that turns white in winter and brown in summer. Another useful strategy is the deposition of thick layers of fat during the short growing season. Fat acts as both an insulator and store of energy.

On Poseidon a number of draconodont species are found in the tundra. Draconodonts of the tundra are divided into endemic herbivores and migratory amphibious carnivores. The resident herbivores are uniformly small and rely on hibernation to survive the long winter. Most have highly cyclic populations. The migratory amphibians have thick layers of fat and generally feed on other migratory sea animals. Several feed exclusively on the eggs of migratory birds or other amphibians.

AMPHIBIOUS BIOMES
TIDAL POOLS

Tidal pools form where there is substantial tidal activity on coastlines dominated by boulders or bare rock. Trapped waters, refreshed through waves and tidal action, act as sanctuaries to a variety of sessile and mobile organisms. Tidepools are found throughout Poseidon. The canyonlands, in many ways, are a form of tidal pool.

ESTUARIES

Estuaries form in sheltered coastal regions, where seawater and freshwater mix. Estuaries vary in their origins and structure, some having a steady flow of seawater with the tide, others with rather sudden tidal bores. On Poseidon, the majority of estuaries are formed as part of a lagoon structure on the larger islands.

Some estuaries develop into tidal muds wetland, most clearly distinguished from other estuaries by the lack of grasses and dominance of large algae. These systems resemble muds shallows, but lack the characteristic reef-building organisms. Tidal muds estuaries host a number of organisms similar to those of the tidal muds reefs.

MARSH

Marshes form on the edges of slow-moving freshwater, resulting in lowlying wetland dominated by grasses. Marshes are common on Poseidon, particularly along river systems. Shifting paths of rivers often mean that marshes are transitional, drying into grassland and then forest, or filling with water.

BOGS

On Earth, regions of slow-moving freshwater can develop into bogs filled with thick mats of acidic mosses. They may form from rivers or blocked ponds.

There are no true bogs on Poseidon, though two biomes resemble bogs in many respects.

Rainforest bogs form from several groups of groundplants typically found in rainforests, which grow into mats of thin vines. These vines develop a highly acidic environment that retards the spread of saprophytes and other plants. The material accumulates into thick mats. A large increase or decrease in water kills off the bog plants and saprophytes lead to a transition to a different system.

Though normally associated with inland rainforest systems, rainforest bogs can be found throughout the tropics of the Pacifica Archipelago, even alongside main rainforests.

Caryatid bogs are found in Darwin's Archipelago and the Endeavor Islands. They are characterized by a thick growth of algae, forming a seaweed-like mat. Tall structures, which are believed to be symbiotic fungal growths, grow through the surface and can reach almost a meter in height. The bogs often have a detailed inner structure, with open spaces or "galleries" above and below the waterline.

Caryatid bogs are typically high in metals and toxic to many animals and plants. Other microorganisms thrive in the environment, along with a variety of insects and amphibians.

AQUATIC BIOMES
SHALLOWS AND SHELVES

Coastal shallows are roughly divided into three types: eastward tropical, westward tropical, and temperate. Shallows are defined by regions where the depth is less than 150 meters. In regions with continental masses, the undersea surface of the continent can extend even further.

Eastward tropical shallows lie to the east of tropical landmasses. They experience quiet and bloom seasons, just like coral reefs. Extensive shallows allow lagoon-like conditions, though stronger currents often run from east to west. These currents bring nutrients into the shallows. Nutrients also flow from rivers into the sea, creating smaller fertile regions.

A wide variety of marine algae and other plants thrive in the shallows. Some rely on breakaway roots and quick growth to survive storms, while others simply drift. The floors are relatively thin in silt, except around river outflows. Concentrations of plant and animal life form around turbulence shadows, where sediment gathers the most.

Species are adapted for larger ranges and more mobility than in lagoons, but the strategies are similar. Amphibians are common, with predators ranging over large territories. Flying organisms do well, as they are able to avoid aquatic predators and cover large territories.

Westward tropical shallows are on the western edge of tropical landmasses. The environment is fertile, fed by runoff from the landmasses and upwelling from the west. Western shallows suffer less from seasonal storms. These factors create a diverse and robust biome. Westward shallows strongly resemble lagoons, and coralline structures often grow in these conditions.

Temperate shallows are mainly found in the Arc of Fire and are dominated by the weather systems described under the temperate shelf biome.

Variable conditions of cool rich waters and warm poor waters, plus the variation in seasonal light cycles, open a niche for fantastically successful kelps. Growing rapidly in high nutrient, high light conditions, the hardy undersea forests of kelp can withstand periods of cooler temperatures and harsh conditions. They form a solid foundation of temperate shallow food chains. Kelp forests also provide hiding places and protection from currents or predators for a wide variety of organisms.

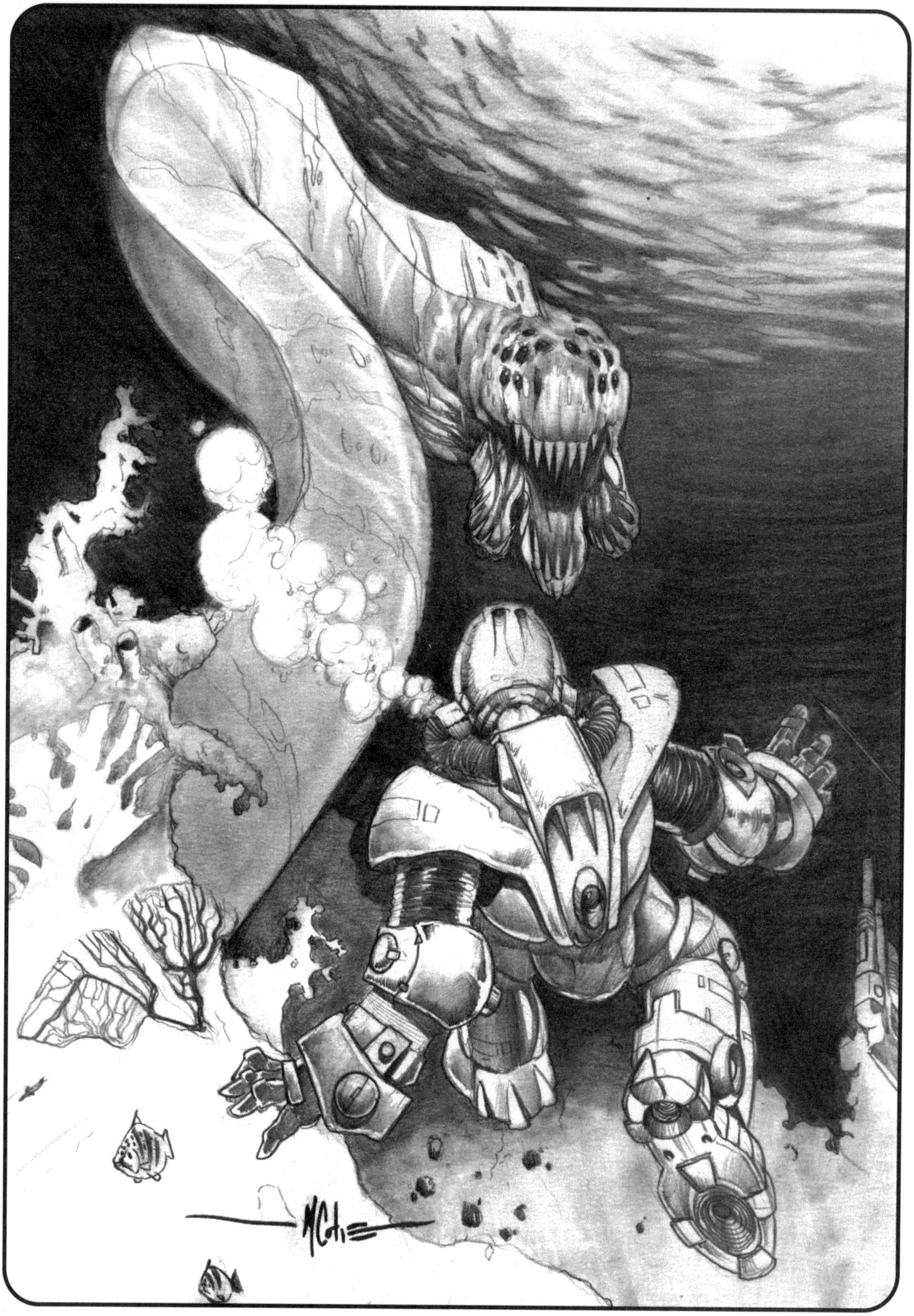

Animal species are adapted for colder waters, forested conditions, and seasonal variations. These adaptations include layers of fat, hiding behavior, attachment behavior or morphology, camouflage in the form of coloration or morphology, rapid breeding and population expansion cycles, and migration. Mammals have quite successfully taken advantage of this ecosystem, as have a number of avian groups. Migration patterns to and from the tundra frequently begin and end in temperate shallows. Many animals summer in temperate shallows, and winter in tropical regions.

A variety of unique worm-like organisms inhabit these ecosystems. Resembling flatworms, velvetworms, and less recognizable animals, each probably represents a new phylum of the animal kingdom. Although some of these organisms have been found in other biomes, they are only found in large numbers in temperate shallows. They occupy niches traditionally occupied by small fish and sessile cnidarians, and many form symbiotic relationships with algae or cyanobacteria.

Some of the largest and most successful fish species are found in temperate shallows, though most are migratory. The prevalence of river spawning among Earth fish is absent from all known fish on Poseidon. Instead, the only comparable examples are some freshwater fish that migrate to the oceans to spawn.

The chittering yellow fly is one of several insects that have adapted to kelp forests. It migrates to the land only to lay eggs that survive the winter. Come summer, young yellow flies return to the sea. They thrive on the many small organisms that proliferate in the surface waters amongst the kelp fronds, including small worms.

Variations
Close to the shore, the coast is dominated by sand and rock. Where wave action is light, the beaches are composed of fine sand. As wave action increases, the sand becomes rockier, eventually giving way to boulders or bare rock. Away from shore, the sea bottom is also layered in sand.

Continental shelves are marked by conditions similar to the shallows. The composition of species and the environment shifts toward the open ocean biome. Strong currents can bring shallow-water organisms further out to sea. A number of mobile animals cross the shelves to cover many shallows.

REEFS
Reef development is fairly well understood. Reef-growing corals, pseudo-corals, and tidal muds organisms grow in the photic layer, giving their photosynthetic partners light to thrive on. Sealevels shift over time, allowing reefs to expand and build huge structures.

The standard model of a coral reef is the fringe reef-barrier, reef-atoll pattern.

Fringe reefs begin as corals and grow in the shallows around an island, usually volcanic. Volcanic islands are rather sudden, geologically speaking, 'floating' on the crust. After they first appear, they slowly sink back, compressing and settling in. Coral grows upward, to maintain exposure to the light.

The shift to barrier reef stage occurs as the ring of coral expands and the island sinks. The outer edge of the reef is exposed to more plankton from oceanic currents—the coral's primary food source—than the inside. The inner edge is also subject to more sedimentary deposits, which hard corals do not tolerate well. These factors, in combination with shifts in sea level, cause the reef system to expand outward. The inner edge builds reef more slowly than the island recedes, and a lagoon soon forms. The reef often extends out of the water, due to shifts in sealevel, allowing the growth of hardy trees and plants.

Lagoons are typically quite shallow, with depths rarely extending beyond the photic layer. A wide variety of marine organisms thrive in lagoons amidst kelp and a variety of plants. These include shellfish, eduropods, soft corals, hydrae, and sea pens. More mobile feeders can use the other organisms or reef surface as protection.

The outer edge has an equally diverse ecosystem. Though more nutrients arrive from oceanic currents, these currents are more vigorous. Benthic organisms have evolved to hold very strongly to the coral. Free-swimming fish and other animals must contend with stronger flows.

Eventually, the island will submerge completely, forming a ring of reefs around a shallow lagoon. This is an atoll. The ecosystems are much like those around barrier reefs. Eventually, the reefs collect sand, forming islands called cays.

Reef systems often show great diversity, as species flow between them is relatively limited.

Reef Builders

Coral and pseudo-coral are exclusively tropical species. Reefs composed only of coral are more common among non-volcanic reef systems, developing from uplift formations or seamounts. Pseudo-coral reefs are generally restricted to volcanic islands, beginning as pure coral reefs that are later colonized. A border of pseudo-corals forms at varying depths. Pseudo-coral reefs achieve a balance between pseudo-coral and coral that is unique to each location. Whether pure or mixed reefs, sponges and other calcareous organisms have a part in their growth.

Tidal muds reefs form in much the same way as outlined above, although they are strictly temperate formations. They are also most common along coastal bays and other older shallow geographical features. Tidal muds organisms thrive on sediment that corals typically avoid, and their growth patterns encourage its concentration.

Reefs and Seasons

Coral and pseudo-coral reefs, unlike those of Earth, show a strong adaptation to seasonal weather.

The quiet season begins with the start of storm season, and brings with it a number of changes in animal species. Pseudo-corals, particularly, develop thicker headplates and may enter a period of inactivity during the worst of the storms. Many species migrate from the reefs, while some sessile organisms develop squatter, current-tolerant forms. This period lasts from early spring to the end of summer, though the timing varies a great deal between locations and even species within one reef system.

The bloom season starts at the beginning of autumn. The storm season is still in full swing, but at this point abundant nutrients have been liberated by previous storm activity. The waters around the reefs are fertile and bring on a rapid increase in the populations of phytoplankton and, soon, all other reef organisms. Sessile organisms often adopt more effective food-gathering shapes, losing the extreme current-hardiness. The seasonal bloom usually lasts until the beginning of winter.

Benthic species have evolved a variety of ways to handle currents and security. Cnidarians, a phylum that includes sea anemones, corals, jellyfish, sea pens, and hydra, are common in benthic formations, as are porifera (sponges). Passive and active feeding strategies allow many sessile organisms to latch onto a particular patch of real estate and wait for food to approach. Coral reefs themselves evolved as an elaborate form of this strategy.

Mobile benthic species rely on clawholds, crevasses, or other attached organisms to assist in fighting the current.

Benthic species on a reef have the advantage of being close to sunlight or food that relies on sunlight, good currents, and safety.

Freeswimming organisms gain the advantage of larger territories, but at the cost of dealing with oceanic currents. Amphibians are common in reefs. Many are migratory and have large ranges between various reefs.

SEAMOUNTS

Seamounts are dormant underwater volcanoes that rise about 1,000 meters and do not break the surface. Seamounts can form as a single mount, called a ridge, or a series of ridges, called a chain.

Seamounts form in one of three ways.

The first is **subduction zones**. The top plate is forced upwards as the other plate melts in the mantle beneath. Volcanoes soon form, creating a line of seamounts.

Hotspots are areas of internal convection, where intensely hot rock wells up against the crust. This often breaks through, creating a volcano. Since the crust moves and the convection currents are relatively stable, both compared to the orientation of the planet, the volcano moves off of the hotspot. After a period of time, the hotspot burns through again. This causes a chain of seamounts or volcanic islands.

Mid-oceanic ridges are the third origin of seamounts. At the center of the plates, convection forces up new material. The plate around this zone spreads, creating a ridge cracked with transverse faults. Volcanoes can grow from particularly weak spots in these ridges.

The difference between seamounts and volcanic islands is a matter of flow rates and time. If a volcano grows long enough, it will break the surface and become an island. However, the initial mass forms "high" on the crust. The crust has not had time to settle under the weight. Over time the crust will give under the weight and the mass will subside. Volcanic islands will often sink back as seamounts, in this way, depending on how big they are.

Seamounts are the site of considerable diversity. Currents accelerate as they move around seamounts, churning up waters from the depths. These deep currents are rich in nutrients, and feed plants and algae in the photic layer. Eddies also form above seamounts, creating an area of concentrated nutrients and reducing the action of currents. These concentrate the biozone, and provide abundant food sources for fish. Rich benthic communities often form, and seamounts of sufficient height can give rise to reefs. Migratory animals often take advantage of these riches.

OPEN OCEAN

Open ocean covers most of Poseidon, and is only disrupted by relatively small continental shelves, seamounts, and volcanic islands. Open ocean is one of the least fertile biomes on Earth, and Poseidon, though enjoying more nutrient-rich waters, is much the same. Life on Poseidon has adapted to utilize the resources of the open ocean.

Surface

The warm waters of the photic layer are separated by a sharp thermocline from colder, deep oceanic waters. This layer is about 200 meters deep and heated constantly by the sun. Most microorganisms remain in the photic zone, as falling to the thermocline means death. This is complicated by wave action and turbulence, and the ocean surface is exposed to enough UV light to kill off many kinds of zooplankton.

Plankton have evolved a variety of ways to survive these challenges. Flagellates of many types have whiptails (thus the name), which they use for propulsion. Larger algae form mats for stability and protection.

Another problem is the need for nutrients. Nutrients tend to leach from the photic layer as plankton dies. Poseidon oceans are generally richer in nutrients than on Earth, but the problem is still acute. Two unique ecosystems have developed on Poseidon to overcome this challenge.

The first is the sargassum island. These thick mats of colonial algae provide a stable home for a vast array of other organisms. They concentrate nutrients and help slow the rate of loss to the ocean floor. In addition, the gathering of material allows more elaborate food chains to develop. Though less robust in temperate climates, they represent a significant proportion of oceanic biomass.

The second is the veil mat. Similar to veil drifts, these organisms form from a cooperation between algae and the veil organisms. With a filmy, filamentary structure and minute gas bladders, they spread thin but relatively durable layers just below the thermocline. Only a centimeter or two thick, veil mat communities can spread for many kilometers. These mats function as a net for material falling from the photic layer, gathering the debris before it can fall further. Since they live below the thermocline, they suffer little predation from zooplankton, and will normally avoid wave turbulence. Veil mats are still at the mercy of currents, and break apart when encountering strong up or downflows.

Veil mats form small gas-filled sacks that are released, punching up through the thermocline and floating to the top of the photic layer. They form tiny structures in symbiosis with algae, although it is unclear whether they incorporate algae or bring algae with them. This forms a cycle in which surface veil sacks drift and then sink, forming new mats.

A variety of freeswimming cnidarians, fish, and some shellfish take advantage of the thinly distributed biomass. Certain large aquatic animals utilize their mobility to more efficiently harvest plankton. Mobile species often benefit from the higher density of life, and therefore more abundant food sources, around veil mats. Sargassum islands have elaborate ecosystems, forming centers of activity in the open ocean.

Benthos

The floor of the open ocean is relatively smooth, broken only by mid-oceanic ridges, seamounts, and volcanic islands. The abyssal plain is covered in a thick layer of ooze. This ooze is caused by organic sediment from the photic layer and from continental zones. It is a major source of nutrients, conveyed back to the surface through cold benthic currents.

Hydrological and meteorological systems create downflow at low latitudes and upflow at high latitudes. This creates extremely cold conditions at the ocean bottom, and matches the Earth's current system. This was not necessarily always the case, although the details of ancient Poseidon hydrology are unknown at present. On Earth, abyssal waters were a relatively balmy 18° Celsius approximately 140 million years ago, probably due to downflow of waters in the tropics.

This convection, of surface waters moving toward the equator and benthic currents moving away from the equator, encourages large temperature variations. A different arrangement of continental shelves could cause the reverse situation, in which the poles are warmed and heat is distributed more evenly throughout the planet. The current situation is rather advantageous for life on Poseidon, with continental shelves concentrated at relatively warm, low latitudes.

Earth's ocean floors are dotted with magnesium nodules, formed through the action of bacteria deep in the oozes and brought to the surface by scavenging worms. Although these are found on Poseidon, the waterworld boasts some elaborate abyssal structures. Many form at the continental rise, creating tubes and horizontal spikes sometimes hundreds of meters long. These structures are formed from metals, calcites, and silicates slowly dissolving into the water. Abyssal storms often cause large pieces to break off. It is believed that a combination of oxygen, organic debris, and erosion from the continental shelves flowing down into the abyssal plain feeds an elaborate ecosystem of bacteria. It is not known how extensive these structures are, but they have been found in almost every similar region.

Other abyssal bacterial structures include slime-domes. These layers are often dozens of meters wide, with "fingerlets" extending far into the abyssal ooze. Acting as centers of scavenging microorganisms, these are interesting due to their ability to form fruiting bodies, spheres of bacteria a few centimeters across. These fruit float slowly upward. It is thought that these are part of an elaborate life cycle or environmental transmission with veil mats, but this has not yet been proven.

The ultimate product of abyssal scavengers and the abyssal environment is dissolved CO_2, bicarbonate, and organic compounds.

Methane hydrate formations found on Earth do not occur on Poseidon. It is possible that slime-domes or other organisms unique to the waterworld tap these formations.

POSEIDON OCEANOGRAPHY

The **Blue Planet v2** *Moderator's Guide* includes an extensive discussion of basic oceanography as it relates to Poseidon (MG 149). The following section provides a short glossary of oceanographic terms, as well as a brief discussion of oceanic phenomena that characters may encounter on the waterworld.

GLOSSARY
ABYSSAL PLAIN
The abyssal plain begins at the bottom of the continental shelves. It is typically smooth, broken only by volcanoes and mid-ocean ridges, and has an average depth of four kilometers. Storms of sediment, turbidity currents, often fall from the shelves. They form massive, slow-moving flows of debris that roll for hundreds of kilometers along the plain.

The waters of the abyssal plain are very cold, below 0° Celsius, much like the abyssal region of Earth. On Earth, this temperature was not always the case, as the abyssal oceans were once much warmer. The warmth was due to geography that caused oceanic currents to drop at the tropics and rise at the poles. Benthic waters became warm, and the planet was more evenly heated. It is not known when, or if, Poseidon had a similar period.

BENTHIC
The term "benthic" refers to animals or regions associated with the bottom of bodies of water or the depths of an ocean. Benthos, benthic animals, often adapt a sessile (nonmoving) existence, or crawl along the bottom. These regions are often rich in nutrients and organic material that has fallen from above. In shallower water, benthic life forms must often contend with currents.

CARBONATE CONSERVATION DEPTH

Calcium carbonate dissolves in seawater, and does so more easily at greater depths. Below this level, no calcium carbonate is deposited and formations are dominated by volcanic materials or silicas.

CIRCUMPOLAR CURRENT

On Earth, a strong oceanic current flows around Antarctica, isolating it from the hydrological and meteorological systems of the rest of the world. This isolation, caused by the lack of landmasses that would break up the current, shifts more heat to the rest of the planet and makes Antarctica much colder than the North Pole.

On Poseidon, there is a circumpolar current around the North Pole, making it extremely cold. Temperatures at the South Pole are more similar to those at Earth's North Pole, due to the movement of currents around the Southern Hope Chain and Arc of Fire.

CONTINENTAL RISE

This is the portion of the continental margin between the abyssal plain and the continental slope. The rise sits atop crustal rocks of the ocean basin. Many of the bacteriological abyssal formations occur in this region.

CONTINENTAL SHELF

On Poseidon, most continental landmasses exist only as shelf, and are divided into core and marginal regions. The core is like the continental shelves, with depths around 100 to 120 meters. Marginal shelves are defined as having depths of more than 120 meters. At about 140 meters of depth, the shelf gives way to comparatively steep continental slope.

CONTINENTAL SLOPE

At the slope, the angle becomes relatively steep, around three to six degrees. The slope sits on continental crustal rocks.

DOWNFLOW

Downflow occurs under several conditions. Winds can push waters toward a coast, driving a volume of water that slips downward. Arid warm weather can evaporate surface waters, increasing their density and causing them to sink. Downflow systems are usually disrupted by freshwater, which can mitigate the arid conditions or disrupt the winds driving the water. On Poseidon, variations in polar melt can alter downflow strength.

EL NIÑO EFFECT

The El Niño effect is a variation in upwelling patterns. Weakening of winds slows upwelling, leading to shifts in temperature and humidity. Since surface waters are not being cycled as quickly, thermoclines increase, surface water temperatures increase where upwelling normally occurs, and regions normally fed by warmer waters become cooler. The increase of humidity and temperature can cause rainfall, further slowing upwelling.

There are a number of variable systems on Poseidon that are similar to Earth's El Niño.

MID-OCEANIC RIDGE

Also called spreader zones, these form in oceanic crust at hot convection zones rising from the planet's interior. Hot material rises to the surface, forcing the crust to move to either side. The ocean floor slowly moves away along a series of ridges that span the entire planet. Transform vaults are large cracks, running perpendicular to the ridge, along which the crust can "slip."

Poseidon is more tectonically active than Earth, and the mid-oceanic ridges spread with more speed. Planetologists believe the mantle underneath the crust is more fluid, partially due to its lighter composition.

Black smokers are formed in the basins within the ridges. Water boils out, dark with chemicals from magma. Some of these substances condense out of the water, accreting and forming exotic shapes.

Ridges are well known for the unusual life that has evolved around them. These chemicals are rich resources for bacteria. The bacteria form symbiotic relationships with other organisms, forming the base of a food chain.

OCEANIC CURRENT

Water at the ocean surface is driven by winds into horizontal currents. These currents can be small and transitory phenomena, or can produce long lasting, cyclical formations. Their boundaries are relatively distinct, creating "rivers" within the ocean.

Cyclical formations are called gyres and can extend over much of a planet. The flow is constrained by continental shelves, and forms distinct belts that convey resources and heat throughout the oceans. Gyres are composed of warm, fast-moving surface currents and cold, slow benthic currents. These currents are driven by downflow and upwell regions.

Shifts in the rate of downflow or upwell alter the speed of the system, and thus affect the distribution of nutrients and heat through affected regions. This translates into climatic change.

Well-defined currents form along continental shelves. In large expanses of open ocean, such as the New Pacific, currents are less well defined and move more slowly.

South polar gyre systems are driven by permanent low-pressure systems at about 50° latitude, near the Challenger Deep. These upwell benthic polar currents and create eastward surface currents.

Along the north and south tropics, numerous weather patterns cause rapid evaporation and downflows. Winds create upwelling regions west of the major tropical landmasses, and in the region between the Southern Hope Chain and the Arc of Fire.

The major surface flows are north along each side of the Arc of Fire, westward across Poseidon's Reach, a west-southwesterly flow west of the Pacifica Archipelago, eastward between Poseidon's Reach and the Southern Hope Chain, and northwest between Darwin's Archipelago and the Endeavor Islands. There are currents elsewhere, but these are the major components of Poseidon gyres.

The major benthic flows are southeast between the Arc of Fire and Southern Hope Chain, south along the southeast side of Darwin's Archipelago, south along each side of the Pacifica Archipelago, west between the Southern Hope Chain and the Pacifica Archipelago, east along the northern tropic of Poseidon's Reach, southeast between Darwin's Archipelago and Endeavor Islands, and westward to the north and south of the Endeavor Islands.

PHOTIC LAYER

The layer of ocean through which light shines. It extends to a depth of 100 to 200 meters, depending on the constitution of the water. Across much of Poseidon, the photic layer is 200 meters deep. The photic layer is generally well oxygenated.

TECTONIC PLATE

Poseidon is rich in light elements, creating a thicker oceanic crust than that found on Earth. This crust is more flexible, however, with a very fluid layer between lithosphere (crust) and mantle. The crust "floats" on denser material, mostly solid and cracked into a number of sections called plates.

Continental material is lighter than the crust and therefore floats on it. The composition of crust under continents is distinct from oceanic crust.

Flow in the liquid material beneath causes these plates to move, rub, and slide under one another.

When plates move away from one another, this is a spreading zone. This is associated with mid-oceanic ridges.

A plate that slides into another will cause one or the other plate to slide underneath, creating a subduction zone. The weight of the top plate will push the edge of the other into the mantle. The crust then melts and floats back to the surface. Material that comes up through the crust forms volcanoes, often in a line along the plate boundary.

Poseidon has 13 major plates, some of which are associated with continents. There are two distinct continental regions that are entirely underwater, the Tranh plate north of Poseidon's Reach, and the small Pacifico-Challenger plate near the equator, from 92° west longitude to 105° west longitude.

The Arc of Fire is one of the most notable subduction zones on Poseidon, caused by the collision of several plates. The oceanic plate to the east is spreading west with some force, into a western and northwestern plate. The dynamics are still being studied, but the result is the volcanism well known to the region.

THERMOCLINE

This is a density barrier in water created by temperature variations, though similar barriers are associated with salinity. In the open ocean, the thermocline forms below the photic layer. The warmth of the sun causes these waters to "float" on cooler waters below.

A thermocline causes sound to shift, due to varying densities. Sonar can bounce off the interface or cause unusual returns, depending on angle and other factors. Unusually layered or turbulent ther-

moclines, such as those near magma vents, can severely restrict the use of sonar.

UPWELLING

A system that causes water to flow up to the surface. The major large-scale form of upwelling is created by wind moving along the surface of water and away from a large landmass. Water is pulled from below to replace the moving surface water.

Upwelling can also be caused by volcanic action, though this is smaller in scope.

OCEANIC PHENOMENA
STEAM SHOWERS

Steam showers were first observed by Victor Drake in the Arc of Fire, and are a rather rare phenomenon. They form from long volcanic ridges running near the shore. Magma flow can become synchronized with sudden influxes of water. The water vaporizes quickly, creating a deadly mass of superheated steam. A crossbreeze then moves the steam onto regular terrain, often ending as a rain of boiling water.

Under most circumstances, the magma beds work more slowly, creating a pleasantly hot rain. Natural hot tubs can be found near these formations.

Several people, usually tourists, are killed each year from steam showers.

TOXIC WIND

These are also associated with volcanic activity. Toxic wind results when large amounts of gases are concentrated, releasing suddenly when disturbed. These winds then kill most living things within range, depending on the constitution of the gasses.

A few of these volcanic structures are associated with pools, and create a combination effect. On Earth, cold pool bottoms can become choked with carbon dioxide due to bacterial growth, concentrated under the barrier of a strong thermocline. In subtropical or higher latitudes on Poseidon, extinct or partially extinct volcanic calderas can create

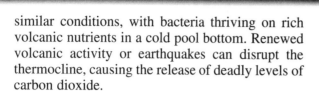

similar conditions, with bacteria thriving on rich volcanic nutrients in a cold pool bottom. Renewed volcanic activity or earthquakes can disrupt the thermocline, causing the release of deadly levels of carbon dioxide.

OCEANIC SLIDES

Volcanic activity and falling rock can cause oceanic slides. More severe than turbidity currents, these result in large surface waves and travel for thousands of kilometers. These waves may reach shore, doing severe damage.

VOLCANIC MUSIC

Submerged volcanoes cause bubbles to form, as magma vaporizes water and volcanic gases escape. This creates distinctive sounds. Active undersea volcanoes can be identified by the pure tones they make.

Cetaceans have referred to these as the "Calls of the Deep Brothers," and can use the sounds to navigate.

EXPLOSIVE SIDEFLOWS

Another phenomenon that is fairly unique to Poseidon is associated with bacteria and volcanic activity. Undersea volcanoes close to continental shelves are commonly inhabited by a variety of bacteria that rapidly mineralize, creating large plugs and caps of heavy rock. These occur most commonly in subduction zone volcanic activity, due to the composition of the magma there.

Over time, these systems create horizontal formations that build in pressure, then explode. The pressure waves created are hazardous, moving mostly horizontally over the ocean floor. This can trigger other explosive sideflows or underwater slides.

VERTICAL INVERSION

As sealevels rise and fall, aquifers and other land-locked freshwater can become submerged under the ocean. This phenomenon is relatively rare on Poseidon, though similar locked freshwater is created by bacteria.

Bacteria form large masses on the floors of continental shelves, eventually getting buried in sediment. Some of these preferentially fix minerals, slowly forming large reservoirs of relatively fresh water. Most of these formations are small, but some have been discovered with a capacity of nearly eight million cubic meters of water.

The most dangerous water inversions occur with nonbacterial freshwater structures, as they are often much larger. An earthquake or mining activity causes a portion of the roof to collapse, releasing freshwater. This water rises rapidly, causing saltwater to flow in from the sides. This turbulence can cause vessels to collide with the ocean floor, or to be pulled into the chamber. A diver is easily injured if pulled across jagged rock. At the surface, freshwater creates turbulence. Large ships can sink into the less dense freshwater and capsize.

Short-range penetrating sonar can discover these pockets of freshwater, but it is a difficult and error-prone process.

RAPID MINERALIZATION EFFECT

This extremely hazardous effect has only been observed a few times, but may be responsible for a number of disappearances. It is associated with volcanic regions at the ocean floor, where water pressures, currents, and topography creates a region of heavily mineralized water. It is suspected that bacteria are also involved.

Divers or instruments in these regions can become the center of a sudden and massive mineralization. A layer of calcite forms over the surface and in water intake systems. It is usually a few centimeters thick, at most, but there is one recorded instance where a diver was encased in a 30-cm thick layer of porous rock.

Normally, calcium cannot accrete at abyssal depths, due to pressure. An unusual and poorly understood combination of factors causes calcium levels to rise sharply in these regions. When the environment shifts, it deposits rapidly out on all available surfaces. Over time it will slowly dissolve again, but in the short term it creates extremely hazardous conditions.

This mineralization causes major damage to propulsion systems, and can also block water intakes. However, the effect has not been observed occurring more than once during a given event, probably due to the depletion of minerals in the water. Also, the layer is relatively easy to break away, though small components and intakes will require hours of cleaning.

POSEIDON METEOROLOGY

BUILDING BLOCKS

Weather systems are dominated by several factors. Planetary rotation, surface heating, surface friction, and Coriolis effect all shape global air patterns.

CLOUDS

Heating occurs in several ways. Clouds have a high albedo, reflecting more sunlight than is absorbed, and partially reflecting light bouncing off the surface back downward. This acts to protect the surface from UV light, preferentially store heat, and prevent overheating of the surface. Heat causes water to increase the humidity of the air, thus increasing cloud cover.

ICE

Icecaps form when more snow and ice accumulate during the winter than melt during the summer. Ocean currents and weather systems affect this process. Once iceshields develop, their high albedo tends to help maintain the ice, reflecting more light than the ocean surface.

HEAT/HUMIDITY

Surface heating provides energy to the entire meteorological system. Humidity increases the heat capacity of the atmosphere, giving weather systems even more strength. Air systems then move in complex ways, composed of several vectors.

Heat causes air to expand and thus rise. Planetary rotation moves the planet under the air, creating an apparent westward flow. Surface friction slows winds near the surface, and imparts motion to water below.

CORIOLIS EFFECT

Coriolis effect arises from the nature of a rotating sphere. Since rotation is constant, the farther a point is from the axis of the planet, the faster it must move to rotate the same arc in the same amount of time. The surface at the equator is moving more quickly eastward than the surface at higher latitudes.

As a weather system moves to higher latitudes, the eastward velocity of the planet's surface decreases, causing the system to apparently "veer" eastward.

PRESSURE

Pressure is a major factor in weather systems. The density of air is interlinked with temperature and humidity. Cooler air can become denser than warmer air. Humid air can hold more heat than dry air. These factors shape the motion of airmasses, from high to low pressure.

COMPLEX SYSTEMS

Much of the complex behavior of weather is derived from the fact that the atmosphere is three dimensional, and is strongly affected by two other systems. Land and sea shape weather, interacting with the basic forces of meteorology. Though Poseidon is simpler in some respects, due to the small percentage of landmass, the systems are still complex.

Hot and humid air will typically rise. This motion causes a zone of continuous low pressure, pulling fresh air along the surface. This is a typical low-pressure system, with air movement along the ground moving into the center, heating up, and rising. As air moves into the system, it imparts a clockwise turn in the Northern Hemisphere and counterclockwise turn in the Southern Hemisphere, due to the Coriolis effect.

This can be confusing. In the Northern Hemisphere, winds moving north veer east. Winds moving south veer west. These winds impart spin on the center, like a hand on a potter's wheel. At high altitudes, the spin is reversed as winds exit.

Strong low-pressure systems are cyclones, and are very common. Most storms are cyclones.

Airmasses can form systems in the reverse manner. Low humidity and cool air cause high pressure. Winds blow out along the surface, pulling high altitude air down into the center. These winds move clockwise in the Northern Hemisphere and counterclockwise in the Southern Hemisphere. They have few clouds. These are known as anticyclones. These form a belt at about 55° latitude, the anticyclone belt, which feeds on low-pressure systems and disrupts them.

Generally, moisture and heat increase the power of cyclones. In the tropics, these factors create massive cyclonic storms, known on Earth as hurricanes. The Storm Belt covers the tropics, at latitudes below 40°.

Cyclones in midlatitudes will move toward higher latitudes and east. Low and high pressures pull or push storms from this general course. Tropical cyclones will move west during their formation and then follow this track toward subtropical anticyclones.

Aridity systems form due to high altitude winds spilling off of the tropics, descending at roughly 40° latitude. As they warm, relative humidity becomes very low. This can create desert conditions, and often causes downflow of oceanic currents. As the airmasses descend, they deflect north and south, curving with the Coriolis effect, increasing westerly winds in the equator and easterly winds at high latitudes. They also pick up moisture, delivering rains to the tropics and temperate latitudes.

At the poles, cold, dry air creates a constant low-pressure zone, creating strong easterly winds.

Though the tropical cyclones of the Storm Belt have garnered the most attention from media and popular culture, there are several important weather systems that have a major impact on life on Poseidon.

POSEIDON RAIN SYSTEM

This system was originally termed the Pacifica Monsoon cycle, but the overall mechanism affects rainfall throughout Poseidon. The Southern Hope Chain and Arc of Fire are part of a distinct seasonal cycle, the Twilight Polar Stream. The overall features of the system are modified by local factors.

There are three identifiable periods in the Pacifica seasonal rains. The seasons were first researched by inhabitants of the Pacifica Archipelago, and have a bias toward their observations and the Southern Hemisphere.

Pacifica Wet Season: Northern spring-summer/southern autumn-winter

This time is frequently referred to as monsoon season. The origins of the major rains lie in the Challenger Deep, in the gap between the Endeavor Islands and Darwin's Archipelago. During the northern summer, most pressure systems collide with aridity systems, draining them of energy. With autumn comes a shift in winds. Southern systems gain energy and move on a more westerly track.

This brings a great deal of rain to the eastern side of Darwin's Archipelago.

The southern end of the Endeavor Islands receives relatively little rain, as most systems track further south. Rainfall is even less for the rest of the islands, though this depends on variations in the strength of the subtropical pressure systems to the east. This is linked to the Butterfly Gap phenomenon.

Moving across Poseidon's Reach, these systems gain a great deal of power and bring heavy, constant rains throughout the Pacifica Archipelago. These systems also bring rain to New Hawaii, as storms rise and cool over the Pacifica Archipelago. Tradewinds moving east pick up strength during this season.

Pacifica Storm Season: Northern autumn-early spring/southern spring-early autumn

This is the most chaotic period of the cycle. Shifting winds bring large variations in weather through Darwin's Archipelago, and some of the heaviest rainfall all year for the Endeavor Islands occurs as energetic cyclones spin northward into them. The aridity systems to the west of the Endeavor Islands show more instability at this time of year, as do the systems in the anticyclone belt north of them.

With this chaos come some of the most powerful cyclonic storms in the Southern Hemisphere. Moving along Poseidon's Reach, these storms can cause huge amounts of rainfall and damage to the Pacifica Archipelago. Some manage to feed systems in the Northern Hemisphere, giving new life and strength to cyclones there.

Along the eastern side of the Pacifica Archipelago, this season is marked by wet, stormy weather. The western side receives rain mainly from systems that make it through the archipelago. This season can also cause the upwelling to the west to drift northward, causing a boom in fishing around Neptune's Cluster and the Sierra Nueva.

Pacifica Dry Season: Northern late summer-early autumn/southern late winter-early spring

During this relatively short period, a chaotic series of storms can bring large amounts of rainfall to New Hawaii and other northern regions. These storms are marked by great irregularity, and there are multiannual cycles of varying activity.

Occasionally these storms wander into the Southern Hemisphere, but this is relatively rare.

The same period in the Southern Hemisphere brings a relatively dry season to the Pacifica Archipelago. Milder, cooler weather springs from the western side, and storms still bring rains throughout, but the activity is generally lessened. There are small-scale, regional variations, depending on airflow patterns.

During this period, Darwin's Archipelago receives relatively little rain. Most of the westerly storms hit the southern end of the Endeavor Islands, moving in a generally northwesterly curve. These intersect with the aridity system west of Endeavor Islands. The rest of the Endeavor Islands receive a fairly steady amount of rain, varying mainly in the constant cyclonic activity tracking across the New Pacific.

THE POSEIDON CONVEYER

One of the most important oceanic current variations, in terms of fishing and aquaculture, is the Lamont-Kandinsky-Hackett cycle, also known as the Poseidon Conveyer effect or the Primary Poseidon Gyre.

The first component occurs around the Arc of Fire. A major upwelling of cold, benthic waters sits east of Albion, in the Southern Hope Chain. These currents, rich in nutrients, flow east and then north along either side of the Arc. Aridity systems to either side of the Arc then cause these surface currents to fall back to the ocean floor.

The second part of the conveyer starts to the east of the Pacifica Archipelago. Surface currents move west, then divide into a northwestern and southeastern current. The northwestern current is strong, encountering a downflow near New Hawaii. This benthic current moves slowly around the archipelago, joined by weaker benthic flows, until it arrives to the western waters off of the Pacifica Archipelago shelf. Here, western winds create an upwelling, bringing the current to the surface.

Changes in weather systems can disrupt the aridity systems flanking the Arc. This is most frequent during the storm season, when powerful cyclonics in the Southern Hemisphere can intersect with them. Usually only the western aridity systems are affected. In any case, when the systems are weakened, it begins the Even Phase of the cycle.

Results

The intersection of cyclones with the aridity systems has the benefit of reducing storm activity in Darwin's Archipelago and the Pacifica Archipelago.

Once these systems are weakened, however, the upwelling west of the Arc of Fire slows down. This backs the system up. The northern flow to the west is weakened, increasing the northern flow to the east. This flow diverts further east, moving away from the Arc of Fire.

On the western coasts of the Arc of Fire, weather is warmer and more humid, but fishing and aquaculture are stricken. Storms are more common, particularly in the north.

On the eastern coast, weather is slightly warmer and fishing is still poor. However, deep oceanic animals thrive far to the east, and deep-ocean fishing booms. This effect is lessened if the eastern aridity system is weakened.

Rainstorms north of the Arc accompany the same weather system that sends cyclonics to the Arc. This can create an El Niño-like effect, slowing the tradewinds that cross Poseidon's Reach. This, in turn, slows down the downflow east of the Pacifica Archipelago and upwelling west of Darwin's Archipelago and the Endeavor Islands. The effect is not acute, but can snowball with other factors.

Timing

How long and when these events occur is still unknown. About four distinct Even Phases have occurred during human occupation of Poseidon, with no clear timing. The storm pattern lasts two to three years, with the oceanographic effects lasting another three years. The eastern current of the Arc moves over longer periods than the western current. The last Even Phase ended in 2193. No Even Phase has been observed where the eastern subtropical system is also weakened, but models suggest strongly that it should occur occasionally.

The timing of the Pacifica component is very long, and it is estimated that the lagtime is on the order of centuries. There is no clear, observable link between when the Even Phase of the Arc of Fire begins and when that of the Pacifica Archipelago begins. This component occurs more slowly and over longer periods than the other, though it is not known precisely how long these periods last. The

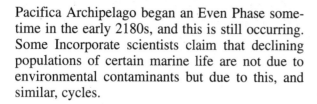

Pacifica Archipelago began an Even Phase sometime in the early 2180s, and this is still occurring. Some Incorporate scientists claim that declining populations of certain marine life are not due to environmental contaminants but due to this, and similar, cycles.

POSEIDON NIÑO EFFECT

This effect is quite similar to the El Niño/La Niña effect of Earth, but further reaching. The warm eastern waters of the Pacifica Archipelago create a rising stream of warm air. This creates a tradewind, blowing at high altitudes eastward. Around Darwin's Archipelago and the Endeavor Islands, the system cools and drops, creating high-pressure systems. This is typically referred to as the Haven Tradewind.

Another tradewind runs along the Challenger Deep, fueled by rising air systems to the east of the Endeavor Islands, running east to the Pacifica Archipelago, and then dropping. The high pressure caused creates strong westward surface winds. This wind is called the Pacifica Tradewind.

Rising warm air near the region where they descend can disrupt tradewinds. This slows the surface winds and increases rainfall in these regions. Both of these effects slow or halt upwelling, and can even create downflows.

The Reach Obstruction, the El Niño effect for the Reach tradewinds, generally starts at the beginning of the northern autumn. Shifting air systems can create slow-moving warm airmasses above the Arc of Fire. Many of these systems divert northeast or southeast, causing increases of rainfall and slowing surface winds. This brings an early end to the dry season for both the Pacifica Archipelago and Darwin's Archipelago, and brings an uncharacteristically heavy wet season to the western side of Darwin's Archipelago. Unfortunately, this also causes the upwelling west of Darwin's Archipelago to lose steam.

The same system causes warm airmasses to form east of Darwin's Archipelago, which drift northward. These interfere with Endeavor's upwelling system, and further contribute to the faltering of the Reach tradewinds, with similar effects on the western coast of the Endeavor Islands.

The six recorded instances of the Reach Obstruction are 2177-2178, 2184-2185, 2186-2187, 2188-2189, 2194-2195, 2196-2197. Observations made previous to 2176 are somewhat speculative, but the frequency is reliably one year in four. Cyclical variations in Reach Obstructions are likely, but have not been documented.

The Pacifica Obstruction is the corresponding effect for the Pacifica tradewinds, though it is rare. During the dry season, an interaction between southern anticyclonic systems and weak southern aridity systems can lead to countercurrents, causing waters to stall west of the Pacifica Archipelago. Warm patches then form in the eastern edges of the Challenger Deep, disrupting tradewinds. The mechanism is somewhat complex, but the ultimate result is to bring an El Niño event to the Pacifica Archipelago. This brings rainfall during the normally dry season, but the western waters become very poor in nutrients.

This event is more rare than the Reach Obstruction, and only two have been conclusively observed. The first was in 2183 and the second in 2190.

TWILIGHT POLAR STREAM

The weather of the Southern Hope Chain and much of the Arc of Fire is not directly part of the Poseidon rain system. These regions are strongly affected by airmasses linked to the south pole.

There are three components of the system. The first is at about 70° south latitude, 60° west longitude, west of the Southern Hope Chain. The second is the Twilight crosspolar airstream. This moves generally northeast from about 60° east latitude, and is partially responsible for the upwelling there. The third component is the downflow system east of the Arc of Fire.

During the southern summers, strong rising aircurrents move south along 170° west longitude, through the Twilight Chain, bringing moderate weather to the islands. It crosses the southern cap, dropping quickly until it reaches the waters east of Albion. This stream and polar melt disrupts local upwelling. The system slows the currents along either side of the Arc of Fire, creating warmer, more humid weather and nutrient-poor waters along the coasts.

Toward the end of summer, a strong current develops north of Albion and moves eastward. The downflow system east and west of the Arc of Fire increases in power, pulling surface currents and kickstarting the system. By autumn, a powerful low-pressure system develops west of the Southern Hope Chain, forming a complex interaction with the anticyclone belt.

Most winters bring strong eastern flows through El Mar Del Sur, cold weather in the Southern Hope Chain, and cool weather throughout the Arc of Fire. Both coasts of the Arc have cool, nutrient-rich waters and relatively dry weather.

The Challenger anticyclonic system is chaotic, however. For reasons that are still unclear, the system can generate powerful cross-polar flows and highly mobile low-pressure systems. This results in a series of strong polar storms. Very cold temperatures and heavy snowstorms buffet the Southern Hope Chain, and often winter storms will collide with Westscape. This can slow down the Arc of Fire current system, creating unusually warm and wet winters.

Typically, one winter in five will cause heavy snowfall in the Southern Hope Chain, and one in 15 will cause snowstorms to reach Westscape. Under normal circumstances, the eastern Challenger anticyclones prevent any cold airmasses from reaching Westscape.

BUTTERFLY GAP

This region of ocean, north of Darwin's Archipelago and west of the Endeavor Islands, is the center of a very chaotic weather system. More stable portions of the cycle are key to the Pacifica monsoon cycle.

A series of aridity systems further west cause downflows, while strong upwelling occurs close to the western edge of the Endeavor plate and along the western edge of Darwin's Archipelago. Storm systems and surface waters flow strongly through the gap.

Even when the Niño effect is not in force, tradewinds form an irregular system. During the northern summer, the tradewinds blow more strongly from the west of the Endeavor Islands, increasing the upwelling and fertile waters. During the other three seasons, the upwelling of the Endeavor Islands depends on airflow from the Challenger Deep, and Darwin's Archipelago enjoys greater winds and upwelling.

This seasonal shift creates a cool summer for the western Endeavor Islands and relatively moist, warm winters for the western regions of Darwin's Archipelago.

Over time, this effect increases the flow of benthic currents to the north and south of the Endeavor Islands. A more noticeable result is that sometimes the same weather that weakens the western subtropical systems will increase the normally weak eastern subtropical systems. If this happens, upwelling forms to the east of the Endeavor Islands, beginning a period of somewhat cooler and calmer weather, as well as a boom of life from the nutrient-rich waters.

Due to this effect, the region tends to alternating years of upwelling strength and poor fishing.

WESTSCAPE SYSTEM

A weak aridity system circulates west of Westscape. The arid winds, combined with high mountains, create the deserts of Westscape. During the Pacifica storm season, this system can weaken as large, moist airmasses collide with it. What little

rainfall Westscape's deserts receive usually falls during this season.

SEASONS BY REGION
PACIFICA ARCHIPELAGO

Weather year-round is generally hot, wet, and stormy. Seasons bring variations in the degree, but the temperature and humidity is high in the tropics and slightly less so in the subtropics.

The dry season is fairly brief, running from late winter to early spring in the southern hemisphere. Weather is dry for the region, and the western regions are mild and cooler. Irregular rainstorms of some strength hit the north. Overall rainfall is distinctly lower.

During Reach Obstructions of the tradewinds, the dry season ends even earlier, lasting only eight to 10 days before giving way to the wet season.

During very rare Pacifica Obstructions, the western half of the archipelago gets unusually warm and rainy weather. This effect lasts well into the wet season. The waters of the western region become nutrient poor, and there are marked drops in fish populations.

The wet, or monsoon, season begins in the southern autumn and runs through winter. The islands are almost constantly drenched in heavy rainfall. Though there are storms, they are generally milder than those of the storm season. New Hawaii sees somewhat more irregular rainfall.

Storm season begins in spring and runs through summer and into early autumn. It is marked by major storms throughout and heavy, though irregular, rainfall. The western side of the archipelago is somewhat calmer.

WESTSCAPE

The weather is similar to that of the rest of the archipelago, with two variations. The Westscape system to the west creates arid conditions, though this is sometimes minimized during the storm season. The Twilight Polar Stream can cause unusual, though brief, snowstorms in winter. This only occurs about one winter in 15, and has happened once since Poseidon's resettlement, in 2188.

ENDEAVOR ISLANDS

Inhabitants of the Endeavor Islands simply divide their years into dry season and Monsoon season.

The general weather is a bit cooler and drier than in the Pacifica Archipelago.

Dry season runs from spring until summer, around the same time as Pacifica's wet season. The southern tip gets occasional rainstorms, sometimes violent ones. The rest of the Endeavor Islands get relatively little rain, for the tropics.

Monsoon season starts in late summer, extends through autumn and winter, ending in early spring. This corresponds to the Pacfica Archipelago's storm season. Constant rain and storms mark this season more evenly throughout the islands.

During the summer, weather is milder and the waters more fertile, due to the Butterfly Gap effect.

At the beginning of the wet season is a period of moderate rains and few storms, with more rain to the south. This corresponds with the dry season of Pacifica, Endeavor Islanders simply consider it the buildup to monsoon season.

During years marked by the Reach Obstruction, the western edge of the islands experiences an unusually rainy and warm autumn, with less fertile waters.

DARWIN'S ARCHIPELAGO

The archipelago is more mild than usual at its latitude, due to cooling effects from upwelling. It also gets comparatively fewer storms than other equatorial regions, due to a number of weather systems to the east. It is still a rather humid, hot region.

Dry season, from late winter through early spring (southern hemisphere), is characteristically dry. The eastern tip sometimes gets heavy rainstorms, but most storms track northeast and miss land.

During the winter, the western edge of the archipelago gets warmer weather and more rain, accompanied by warm, nutrient-poor waters.

Storm season, from spring through early autumn, brings extreme weather and heavy rains.

Wet season lasts from autumn through winter. There is frequent rainfall, with the eastern edge of the archipelago receiving the most.

During periods of Reach Obstruction, the western side becomes warm and rainy during the spring.

This is accompanied by nutrient-poor waters to the west.

ARC OF FIRE

The northern edge of this region, particularly near the Plesset Straights, sometimes shares the weather patterns of Darwin's Archipelago. The northern regions have drier but more irregular weather than the islands south of the southern tropic. The southern region is dry and temperate.

Summers are warm and humid, with nutrient-poor waters on both sides.

Winters are cool and dry, with nutrient-rich waters. Occasionally the Twilight Polar Stream can cause warm and rainy winters, as well as nutrient-poor waters along either side of the Arc.

SOUTHERN HOPE CHAIN

This region is cold or temperate, and rather dry.

Summers are cold and dry to the east, warmer and less arid to the west.

Winter is very cold, with a slight moderating effect caused along El Mar Del Sur. One winter in five brings severe polar ice storms.

Spring can bring rainfall, particularly toward the west, from easterlies spilling off storms in the Pacifica Archipelago.

ATMOSPHERIC PHENOMENA

While not strictly meteorological, there are a number of environmental phenomena that are common to Poseidon.

POLAR LIGHTS

Solar wind is a plasma composed of ionized hydrogen. This outflowing plasma interacts with the magnetosphere of a planet, forming a huge charged "tail" of particles away from the sun. The particles form a dynamo, with charged particles circulating between a positive pole at the planet's "dawn" and a negative pole at the planet's "evening."

Cycles of solar flares cause surges in the solar wind. These disrupt the dynamo, making it constrict. At the top of the planet's atmosphere, the ionosphere is composed of ionized atmospheric gases. These will conduct the bunched-up particles, resulting in an electrical short. The particles flow along the planet's magnetic field lines, diving toward each pole.

The current of electrons through atmospheric gases creates the observed Polar Lights, as they are called on Poseidon. The greater tilt of the planet and comparatively weaker magnetosphere results in more dramatic and beautiful lights.

The beauty is also a danger. Polar lights are the visible effect of a massive flow of particles into the planet. This can knock out large power systems and play havoc with instruments, particularly for craft high in the atmosphere. Ionization of the atmosphere can disrupt communications over long distances. The surges in solar activity associated with the polar lights are also hazards for spacecraft.

AURORAL COLUMNS

These are a particularly dangerous and powerful variation of the Polar Lights. The ozone layer of Poseidon is a bit thicker than that of Earth. At certain points of the solar cycle, it is believed, a particularly large series of solar flares hits the planet, when one polar cap is oriented most toward the sun. With the planet's significant tilt and relatively weak magnetosphere, the tail is flooded and then lets loose with a massive, sudden flux.

Auroral columns extend from the top of the atmosphere almost to the planetary surface and are often accompanied by lightning and other discharges. They can be seen for thousands of kilometers. They can also ionize the atmosphere over much of the planet, causing communications blackouts and damaging power systems.

Thankfully, auroral columns are fairly rare, having only been reliably observed three times since Poseidon was first discovered. All three instances struck the north pole, leading GEO and Incorporate officials to declare that the phenomenon is only associated with that pole. Planetologists warn that there is no conclusive evidence that this is true. No steps have been taken to protect against a southern auroral column.

FIELD GUIDE

CHAPTER

03

ANGEL WINGS (*Poena angelus*)

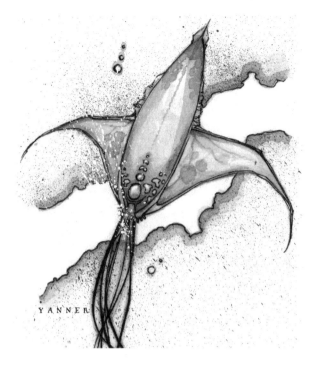

YANNER

Angel wings are small, fragile, planktonic invertebrates commonly found in Poseidon's warmer waters. These animals are ctenophore analogs, and have flat, transparent bodies and pairs of wing-like paddles that give the species limited maneuverability. When they catch the light, iridescent colors shimmer across the paddles, ostensibly giving the species its name. Angel wings typically hang vertically in the water, trailing a short, thin mass of tentacles as they drift with the current.

BEHAVIOR

Angel wings are planktivores, consuming the tiny organisms that get caught in the sticky coating covering their trailing tendrils. They are generally not a danger to humans, but bear mention in this report for a troublesome aspect of their reproductive biology.

During their year-round breeding cycles, angel wings produce small, sticky egg clusters on the distal ends of their tentacles. When these tendrils come in accidental contact with another organism, the tendril tips and their egg clusters break off, hitching a ride on the passing creature. The eggs shortly hatch and the angel wing larvae burrow into the skin of the host. There they reside for several days, growing only slightly, but collecting vital organic compounds from the host that adult angel wings are apparently unable to provide. When suf-

ficient quantities of these compounds are collected, the tiny larvae squirm out from the host's tissues and become free-living plankton.

Angel wings represent a potentially serious threat to human hosts, but one that is easily dealt with if the infestation is caught in time. Angel wing larvae infest humans in the same way they infect indigenous animals. The compounds they seek, however, are apparently absent from the human biochemical makeup. When not supplied with the nutrient, angel wing larvae fail to emerge, and after approximately a week they die. The necrotic parasites can subsequently cause a number of complications including fast fungus (MG 168) infections, gangrene, and various other toxicity syndromes.

Virtually every native on Poseidon has been infected with angel wing larvae at some point in their lives, and many have been infected more than once. Consequently, the cure is well known across the archipelago, at least in areas with a high native population. Though unpleasant, the cure is simple and completely effective. The infected individual must coat the infested region of skin, marked by an irritating rash, with a paste of freshly ground fish meat. Any species will do, as the indigenous flesh apparently provides the larvae with the mystery nutrient they seek. The fish paste poultice must be replaced every few hours, but after three or four days the larvae crawl out, the rash disappears, and the host is parasite-free.

Range	Tropical and semi-tropical waters planet wide
Habitat	Photic zone
Length	10 to 18 centimeters
Weight	15 to 25 grams
Frequency	Common
Resource Value	None
Threat Level	Low
Attacks	None
Damage Rating	None
Movement	Drifts with current
Build	-28
Fitness	-2
Agility	-2
Awareness	-8
Will	0
Endurance	0
Reflexes	-5
Strength	-15
Toughness	-8
Armor	None

AURORA BORIALGAE

(Autus fervens)

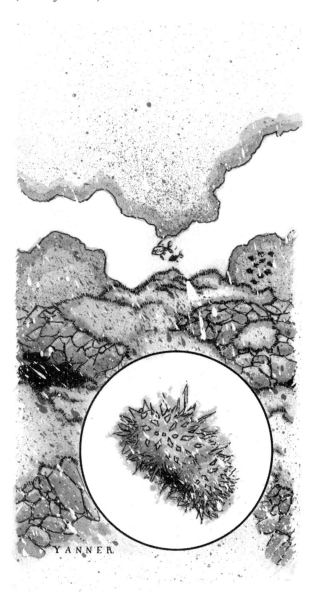

YANNER

Aurora Borialgae is the unfortunate common name for one of the more spectacular species of reef-building organisms on Poseidon. In the Pacifica Archipelago, borialgae occurs only in the Westcape region, though biologists have reported a wider, tropical distribution.

Borialgae is actually a protist analog, and has more in common with plants than terrestrial coral polyps. It grows in only very shallow, nutrient-rich waters, and is most abundant at sites enriched by deep-ocean upwelling. The species is a colonial organism that grows in massive, monogenetic patch reefs that can stretch for dozens of kilometers. The individual organisms are small, fleshy clusters that surround themselves with crusty, interconnected, calcitic shells, extracted ion by ion from Poseidon's mineral rich waters.

The algae varies in color from dark purples, browns, and greens to gold, yellow, and pale orange. The calcium shell is pale and translucent, but trace minerals presumably washed from the Westcape mainland are incorporated into the calcium compounds, giving the reef structure itself a rusty iron hue.

The borialgae reef material is relatively soft and crumbles easily, giving the growths extremely sharp edges and creating a severe hazard for any swimmer or cetacean unfortunate enough to brush against the reef.

BEHAVIOR

Borialgae demonstrates a unique behavior that has made the species well known, even back on Earth, and has lead to a growing tourist industry during the organism's short summer reproductive season. Hundreds of natives from Westcape and thousands of tourists from Dyfedd come by catamaran, yacht, and VTOL to witness the unique show offered by the region's Skyscraper Reefs (MG 107).

Every season, fully one third of the individual plants comprising each reef bioconcentrate dissolved magnesium from the surrounding seawater and store it in tiny pockets within the reef shell structure. In conjunction with the seasonal release of gamete-like spores, some unknown environmental stimulus causes an equally unknown chemical mechanism to oxidize the concentrated magnesium. The tiny flares provide a spectacular nighttime light show that races up and down the length of each reef, turning the darkened waters into a fairy world of wavering glow and shimmering color. Native and newcomer visitors alike are often moved to tears by the beautifully eerie sight.

How the individual colonies synchronize their flares, what controls which individual plants collect magnesium, when a given reef lights up, or even what the purpose of the natural illumination might be are all open to speculation. Biologists at HISTOS (MG 114) in Dyfedd are studying the phenomena, but are currently at a complete loss to explain it.

Range	Tropical waters planetwide
Habitat	Shallow, nutrient-rich waters
Length	Individuals up to 2 centimeters in diameter, single colonies up to 35 kilometers along longest axis
Weight	Up to 6 grams per individual
Frequency	Rare
Resource Value	Commercially important to the tourist trade in Westcape
Threat Level	Low; hazard to swimmers
Attacks	Accidental impact
Damage Rating	2
Movement	N/A
Build	N/A
Fitness	N/A
Agility	N/A
Awareness	N/A
Will	N/A
Endurance	N/A
Reflexes	N/A
Strength	N/A
Toughness	N/A
Armor	None

BAD MOJO (*Magus malum*)

The mojo is a large species of predatory fish known for its exceptional speed and singular huntsmanship. The mojo is streamlined with bright, silvery skin, a well-muscled and shallow body, and a stiff lunate tail. The animal's primary jaws are long and narrow and lined with dozens of serrated teeth. The species lateral jaws are wide and sport razor sharp bony spurs along their outer edges. The mojo is one of the fastest fish species on the colony world, and in the shifting light of the open ocean mojos seem to fade in and out like ghosts as their silver hides reflect the colors around them.

BEHAVIOR

The mojo is a predator with a unique niche. The fish specializes in preying on other predators, attacking when its target is distracted by its own hunt or struggling food. Mojos hunt in pairs or trios, swimming near the surface and following schools of baitfish. When other predatory species descend on the bait, the mojos attack, streaking out of the glare of the overhead sun like surprise dive-bombers. They race past their unsuspecting targets at speeds in excess of 60 kilometers an hour. They slip past so closely that the razor-like spurs along their lateral jaws slice into their prey, causing

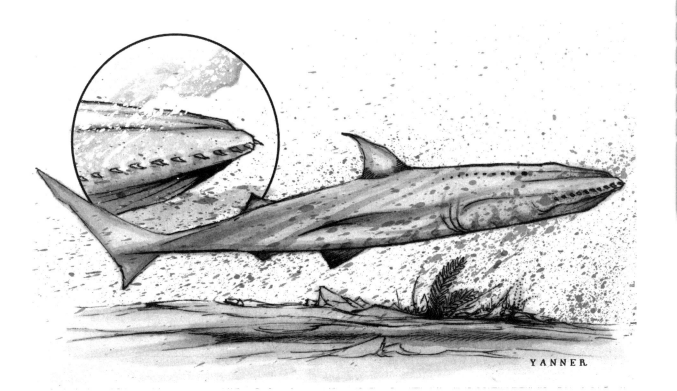

YANNER

severe muscle damage that leaves the unsuspecting fish crippled and bleeding. The mojo usually makes a second and third pass, then circles around to tear large mouthfuls from the now helpless predator-turned-prey.

Though bad mojos seem to prefer hunting animals significantly smaller than themselves, they have been known to attack larger prey, including humans. Though these attacks are rare, they have been documented and are usually lethal. Spear fishermen, native hunters, and biologists collecting specimens are advised to be wary of these animals. Most such attacks on humans have come as might be expected, while they were distracted with their own struggling quarry.

Newcomers have taken to calling these fish "marshals" in place of the native name. The name is apparently an anthropomorphic comment on the species' ruthless dog-eat-dog tactics. Though reportedly the marshals themselves consider the slang an apt comparison, the Justice Commission officially discourages GEO personnel and their associates from using the name.

Range	Temperate waters of the southern hemisphere
Habitat	Pelagic surface waters
Length	1.5 to 2.3 meters
Weight	Up to 80 kilograms
Frequency	Rare
Resource Value	Medium; the species is tasty but difficult and somewhat dangerous to catch
Threat Level	Medium; attacks on humans are rare but potentially lethal
Attacks	Slash 5, Bite 3
Damage	Slash 5, Bite 3
Movement	10/32
Build	4
Fitness	3
Agility	1
Awareness	2
Will	3
Endurance	5
Reflexes	1
Strength	3
Toughness	2
Armor	1

BASILISK (*Lacerta infucatus* var.)

The basilisk is certainly not the fearsome creature its mythical name implies. In fact it is quite the opposite and is seemingly harmless to anything but the occasional insectoid. The basilisk is a common reptiloid found throughout the tropical and subtropical regions of the Pacifica Archipelago. It is similar in form and ecology to Terrestrial iguanas, though the various species are brightly colored and typically much larger than their Earthbound analogs. Their remarkable rainbow pigmentation is likely a form of warning coloration keying potential predators to the animal's foul tasting and mildly toxic hide.

BEHAVIOR

The basilisk is primarily a vegetarian, eating a variety of plant life including various toxic species without ill effect. It is probable that its own toxic nature is the result of metabolic incorporation of these plant poisons. Basilisks also include insects as a nutritionally important part of their diet, and are uniquely adapted to preying on them. These animals produce saliva with a sweet, flowery fragrance, which when combined with their bright coloration, seems sufficient to dupe nectar-feeding insects into approaching close enough to be snagged from the air. Basilisks have long, flexible necks well adapted to sudden lunges, and when hunting insects they sit with heads cocked upwards, mouths agape. When foraging insects come too close, basilisks snap their necks out with a blinding lunge few insects can escape.

In all other movements, basilisks are slow and torpid. They are uniquely docile and when not feeding they typically spend their time basking in the sun. They have few predators, even in Poseidon's hungry ecology, and this is likely due to their borrowed toxicity. Basilisks are long lived and slow growing, and except for the breeding season, during which they gather in large, swarming masses, they appear to be solitary animals.

Their beautiful coloration, pleasant odor, and docile nature have made basilisks popular pets among natives and frontiersmen. In many villages and outposts it is not uncommon to see these lizards lounging on porch rails, roof beams, chair backs, or even in the laps of children. Though their innate intelligence is low, they respond contentedly to stroking and petting and so unintentionally illicit affection from humans.

Range	Tropics and subtropics throughout the Pacifica Archipelago and likely planetwide
Habitat	Primarily tree-dwellers common in jungle, coastal scrubland, and mountain forest
Length	0.5 to 2.1 meters, including their long tail
Weight	0.25 to 16 kilograms
Frequency	Common
Resource Value	Valued as a pets in native culture, and if carefully skinned so as not to contaminate the flesh with hide-borne toxins, the meat is light and tasty
Threat Level	Minimal
Attacks	Bite 2
Damage Rating	1
Poison	Induces vomiting and intestinal pain
	Onset Time 10 minutes
	Duration 3 to 4 hours
	Damage Rating 1
Movement	0.1/1.0

Build	-3
Fitness	0
Agility	-1
Awareness	-1
Will	0
Endurance	0
Reflexes	2
Strength	-1
Toughness	0
Armor	None

BIG ROUND THING (unclassified)

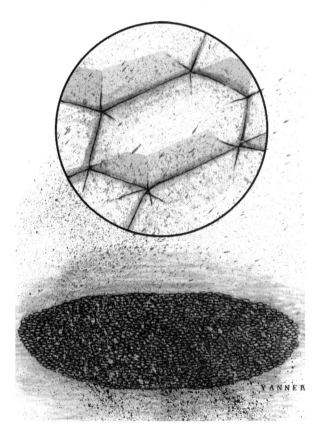

BRTs, or rounders as most natives call them, are another of the seemingly endless ecological enigmas found on Poseidon. Featuring a structure and biology as unlikely as their name, these creatures are enormous, often reaching diameters in excess of 100 meters. At their thickest, however, rounders seldom exceed one meter from their dorsal to ventral surfaces. The central portion of the organism typically consists of several overlapping, staggered layers of subunits that pare down to a single ragged layer at the creature's margins.

The body of the organism is extremely tough and rubbery, and the surfaces are coated with a thick

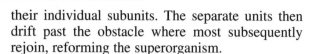

slime that apparently helps prevent encrusting growths from taking hold. The upper layers of tissue contain large patches of mottled, dark brown pigments that are light sensitive and conduct a form of photosynthesis. The spaces between these patches are translucent, and almost transparent in places. The lower layers of tissue contain much less pigmentation and are typically pale reds and yellows. When a rounder is viewed from below, with bright sun above, the effect is impressive. The organism looks like a muted, living stained-glass window, appearing to cast countless wavering beams of subtly colored light into the depths.

BRTs appear to be some form of superorganism that is actually a collection of smaller units that some biologists argue should be classified as separate species. These subunit organisms are seldom encountered independently, however, and in captivity quickly enter a state of dormancy that invariably precedes death. This implies that the organism is not simply a colony of individuals, but an organic manifestation of the physiological interdependence of its smaller units. There are a variety of these subunit forms, though beyond subtle differences in shape and coloration, the uninitiated find them difficult to tell apart.

Most subunits are multisided polygons with rounded corners. The most abundant units are hexagonal and rarely exceed two meters in diameter. Ecologists classify the individual subunits by their shape and position within the greater structure—rim units, dorsal units, ventral units, visceral units, and so forth. Dorsal units contain the majority of the photosynthetic pigments, while the translucent ventral units support tiny feeding papillae that gather microscopic organisms and dissolved nutrients from the water. In addition to numerous structures whose functions are not currently understood, the visceral units contain grape-like collections of air bladders used to regulate buoyancy.

BEHAVIOR

Big round things are drifters, making them planktonic organisms despite their incredible size. During the day the creatures bask at or very near the surface, feeding on the much smaller phytoplankton. At night, the organism submerges, disappearing into the depths. Though confirmation is still forthcoming, biologists speculate that the organism sinks to the sea floor where it can absorb nutrients absent at the surface. Rounders that drift ashore or encounter storms readily break up into

their individual subunits. The separate units then drift past the obstacle where most subsequently rejoin, reforming the superorganism.

Virtually nothing is known about rounder reproductive biology, as the mechanism has yet to even be identified. The creature also remains unclassified as debate continues over its phylogeny. Many advocate its inclusion in the plant-animal crossover kingdom suggested in the GEO's recently proposed Poseidon taxonomy.

BRTs themselves are of little economic value to either natives or colonials. They do, however, attract a number of valuable aquatic and avian species looking for temporary shelter or food. These transient communities are favored hunting grounds for native spear fishermen and curious biologists.

Rounders pose little threat, but when near the surface they can be navigational hazards. Though a collision with a BRT will seldom damage a boat hull, the individual subunits that often break free with the impact can clog MHD drive tubes. Note also that big round things are a favorite food for greater whites (MG 171), and congregations of rounders in current eddies or along drift lines often attract these dangerous animals.

Range	Planetwide
Habitat	Surface waters, typically adrift along the margins of major currents
Length	Up to 120 meters in diameter
Weight	90 to 110 metric tons
Frequency	Uncommon
Resource Value	Medium; valuable as hunting grounds and as a scientific curiosity
Threat Level	Low
Attacks	None
Damage Rating	N/A
Movement	Drifts with current
Build	N/A
Fitness	N/A
Agility	N/A
Awareness	N/A
Will	N/A
Endurance	N/A
Reflexes	N/A
Strength	N/A
Toughness	N/A
Armor	N/A

BLOOD HUNTER (*Venator cruentus*)

YANNER

Blood hunters, or hunters as they are more commonly called, are voracious fish analogs that inhabit the shallow coastal waters of Poseidon's tropics. These fish are most appropriately compared to the now-extinct piranha species of Terrestrial South America. They are dark green to black with an iridescent sheen in bright light. They are sleek bodied, fast swimmers with two rows of exceptionally sharp slicing teeth on each of their four jaws.

BEHAVIOR

Hunters swim in large, tightly packed schools of several thousand animals. They patrol coastal shallows in a constant search for prey and their particular attraction to the scent of blood is likely the reason for their common native name. They are keen cooperative predators that kill even the largest animals. A typical school of hunters can flence a lesser white (see page 85) to the bone in seconds, instantly turning the surrounding water into a bloody froth of swarming fish and drifting bits of tissue.

Hunters tend to swim near the surface, and are so closely packed that from above they look like a single, larger animal. In such schools individuals constantly break the surface, churning the water and leaving a notable wake. This is often the only warning before hunters attack, and even the youngest native children watch warily for such sign.

Fortunately, blood hunters are a relatively rare species and where they do occur they seem staunchly territorial. In the rare event that one school strays into the territory of another, the defending school is quick to attack. The result is typically a bloody decimation of both schools that leaves each so depleted neither is able to hunt effectively. Strangely, a single new school typically reforms from the remnants of the originals. Biologists think these occasional territorial battles may be a natural culling in response to overpopulation, where the end result is an ecological boon of increased genetic diversity, reduced competition, and larger territory.

Range	Tropical waters planetwide
Habitat	Shallow coastal waters, commonly bays, marshes, and estuaries. There are reports that some tropical rivers may support smaller schools of freshwater hunters, but such reports have yet to be verified.
Length	Up to 30 centimeters
Weight	0.35 kilograms
Frequency	Rare
Resource Value	Minimal; though edible, they are considered too dangerous to fish
Threat Level	Extreme
Attacks	Bite 4
Damage Rating	2
Movement	6/15
Build	-20
Fitness	4
Agility	4
Awareness	2
Will	2

Endurance	5
Reflexes	3
Strength	-8
Toughness	-4
Armor	None

BUBBLE ARRAY (unclassified)

The bubble array is a bizarre aquatic creature, and one for which there is no suitable Terrestrial analog. Bubble arrays consist of a multitude of transparent spheres, clustered together to form a long trailing mass. A mature array can be almost 70 meters in length, consisting of a symmetrical assembly of spheres at the front that tapers into a long train of single interconnected bubbles at the end. The spheres range in size, with the anterior bubbles reaching almost a meter in diameter, and the tail bubbles as small as a quarter of a meter. The bubble membranes and the tissue-fluid amalgam filling them have almost the same incidence of refraction as seawater, and so the organism is virtually invisible from any distance greater than a few meters.

BEHAVIOR

Bubble arrays are essentially planktonic organisms, able to swim only with the current or in the calmest waters. Most of the anterior bubbles support clusters of long spine-like protrusions that paddle in tiny circles, driving the creature forward in a slow, randomly undulating motion reminiscent of a dragon in a Chinese festival. The rotating spines can be more than half a meter long and may reflect bright light with a colorful iridescence. The shimmer from these spines is often the first evidence of the creature's presence.

A bubble array swims slowly through the water collecting zooplankton and other small marine animals within the interstices of its individual bubbles. Acidic secretions within these pockets and dead end canals quickly dispatch and then slowly dissolve the prey into basic organic compounds. This nutrient rich fluid is absorbed through the surface of the inner spheres and apparently distributed from there throughout the mass of the creature.

The bubble array is likely a distant relative of the blimp (MG 164), but one that has evolved a different use for the hydrogen it electrolyzes from seawater. Unlike the blimp, which uses the hydrogen it products as a lifting gas, the array uses its hydrogen to produce hydrochloric acid. This acid is

secreted into the enclosed channels of the array's body where it is used to kill and digest the array's food. The acids are also used to protect the creature itself from predation. The acids it secretes are concentrated enough to burn on contact, making the array a painful mouthful for even Poseidon's biggest predators.

As benign as the bubble array may appear, care should be taken to avoid physical contact with one. The acids the creature ejects as a defensive measure will damage bioplastic equipment and readily burn exposed skin.

Range	Temperate waters planetwide
Habitat	Photic zone
Length	Up to 70 meters
Weight	1.25 to 2.0 metric tons
Frequency	Uncommon
Resource Value	None
Threat Level	Low; use caution to avoid chemical burns
Attacks	None
Damage Rating	N/A
Movement	1
Build	40
Fitness	-6
Agility	-30
Awareness	-20
Will	0
Endurance	-3
Reflexes	-25
Strength	N/A
Toughness	9
Armor	None

CHUB (*Victus facilis* var.)

YANNER

Chubs are small unlikely creatures and are compared most frequently to Terrestrial rabbits. There are many known species varying in size, coloration, and behavior, but the similarities are greater than the differences. Chubs are small creatures with no defenses and the unfortunate lot of serving as prey for even the most timid of Poseidon's carnivores. Chubs are furless, but their bare skin is soft and has tiny wrinkles that give it a velvety texture. They have six legs with large digging feet, but they are still relatively clumsy and slow animals.

BEHAVIOR

Chubs are herbivores feeding preferentially on seeds and fruits that fall to the ground, but they will consume just about any plant material available. They have limited climbing ability, and are restricted to the lower underbrush where they scrabble around foraging for food. Chubs are burrowing animals, and their simple warrens seem to be their only defense against, and the only reason they have survived in, Poseidon's unforgiving ecology.

Chubs are considered cute, at least by Poseidon standards where scales, poisons, and webbed feet are the norm. They also have the unfortunate luck of being quite flavorful, their meat having a natural buttery flavor. Even though their small colonies occur naturally only in the coastal scrubland of the Westcape region, chubs have become a favorite pet and meat source, and are common livestock in native settlements throughout the archipelago.

Range	Natural populations occur only on the islands of the Westcape region, though transplanted chubs have established viable colonies throughout the Pacifica Archipelago where they have escaped native livestock hutches.
Habitat	Dry coastal scrub forest
Length	20 to 25 centimeters
Weight	0.25 to 0.75 kilograms
Frequency	Common
Resource Value	High; though there is little meat on each animal, chub flesh is delicious. Their cute appearance and timid demeanor also make them popular pets among native children.
Threat Level	None
Attacks	None
Damage Rating	N/A
Movement	2/5
Build	-20
Fitness	2
Agility	-1
Awareness	1
Will	-2
Endurance	0
Reflexes	0
Strength	-9
Toughness	-5
Armor	None

CUP SUCKER (*Crusta crocinus*)

YANNER

The cup sucker, or wound snail, is a mollusk analog that is a favorite tool of the native healer's trade. The snail is tiny, with a simple, cup-like shell. The shell is bright yellow, warning potential predators of the animal's toxic body fluids. The snail's foot is an equally bright purple with dull, rust-colored spots. Cup suckers are found in tide pools, muds, and sands of the intertidal zone where they play the unique ecological role of mutualistic fungivores.

BEHAVIOR

Cup suckers seem to prefer a diet of fast fungus (MG 168), and if the growth is readily available, they are content to consume only the fungus. They are commonly found in great numbers on decaying carrion, along the beach drift line, or anywhere else that abundant organic material supports a rich fast fungus crop.

Cup suckers are also known to attach themselves to injured animals, where they feed on the fast fungus that typically infects the injured tissues. Apparently, the wound snail's presence reduces the physiological stress on the host organism, sparing it a fast fungus infection that could possibly turn a minor injury into a life threatening condition.

The snail's service is not free. As it feeds on the fungus within the wound, the snail also draws nourishment from the host's body fluids. This drain is physiologically negligible, and has little detrimental effect on most host animals. The snail, however, uses the additional nutrients to produce a tiny cluster of eggs and attaches the cluster to a patch of the host's healthy hide. When the injury is sufficiently healed that further fungal infection is unlikely, the snail simply lets go and drifts away. The sail departs but the small egg sack remains attached to the host's skin for several days before also drifting free. The apparent ecological significance is that the cup snail's young are dispersed to new habitats.

Native healers have been using cup suckers since before the Abandonment to keep open wounds, abrasions, and burns clear of fast fungus infections. Most healers keep small colonies of the mollusks on hand to service their patients, and claim that the tiny animals have been responsible for saving thousands of lives over the years.

The colonial medical establishment has even started to accept the species as a viable tool in the battle against fast fungus infection, and has begun using the snail in abnormally resistant or extreme cases. Recent medical research at the Haven Institute of Science and Technology has suggested that there may be more to the snail's medical value than its appetite for fast fungus. Antibacterial compounds in its mucosal secretions may also help disinfect the wounds it cleans. If these preliminary findings bear out, the researchers hope to develop a line of antibiotics better suited to combating Poseidon's more drug-resistant bacteria species.

Range	Tropical waters planetwide
Habitat	Intertidal zones
Length	Up to 1.5 centimeters in diameter
Weight	5 grams
Frequency	Very common
Resource Value	High; valued as native medical treatment for fast fungus infection
Threat Level	None

Attacks	None
Damage Rating	N/A
Movement	N/A
Build	-40
Fitness	0
Agility	-15
Awareness	-5
Will	0
Endurance	0
Reflexes	-10
Strength	-20
Toughness	-10
Armor	None

DUNE CREEPER (*Paliurus defendo*)

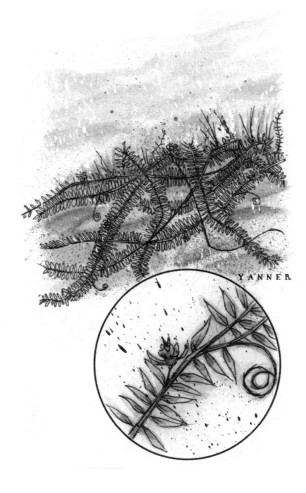

Dune creeper is a common, slow-growing plant that is a highly valued resource in many native villages. The vine has deep and bushy roots that do a good job of holding sand together against erosion, helping to build beach dunes and berms. The stalk of the plant consists of long, ropy runners with small green leaves and tiny sand-colored flowers.

The runners are thin, but tough, and branch out in all directions, further protecting the beach from the forces of wind and water. The runners and leaves alike are a dark green that appears almost black.

BEHAVIOR

The plant is a halophyte, able to grow in the salty conditions of the shoreline water table. As the plant absorbs salt water through its roots, active transport in the runner tissues concentrates the salts in individual, sacrificial leaves. As the salts accumulate, these storage leaves slowly die, turning a pretty gold color before falling off the vine, taking the excess salts with them.

Every few meters, dune creeper runners send advantageous roots deep into the loose sand. These root systems secure the plant against storm winds and become nodes for new runner outgrowths. In this way, a single individual plant can leapfrog its way across the top of the beach, covering the ground in a maze of tendrils and colonizing a whole shoreline.

Dune creeper helps stabilize beach sand against erosion, and therefore helps to establish relatively rich ecological communities that would otherwise be unable to form in such an arid and salty habitat. Crustacean analogs and other invertebrates find shelter and food among the vines, eating both the plant itself, as well as each other. Other plants root in the more stable soil under the creepers outstretched vines, and benefit from the water its extensive root system holds near the surface and the natural fertilizers the other hangers-on leave behind.

Since the early years of the Abandonment, Poseidon's natives have made dune creepers a useful part of their architecture. Where creeper grows well, it can be coaxed to climb pilings, support beams, walls, and up over rooftops. On this stable substrate the vine does especially well, growing thickly. If the climbing plants are well tended, a small building can be completely encased with creeper in just a few years. The growth dramatically improves the structural integrity of small wooden buildings, often helping them to withstand even cyclonic winds. The plant helps waterproof covered structures, and keeps them cooler in the hot sun. It is also documented that creeper-covered buildings suffer less from the ravages of fast fungus (MG 168) as well. Where creeper has been extensively utilized in the local architecture, native dwellings often take on a wilder air, and seem more a part of their natural surroundings than artificial constructs of a human community.

Range	Subtropical regions
Habitat	Arid coastal dunes
Length	Individual plants can reach several hundred meters in length.
Weight	Up to 0.25 kilograms for an individual runner
Frequency	Common
Resource Value	High; native children collect edible invertebrates from the associative communities creeper supports. The plant is cultivated to stabilize the sands around beach communities and to structurally reinforce native buildings.
Threat Level	None
Attacks	None
Damage Rating	N/A
Movement	N/A
Build	N/A
Fitness	N/A
Agility	N/A
Awareness	N/A
Will	N/A
Endurance	N/A
Reflexes	N/A
Strength	N/A
Toughness	N/A
Armor	None

ECHO/FISH (*Piscis refero*)

Echo/fish is the Interspecies (PG 235) name for a group of related fish species that are the preferred natural prey of dolphin natives and colonists alike. With dolphin sound-picture names like soft/swift/diver/twitch/soft and bony/rough/speeder/juice/bony, it is easier for humans to simply lump these similar species together under one name—echo/fish. Fins find the inability of humans to readily distinguish between these species baffling, and always seem ready to offer endless discourse on the nuances of their acoustic signatures, swimming habits, and textural variations. Cetacean psychologists believe that this ongoing discourse is a subtle commentary on human physical limitations that fins find endlessly humorous.

Echo/fish range in size up to a quarter of a meter and share basic elements of shape and color. Most species are some version of silver, gray, or brown, and have what could be considered the archetypal body form for Poseidon fish. Most live in large schools and are found throughout the Pacific Archipelago and beyond.

BEHAVIOR

These species form large, dense schools that range along island coastlines in predictable distributions. Echo/fish are abundant and prolific, reproducing year round and quickly replenishing any depletion of their stocks. Echo/fish are readily stunned by dolphin sonar attacks making them easier to catch. Human fishermen do not compete with fins over these stocks. Echo/fish are relatively bony and therefore more troublesome to prepare than other common species. Dolphins, on the other hand, typically swallow their prey whole and so do not seem to mind.

Fin and human spiritualists claim that such ecological hunting habits are in keeping with the underlying tenets of the Whalesong (PG 231). Others claim that making ecological considerations in the utilization of natural resources is simply responsible citizenship.

YANNER

Range	Temperate to tropical waters planetwide
Habitat	Continental margins and coastal shallows
Length	10 to 25 centimeters
Weight	0.4 to 1.8 kilograms
Frequency	Abundant
Resource Value	High; preferred food fish for dolphins
Threat Level	None
Attacks	None
Damage Rating	N/A
Movement	3/8
Build	-20
Fitness	2
Agility	2
Awareness	0
Will	0
Endurance	3
Reflexes	1
Strength	-9
Toughness	-5
Armor	None

GLADIATOR CRAB
(*Cancersimila preliator*)

The gladiator crab is a large crustacean analog whose name comes from its single-minded territoriality. The animal is believed to be a close relative of the digger crab (MG 167) and is the most heavily shelled and densely muscled of Poseidon's many crustacean species. Sporting comically large chila, or pinching claws, and an unusually thick carapace, the gladiator is a formidable animal that is typically eaten by only the largest and most determined predators.

Gladiator crabs have iridescent shells that shimmer with the colors of mother of pearl. Constant tunneling through the sand keeps gladiator shells clear of algae and other growths, and serves to polish them to a bright sheen. Besides its oversized fighting claws, the gladiator has four thick walking legs, each tipped with splayed protrusions that give the animal an unusually good grip in the wet sand of its burrow and the intertidal zone where it hunts.

Gladiator crabs are edible, and considered delicious. Their dangerous territoriality and thick shell make them both difficult to find and still harder to kill. As a result, they typically go unhunted in favor of their thin-shelled cousins.

BEHAVIOR
Gladiators are one of the most aggressively territorial animals known to biologists. Unlike most other species, whose combatants typically submit and retreat before serious injury occurs, gladiator crabs invariably fight to the death. Female and male crabs alike stake out and protect individual territories, defending them against all trespassers, and most aggressively against their own kind.

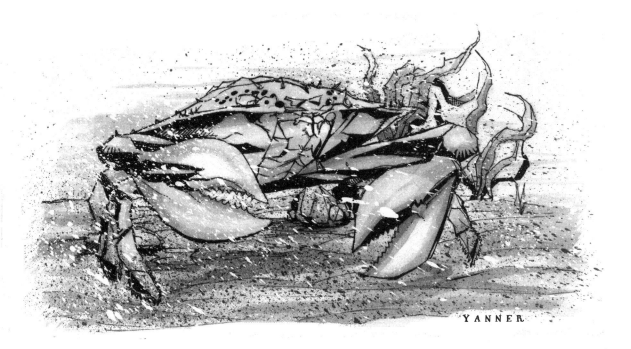

YANNER

A gladiator grab that catches another of its species on its territory will attack without hesitation and fight until it has killed the invader, been incapacitated, or itself killed. Gladiator's shells are so thick that such battles can last over an hour before one combatant manages to breach the carapace of the other, or sever enough of its opponent's limbs to render it immobile.

If the victor has enough energy left after the battle, it will drag the vanquished crab back to its burrow where it consumes the remains. On the other hand, the victor itself is sometimes so spent after a fight that it dies of exhaustion, or succumbs to a predator it might otherwise have been able to fend off.

Gladiator crabs never associate peaceably with each other, even during their short breeding season. During a two-week period, female gladiators dig deep nests just above the high-tide line along the borders of their territories. After burying their eggs, they mark the area with potent pheromones that apparently only attract male gladiators. Males prowl their own territorial boundaries looking for these nests, which they dig up, fertilize, and then rebury.

Misguided native children and mean-spirited adults, both native and otherwise, often stage combats between gladiator crabs. The adults set up betting tournaments in aquatic imitation of Terrestrial cockfighting, and in the native quarters of many colonial settlements Incorporate slummers and thrill-seeking tourists are making gladiator fights big business. Some fight rings have become so lucrative that they have reportedly attracted the attention of organized crime, which in turn has attracted the attention of the GEO Justice Commission.

Range	Throughout the Pacifica Archipelago
Habitat	Sandy to semi-rocky intertidal zones
Length	Up to 0.85 meters
Weight	Up to 12 kilograms
Frequency	Uncommon
Resource Value	Valued for its flavorful meat and used in animal-fighting tournaments
Threat Level	Medium
Attacks	Pinching claws (x2) 4
Damage Rating	4
Movement	1/3

Build	-12
Fitness	0
Agility	-5
Awareness	-2
Will	0
Endurance	0
Reflexes	-3
Strength	-6
Toughness	-3
Armor	5

GLASS CORAL (*Crystalus perspicuus*)

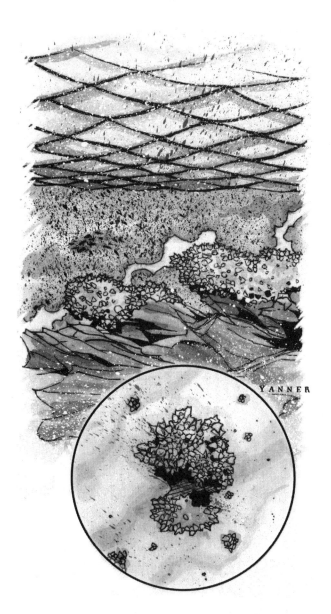

YANNER

Glass coral is arguably the most spectacular life form on Poseidon, and without a doubt the most beautiful. Like Terrestrial reef-building coral and several of the other reef organisms on the water-world, glass coral is a colonial animal that forms vast mineral structures on the seafloor. Unlike other reef species, however, glass coral utilizes silica, extracted from Poseidon's silicon rich waters, to form its unique shell structure almost entirely out of natural glass. Glass coral is apparently a member of the same evolutionary line as borealgae (see page 64), but the individual organisms are significantly smaller, and though they contain functional photosynthetic compounds, they are relatively transparent.

BEHAVIOR

What makes glass coral reefs so spectacular is the sheer beauty of their structure. The mineral skeleton the algae lays down is a natural glass that varies from translucent to entirely transparent. Trace amounts of locally abundant minerals and various organic compounds are incorporated into the lattice structure of the reef material itself, lending the finished glass a variety of swirled and exotic colors.

As beautiful as this may be, the most breathtaking sight occurs when the bright Serpentis sun hits the reef at just the right angle and the light is shattered into a million shimmering fragments—an alien rainbow of colors never seen on Earth. The flowing lens of the surrounding water interplays with the natural prisms, irregular forms, and colorful imperfections of the glass to create a stunning, almost supernatural light show. Even the highest resolution holographic equipment seems unable to capture the true nature of the display, and only first-hand experience allows for true appreciation. Scientists and artists alike are enthralled by this species, the former in speculation about the purpose of such adaptation, the latter simply in awe of the chromatic majesty.

Glass coral reefs are particularly hard structures with razor-sharp edges and dagger-like protrusions that are serious hazards to errant boat hulls and unwary swimmers. Despite the obvious threat to harvesters, the natives value glass coral for more than its inherent beauty.

Some of the organic compounds secreted into the reef structure by the algae analogs make the otherwise brittle natural glass remarkably durable. Since the earliest days of the Abandonment, natives have used glass coral fragments to make a variety of useful tools, including needles, scrapers, awls, and blades of all sizes. Well-made glass coral knives are efficient and valued possessions, and a native tradition has developed of passing on such blades as family heirlooms. Some craftsmen have become so skilled and their designs so elaborate that their knives have begun to claim thousands of scrip from collectors in Haven and among the Incorporate.

Glass coral reefs are also becoming tourist attractions in some regions. Local native villages and a few colonies are seeing increasing numbers of day trippers and weekenders coming to see the reefs, and in the Haven Cluster several guide services have begun offering trips planned around glass coral dives.

Range	Tropical waters planetwide
Habitat	Nutrient-rich waters
Length	Individuals up to a centimeter in diameter, single colonies up to 3 kilometers along longest axis
Weight	Up to 2 grams per individual
Frequency	Uncommon
Resource Value	Important source of tool and artistic materials to natives, and of increasing regional import in the tourist trade
Threat Level	Medium; extreme hazard to unwary swimmers and helmsmen
Attacks	Accidental impact
Damage Rating	4
Movement	N/A
Build	N/A
Fitness	N/A
Agility	N/A
Awareness	N/A
Will	N/A
Endurance	N/A
Reflexes	N/A
Strength	N/A
Toughness	N/A
Armor	None

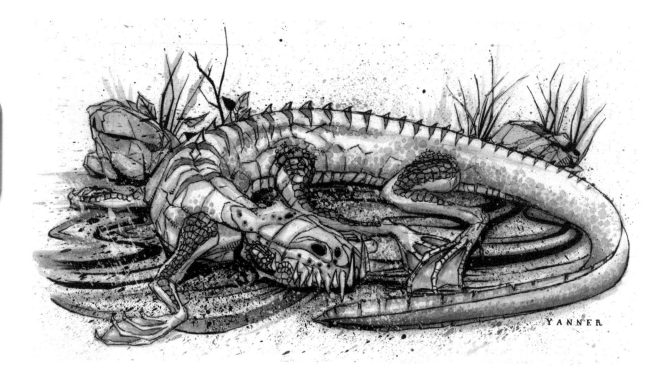

YANNER

GRENDEL (unclassified)

Little is known about this species—except that it is extremely dangerous. It is unclear even what its phylogeny may be and most information about it should be considered speculative. Grendels, named presumably after the deadly creature of the Beowulf story, are likely relatives of the marsh devil (MG 177) of the Sierra Nueva region, but a genetic comparison has yet to be made. Reports indicate that grendels grow larger and are even more aggressive than their suspected cousins, and therefore pose an even greater threat.

Like marsh devils, grendels are large, six legged, carnivorous amphibians. Their coloration is mottled, varying from brown to muddy green, and most bear vertical stripping akin to that of Terrestrial tigers. Their bodies are low slung and muscular, and their flat, angular heads support powerful jaws. Their teeth are actually not individual structures, but serrations extending from the bony plates of their jawbones. The structures are poorly suited to chewing, but allow adult grendels to remove up to 20 kilograms of flesh with a single snapping bite.

To date, grendels are known only from the central hills and savannas of New Jamaica, but biologists suspect their actual range may be more extensive.

BEHAVIOR

Grendels apparently spend most of their time submerged, buried in the muds of marsh and streambeds. They are active, nocturnal hunters and typically take to dry land in pursuit of food. These animals are deliberate stalkers, relying on uncanny speed rather than subtlety to catch their prey. Their appetites are formidable and grendels consume a broad range of aquatic and terrestrial prey, including members of their own species. Grendels usually eat their prey where it falls, but have been known to drag it back to favored water holes for safekeeping.

Special note should be made regarding the unusual speed of these creatures. The muscle structure and metabolism of marsh devils allows for powerful bursts of over 30 kilometers per hour over even terrain. Holo footage and preliminary studies of grendel muscle structure indicate that grendels may be capable of speeds in excess of 40 kilometers per hour.

Infant grendels hatch from large globular egg clusters as miniature versions of adults—teeth, appetites, and all. Large hatchings are frightening events, making the marshes and rivers of central New Jamaica exceptionally dangerous during the grendels' early summer breeding season.

The residents of Bright Savanna (MG 141) have suffered significant loss of life, livestock kills, and property damage as a result of larger hatchings, and most of the information in this field guide concerning grendels comes from reports made by the authorities there.

Range	New Jamaica, though the actual range may include all of the Zion Islands
Habitat	Freshwater rivers, marshes and riparian savanna
Length	2 to 3 meters
Weight	300 to 400 kilograms
Frequency	Rare
Resource Value	None
Threat Level	Extreme; there are numerous verified reports of lethal attack on humans and livestock
Attacks	Claw (x2) 7, Bite 5
Damage Rating	8, 8
Movement	12/24; though always quick, grendels can only maintain their top speed for 6 rounds
Build	7
Fitness	3
Agility	2
Awareness	2
Will	2
Endurance	5
Reflexes	3
Strength	5
Toughness	3
Armor	3

HELLBENDER (*Os venenifer*)

Hellbenders are named after the large Terrestrial salamanders they vaguely resemble. Unlike their namesake, Poseidon hellbenders are hexipeds and have a dozen ruddy-colored eyespots along the length of their marbled brown backs. The animals have feather-like external gills and rudimentary but functional lungs. Their tails are long and laterally compressed making them powerful swimmers. Their feet are long toed and tipped with small claws that also make them able climbers.

Hellbenders have large splayed heads with wide primary and narrow lateral jaws. The flesh covering their lower jaw is wrinkled and bulging, and contains not only the glands that produce their potent neurotoxin, but also their unique delivery mechanism for that venom.

BEHAVIOR

Hellbenders are found in both fresh- and salt-water environments. They prefer slow-moving rivers and salt creeks from which they can climb into overhanging vegetation and lay in ambush. Benders will cling motionless to low branches for hours until a suitable victim strays close enough to attack.

Hellbenders are a remarkable example of parallel evolution. The loose, elastic flesh of the bender's lower jaw is lined with tubular structures that can be forcibly filled with body fluids, forming a projecting tendril that can strike a target up to a meter and a half away. This hydraulic appendage is similar in shape and action to the insect-grabbing tongue of some Terrestrial reptiles and amphibians. Instead of a sticky pad, however, the bender's appendage is tipped with three small hypodermic

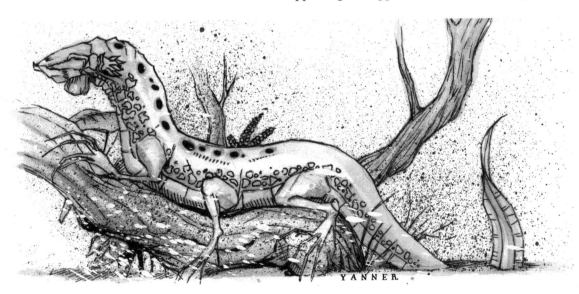

YANNER

spines. These spines inject a potent dose of venom upon contact, penetrating all but the thickest hide.

Even the largest victims usually succumb quickly to the hellbender's lethal neurotoxin, first to general paralysis and then minutes later to cardiopulmonary failure. If the prey is small, the bender typically drags it into the water and consumes it at leisure. If the victim is larger, the hellbender will often eat its fill and then retreat to the relative safety of the water to digest its meal. Some days later it will return to its ambush perch where it targets one of the scavengers its kill may have attracted, and strikes again. This sequence of killing, eating, digesting, baiting, and killing again may continue for weeks. Large piles of bones and rotting remains alongside muddy riverbanks are fair warning that a hellbender is laying in ambush.

Range	Semi-tropical regions throughout the southern hemisphere
Habitat	Riparian zones and estuary tidal creeks
Length	Up to 1.2 meters
Weight	3 to 4.8 kilograms
Frequency	Rare
Resource Value	Low; native hunters sometimes capture hellbenders alive and milk them for their venom, which they use to tip spears and arrows
Threat Level	Medium; benders do not often attack humans, but care should still be exercised when their presence is likely
Attacks	Tendril 5
Damage Rating	None
Poison	Neurotoxin
	Onset Time 30 seconds
	Duration 15 minutes
	Damage Rating 8
Movement	1/3
Build	-16
Fitness	2
Agility	2
Awareness	-2
Will	0
Endurance	1
Reflexes	0
Strength	-7
Toughness	-3
Armor	None

JELLYROLL (unclassified)

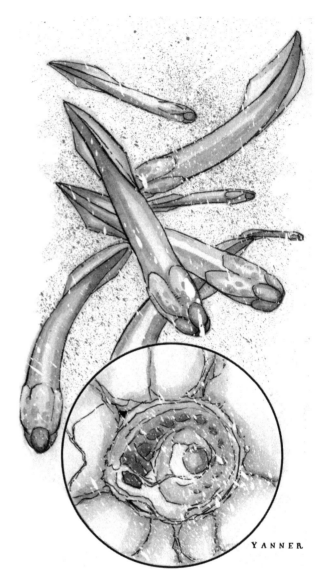

YANNER

Another of Poseidon's more enigmatic species, it is not even clear whether the so-called jellyroll organism described here is the larval or adult creature. Jellyrolls are encountered in two forms. The most common is in globular egg clusters that wash ashore throughout the archipelago. The second is as individual organisms buried in the sands of the upper surf zone. Jellyrolls are small lancelet-like invertebrates that may represent the evolutionary precursor to Poseidon's ubiquitous fish species. They are tiny animals, seldom more than a centimeter or two in length. They are almost translucent, have rudimentary eyespots, and what appears to be the first evolutionary stages of the four-part mouth structure of modern Poseidon fish.

Though developmental studies seem to imply that the organism is the larval form of some larger creature, scientists have been unable to artificially initiate metamorphosis in the laboratory. Native biologists have also been thus far unable to suggest an organism that could represent the adult.

BEHAVIOR

Jellyroll egg masses drift ashore throughout the summer months. As the surf washes the clusters against the beach face, they slowly fragment as they roll up and down the sand. The clusters break apart, hatching and spreading the tiny organisms all along the beach. The animals quickly burrow into the sand where they feed on tiny benthic invertebrates. Here they spend some indeterminate period of time before an unknown environmental key triggers further development and they disappear out to sea.

Though almost tasteless, jellyrolls can be a valuable source of protein, especially in survival situations. Where they are abundant, natives collect jellies as soon as they wash ashore and boil them to denature their toxic proteins and render them edible. The resulting syrup can be eaten as is, or can serve as a nutritious base for stew. Care must be taken when collecting jellies, however, as their egg tissues contain a variety of caustic enzymes that burn to the touch and cause life-threatening allergic reactions in many humans.

Various research and development teams have recently become keenly interested in jellyrolls. Rather conclusive studies have determined that though the free-swimming jellies are subject to normal levels of predation, the egg clusters are not consumed by any known species. Most suspect that the caustic enzymes contained in jellyroll egg tissue are responsible for their immunity from predation and feel that there may be profitable biotech applications for such chemicals.

Range	Found seasonally throughout Poseidon's tropical waters
Habitat	Egg cases can be found along any shoreline, but the larva are found only in sandy surf zones
Length	Egg cluster is a globular mass 6 to 8 centimeters in diameter; larva are 1 to 2 centimeters in length
Weight	Egg clusters are 1.0 to 1.3 kilograms, larva are 0.75 to 1.2 grams
Frequency	Seasonally common during mid summer
Resource Value	Useful source of edible protein, and potentially valuable to the biotech industry
Threat Level	Low
Attacks	None
Damage Rating	N/A
Poison	Enzymatic irritants that cause chemical burns and possibly allergic reactions
	Onset Time Immediate
	Duration Until affected area is chemically neutralized
	Damage Rating 2
Movement	Negligible
Build	-24
Fitness	2
Agility	0
Awareness	-8
Will	0
Endurance	1
Reflexes	-4
Strength	-11
Toughness	-5
Armor	None

JUMP JUMP (*Tripudio tripudio* var.)

Jump jump is the native name for a group of common, edible fishes that form large schools throughout the Pacifica Archipelago. These animals range in size, but seldom exceed two kilograms. They are nondescript and silvery, though some have reddish or yellowish hues to their fins. They stand as examples of typical Poseidon fishes, and have little to distinguish them save their abundance, and their resulting importance to the native subsistence fishery.

Jump jump is a staple of the native diet, comprising more than 35% of the fish meat consumed in most villages. Jump jump flesh is yellowish and flaky when cooked and has a nutty flavor that is an acquired taste for most non-natives. Soaking the uncooked meat in clean salt water makes the fish more palatable to the average newcomer, but is considered a crime by native cooks.

BEHAVIOR

Jump Jump is a schooling fish that forms massive shoals that often span kilometers. This makes the species susceptible to gill nets, purse seines, weirs, and cast nets, as well as cetacean herding parties. Only the largest species seem interested in baits or lures, and even then catching them on tackle is more often for sport than sustenance.

Range	Temperate to tropical waters planetwide
Habitat	Continental margins and coastal shallows
Length	25 to 40 centimeters
Weight	0.4 to 2.2 kilograms
Frequency	Abundant
Resource Value	High; by weight, more jump jump is eaten in traditional native villages than any other meat
Threat Level	None
Attacks	None
Damage Rating	N/A
Movement	4/11
Build	-23
Fitness	3
Agility	2
Awareness	-2
Will	0
Endurance	3
Reflexes	0
Strength	-10
Toughness	-5
Armor	None

KEEL VINE (*Vinea carpo*)

YANNER

Keel vine is a troublesome aquatic growth for which even native Poseidoners have failed to discover a use. Keel vine is a thick-stalked, kelp-like algae that is common in protected temperate shallows. The algae has bright orange fronds with mottled brown stalks, and grows in large anchored patches that form semi-submerged rafts at the water's surface.

BEHAVIOR

Keel vine fronds are covered with tiny barb-like growths that are quick to grab hold of a passing animal's hide or a boat's hull—sometimes even modern bioplastic. In smaller clusters the passing object easily breaks free and serves to disperse hitchhiking reproductive tissues to new habitats. In larger clusters, however, the vines can be so entangling and cumbersome as to hold a creature, or even slow moving boat, dead in the water. Breaking free is problematic and can be life threatening as there have been numerous human and cetacean drownings attributed to keel vine. Luckily the algae's bright color is a useful warning notable by even the most inexperienced newcomer.

Range	Temperate waters planetwide
Habitat	Shallow, nutrient-rich waters
Length	Up to 20 meters in length
Weight	5 to 8 kilograms per frond
Frequency	Common
Resource Value	None
Threat Level	Medium, but only to the unaware
Attacks	Grapple 3
Damage Rating	Potential drowning
Movement	N/A
Build	N/A
Fitness	N/A
Agility	N/A
Awareness	N/A
Will	N/A
Endurance	N/A
Reflexes	N/A
Strength	N/A
Toughness	N/A
Armor	N/A

The subtle rules that govern evolution dictate that large animals do not evolve on small landmasses, hence the distinct lack of any large, wholly terrestrial species on Poseidon's islands. This ecological rule does not hold true for marine environments, however, hence the proliferation of such fantastically huge species in Poseidon's oceans. The supportive buoyancy and the biological productivity of the ocean conspire to allow organisms to reach enormous sizes, and the ultimate example of this evolutionary extreme is the leviathan.

Named after the monsters of ancient maritime myth, the leviathan is the largest non-colonial organism ever discovered, actually exceeding what biologists thought were the physiological limits for a multicellular animal. Despite their size, leviathans are fish and are bigger even than their greater white (MG 171) cousins.

Their bodies are long and covered with encrusting marine growths. They have rough hides that, unlike the degrading skins of greater whites, act as armor against invading parasites. Typical coloration is light gray with dark lateral streaks running the length of their bodies. Enormous, dark eyespots line their dorsal surface, but how well they see is a matter of debate. Leviathan heads are compressed dorsa-ventrally, appearing flattened, wide and shovel-like. Their reduced jaw structures surround gaping maws up to 10 meters across, allowing them to filter plankton from over five million liters of seawater an hour.

LEVIATHAN (*Picis ingens*)

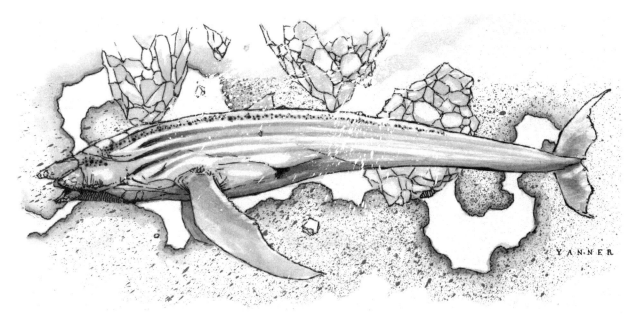

YANNER

BEHAVIOR

Leviathans are planktivores and survive solely by filter feeding. There is simply no way that the species could support its massive body by consuming anything from a higher trophic level—there would not be enough biomass. Their dependence on abundant plankton restricts leviathans to colder temperate and polar waters where plankton populations are highest. As a result, leviathans were not discovered until after Recontact, despite their size. Ecological processes keep populations necessarily small, allowing the animal to remain a secret until the more extensive exploration of post-Recontact revealed its existence.

Leviathans swim slowly along in a never-ending quest for calories. When local plankton blooms allow, a leviathan may remain in a given area for some time, grazing in ever widening spiral patterns. When plankton populations are more disperse, the animal will travel hundreds of kilometers in a single day, eating continuously. The only time the species leaves the plankton-rich photic zone is to make periodic dives to the seafloor. They appear to do this every few days, and biologists speculate, based on collected fecal samples, that the species may actually swallow mouthfuls of mud gouged from the seafloor. Such sediments often contain thick mats of energy-rich bacteria as well as important nutrients. Since leviathan breeding behavior has never been documented, many scientists speculate that mating may also occur during such benthic excursions.

To date, all information on leviathans has been gathered though observation and remote probes. The animals are so rare and inhabit regions so far outside colonial population centers that Poseidon's ecology has recycled deceased leviathans before their corpses could be discovered. A research group at the Haven Institute of Science and Technology has a standing reward of 50,000 scrip for information that leads them to a fresh leviathan corpse. Their interest in studying these animals up close is so keen that the team has a high-speed VTOL waiting on 30-hour standby. With the plane and its cargo of custom-built medical robots, the crew can be on site and conducting a necropsy anywhere on the planet within eight hours. To prevent poachers from purposefully killing one of these rare animals simply to claim the reward, the researchers' offer stipulates that the leviathan must have died of verifiably natural causes.

Range	Temperate and polar waters planetwide
Habitat	Photic zone, with period benthic dives
Length	The largest specimen ever observed was 131 meters in length
Weight	Estimates suggest an adult weight of up to 280 metric tons
Frequency	Rare; global population estimates vary, but none exceeds 600 individuals
Resource Value	High; the species is the subject of intense scientific curiosity
Threat Level	Medium; collisions could cause severe hull damage and may elicit dangerous defensive behavior
Attacks	Breach 6
Damage Rating	50
Movement	4/7
Build	50
Fitness	4
Agility	-10
Awareness	2
Will	0
Endurance	4
Reflexes	-4
Strength	27
Toughness	14
Armor	8

LESSER WHITE (various)

YANNER

The collective term "lesser white" refers to any of the much smaller relatives of the greater white (MG 171), and includes Poseidon's ecological analogs to Terrestrial sharks. There are over 50 classified species, and biologists estimate there are likely hundreds more. Many are common and significant both ecologically and economically. Many are well known to the natives and carry common names like surf cutter, black back, and woe-am-I. These animals vary greatly in size, behavior, and superficial physical characteristics, but they share a basic anatomy and predatory ecological role.

Though significantly smaller than their enormous cousins, lesser whites are similar to greater whites in their eel-like body form and four part-mouth structure. They vary broadly in color, and ironically, few are even partly white. Though varied, typical coloration is cryptic, adapted to their predatory role. Most species have anterior steering fins and one or more posterior propulsion fins that are more extensions of their long bodies than actual caudal fins. Their skeletons are comprised of stiff connective tissue templates variably ossified with inor-

ganic salts apparently extracted from the surrounding seawater. Unlike their huge relatives, most species of whites do not shed their skin, but instead are covered with ridge-like dermal scutes that are hardened with long and complex protein chains.

BEHAVIOR

Though most lesser whites are predators, some fill scavenger and herbivore niches. Whites have hundreds of sharp cutting teeth and seemingly endless appetites. Some hunt from ambush, while others stalk and attack prey from below. A number of species hunt in cooperative, pack-like schools that can be more frightening than their bigger cousins when on the attack. Whites are found in just about every marine habitat on the planet and there are at least three known freshwater species. Though superficial behaviors and physical traits vary, lesser whites represent an ecologically important collection of species and a considerable threat to humans plying Poseidon's seas.

Range	Planetwide
Habitat	Known from all marine habitats and several freshwater and river systems
Length	0.5 to 24 meters
Weight	2 kilograms to 16 metric tons
Frequency	Common
Resource Value	Prized and flavorful food source; many colonial restaurants have begun featuring white meat, and commercial fisheries are currently pressed to meet demand
Threat Level	High; there are numerous verified reports of unprovoked predatory attacks on humans and cetaceans
Attacks	Bite 8
Damage Rating	8 (average species)
Movement	7/18
Build	-10 to 8
Fitness	4
Agility	-2 to 2
Awareness	-2 to 2
Will	0 to 4
Endurance	2 to 6
Reflexes	-2 to 2
Strength	-3 to 6
Toughness	-1 to 3
Armor	0 to 2

NIÑO MUERTO (*Parvulus mortuus*)

YANNER

Niños muertos, or "dead children," are a rare but extremely dangerous terrestrial predator found in Poseidon's tropical and semitropical forests. This animal seems like a morphological cross between a Terrestrial baboon and a hyena, though larger and somewhat leaner than either. There is some speculation that the species may be related to squealers (MG 188), but unlike their possible cousins, niños are fierce predators that should be avoided at all costs.

Niños get their name from their haunting, ululating hunting calls which sound distressingly like crying children, and echo through the forest when a pack is on the prowl. Niños muertos are lithe but very strong and are covered in course bristling fur. Their hides are a mottled black and gray, which makes for extremely effective camouflage in the dappled sunlight and shadows of the jungle's lower canopies. Niños have narrow heads and long jaws supporting large canines and numerous carnasial

teeth. Their limbs are gangly, and like squealers, they have extra joints. Their digits are tipped with talon-like claws, and though not poisonous themselves, the claws are typically covered with saprophytic bacteria that can cause deadly infections in any organism lucky enough to survive a nino's attack.

Adult niños have sticky musk glands located just under their jaws, which produce a thick, oily secretion that they groom into their fur. The oil is likely a water repellent for the animal's coat, but the musk has a uniquely strong and foul odor reminiscent of rotten meat. The odor is thought to be some sort of olfactory tag for the members of a given pack, and the odor is so strong it permeates the air around the animals' temporary roost sites. The fetid smell is often the only warning that the species has moved into a given area.

BEHAVIOR

Niños muertos are effective pack hunters and few terrestrial organisms can escape a niño attack. Children are semi-arboreal and use trees to great effect when stalking their prey. A hunting pack will move through the canopy, leaping from tree to tree calling loudly back and forth as they do. Their calls seem intended to spook their prey and send it into panicked flight. Working together to surround and cut off the fleeing animals, attacking children leap onto prey from above, mobbing and bringing down even the largest creatures. Such attacks are vicious, bloody, and singularly lethal.

The appearance, ferocity, and eerily intelligent behavior of niños muertos have served to give the creatures a fearful reputation among Poseidon's natives. They are often the bogey man in stories meant to keep native children away from the jungle, and when ninos approach inhabited areas, villagers are forced to actively hunt down the nomadic packs, driving them away, or more often eradicating them with poisoned baits, traps, and guns.

Range	Currently known only from the jungles of the Channel and Zion islands, and the mountain forests of Prime Meridian
Habitat	Multi-canopy forests
Length	1 to 1.7 meters
Weight	60 to 75 kilograms
Frequency	Rare
Resource Value	None

Threat Level	High; natives report numerous fatal attacks on livestock and humans
Attacks	Claw 4, Bite 4
Damage Rating	3, 6
Movement	6/12 on the ground, 4/9 through the trees
Build	0
Fitness	2
Agility	3
Awareness	3
Will	2
Endurance	2
Reflexes	3
Strength	2
Toughness	1
Armor	None

PHARIUM (*Pharium solitas* var.)

Pharium (PG 23) is a low, ground-hugging growth with numerous small round leaves and simple, wind-pollinated flowers. The stems are thin and ropy with small curling runners that end in tough, nut-like seedpods. The pods rest on or dangle just above the ground and each contains several dozen small black seeds.

BEHAVIOR

Wild pharium is a fickle plant and grows well only under bright, warm, and dry conditions. The original species is supposed to have come from the plains of Prime Meridian but colonial records are unclear on this point. The various strains now in cultivation grow under a variety of conditions and have been bred in part to suit local environments across the archipelago.

Though pharium is a contraband substance in most colonial settlements, it is nonetheless an important component of Poseidon's economy. Natives have been using the plant as a recreational drug since the early years of the Abandonment. Despite occasional cases of psychological addition, the use of native pharium has always been considered harmless and has become an accepted part of native culture and spiritualism. Since Recontact, however, the breeding of more potent strains has created pharium derivatives that provide dangerous highs and debilitating physiological addiction.

If chewed or smoked, the leaves of native pharium provide the user with a soft, almost imperceptible buzz that takes the harshness out of physical sensations and replaces it with a warm sense of well being that lasts an hour or two. Alternatively, the seeds can be ground into a course powder and smoked over a flame or mixed with conventional tobacco. The effect of the seeds is similar to that of the leaves, but with two or three times the potency and duration. A native pharium high is easy to hide and has little effect on a person's physical abilities. Mental abilities are marginally depressed, but recovery is quick and there is no discernible crash.

YANNER

Strain-derived pharium, or derivative as it is called on the canals of Poseidon's urban centers, is a different story. The various subspecies from which D is harvested have been bred for potency and effect, and several are full-modification jobs straight out of high-end genetics labs. Most derivative has effects similar to but more powerful than those of native pharium. Most are temporarily debilitating, causing profound lethargy and semiconscious states lasting several hours. Users claim the intense sensations they experience are mentally expansive and physically pleasurable, and that post-high crashes are defined by nausea, headaches, and temporary sensory nerve dysfunction.

Some D variants are more potent still, and sometimes cause delusions and paranoia that in turn can lead to psychotic episodes and violent behavior. It is the recent proliferation of such strains, and the rash of violence they have caused, that has motivated the Justice Commission's crackdown on pharium dens operating within GEO jurisdiction. This recent effort has brought law enforcement agents into conflict with organized crime, especially in the larger cities. The pharium trade is big business and groups like the Gorchoff syndicate are not willing to give up their operations without a fight.

Range	Currently found throughout the Pacifica Archipelago
Habitat	Varies by strain
Length	Up to 0.4 meters high
Weight	0.15 kilograms per plant
Frequency	Uncommon
Resource Value	High; valued by traditional natives as a recreational drug; bred and sold as a cash crop by organized crime
Threat Level	Low
Attacks	None
Damage Rating	N/A
Poison	Some derived strains only, neurotransmitter inhibitor Onset time 30 seconds Duration 4-5 hours Damage Rating 2
Movement	N/A
Build	N/A
Fitness	N/A
Agility	N/A
Awareness	N/A
Will	N/A
Endurance	N/A
Reflexes	N/A
Strength	N/A
Toughness	N/A
Armor	N/A

POSEIDON POTATO

(*Victualia amplus*)

The Poseidon potato, or popo as it is more commonly called, is one of the most economically important plants on the colony world. Though not much like a potato at all, in fact not even a tuber, the popo is so called because of its ubiquitous role in native cooking.

Colonial records report the use of the plant as a food staple several years before the Abandonment, and describe numerous methods of preparation from even those earliest years. After the Abandonment, the popo became a vital agricultural crop, especially in regions were the native ecology made growing introduced Terrestrial plants difficult. The Poseidon potato has become such a prevalent food in native culture that it is even featured in the growing body of native folklore. Stories claim that the Storm Widow herself is responsible for discovering the plant, and several of the more popular popo recipes are attributed to her kitchen.

Records indicate that popo was actually first discovered in the Zion Islands, but quickly spread to other centers of human habitation. The plant can now be found growing wild on almost every island of the Pacifica Archipelago that has experienced even the most temporary habitation. This wide distribution is a testament to the intrinsic importance, and inherent hardiness, of the species.

Popo plants are low, thick-stalked growths with a vine-like form similar to Terrestrial squashes. The stems are rust colored with thick, pulpy leaves. The leaves are shiny and dark green with darker purple around their edges, and the fruits grow in clusters of three suspended just above the ground. The fruits are covered with a thin, skin-like rind that is the same dark purple as the leaf edges, but swirled with rusty streaks.

The meat of the fruit is salmon colored and firm near the surface, turning softer and pulpier toward the center. Each layer has a distinct flavor, and dozens of uses in native cooking. There are three hard seeds at the fruit's core, and even these have culinary applications.

BEHAVIOR

Both the plant's leaves and the rind contain chemicals that readily induce vomiting in almost all of Poseidon's herbivorous species, but seem completely harmless to humans and their introduced livestock. It is obviously these compounds that help the plant survive Poseidon's hungry ecology in such a variety of environments. The few animals that do consume the fruits use sharp teeth, beaks, or claws to first expose the meat and then carefully eat only the inner layers. These species are inadvertently responsible for distributing the plants small seeds to new habitats.

Popo fruits provide four distinct food products, which in turn are used in literally dozens of popular recipes. The rind is used to make a variety of native snacks, and though it provides little nutritional value, it is never wasted. The firmer, outer layer is the greater part of the fruit and is most similar in texture and culinary versatility to Terrestrial beets or squash. The inner layer is soft and pulpy. It is easily separated from the rest of the fruit and can be used like Terrestrial tomatoes. The seeds are dried, ground into a coarse powder, and used as a spice. The flavor is elusive but light and pleasant, and has become a hallmark of native cooking.

The entire plant can be eaten raw or cooked, but raw it has a rather bitter flavor that most find unpleasant. The cooked flavors of both fruit layers are similar but the inner layer is significantly stronger than the outer. It is difficult to describe the flavor of popo, as there are no apt Terrestrial comparisons. Most simply consider the taste another of the unique aspects of Poseidon, one a person can only experience firsthand.

Range	Throughout the Pacifica Archipelago, though that distribution is an artifact of the human colonization effort
Habitat	Suitable growth habitats seem limited by only a minimum soil moisture content
Length	8 to 10 centimeters in diameter
Weight	0.2 to 0.3 kilograms
Frequency	Abundant
Resource Value	High; the popo is a staple of native cooking, and many colonial historians believe it

may have been responsible for the survival of many satellite communities during the hardest years of the Abandonment. Economists compare the Poseidon potato to Asian rice crops as an indicator of their food market value.

Threat Level	None
Attacks	N/A
Damage Rating	N/A
Movement	N/A
Build	N/A
Fitness	N/A
Agility	N/A
Awareness	N/A
Will	N/A
Endurance	N/A
Reflexes	N/A
Strength	N/A
Toughness	N/A
Armor	N/A

POSEIDON SARGASSUM

(*Thalassinus* species)

Thalassinus is a genus encompassing a variety of floating marine algae collectively called Poseidon sargassum. The different species show variation in coloration, frond and bladder size, as well chlorophyll chemistry, but the differences are subtle and generally only relevant to biologists and foraging natives. The algae analogs range in color from green to red to brown, with large patches of each species growing intermingled with others. All species develop gas bladders ranging is size from three to 15 centimeters, which fill with the oxygen produced by the organism's photosynthetic metabolism. The fronds are generally small, and overlap each other, dangling, entwining, floating, and climbing towards the sun.

BEHAVIOR

Most species extend small tendrils that cling to surrounding vegetation, drawing the floating masses together into vast living rafts called sargassum islands (MG 154). The tendrils play a continuous game of king-of-the-hill that draws new sprouts and fronds up onto adjoining plants as each vies for maximum exposure to the sun.

The constant battle is misleading, however, as each plant is decidedly dependent on its apparent competitors for the collective ecological good of the raft. Together the interlocked plants resist waves and storm winds, capture nutrients, and attract animals that further fertilize the growths. The interconnected masses provide ready growth substrates and sources of spores for sexual reproduction. Their collective bulk also means that grazing animals are not as likely to devour the entirety of any one plant, offering the individual growths the same protection fish gain from schooling.

Aside from the various hunting and foraging benefits Poseidon's natives garner from sargassum rafts, the algae species themselves are a valuable resource. Though most species are edible, many offer trace nutrients that are hard to come by in other indigenous foods. Where wild sargassum is not abundant, many villages have large net-bound pens in which they cultivate the algae. Most sargassum species are used in native cooking but some are particularly suited to feeding livestock such as weedeaters (see page 101), pigs, and goats. A few species of sargassum have medicinal uses, primarily as topical antibiotics. High concentrations of iodine and various bioaccumulated salts offer readily available treatments for minor fast fungus (MG 168) and bacterial infections as well

as afflictions ranging from diaper rash to upset stomach.

It has recently been discovered that these plant-like species share closer genetic similarities with analogous Terrestrial species than any other organisms on Poseidon. This discovery has sparked heated scientific debate, and many research labs are hoping the species might provide the information needed to explain the mysterious genetic commonality of Earth and the colony world.

Range	Tropical and subtropical waters planetwide
Habitat	Surface waters
Length	10 centimeters to 12 meters
Weight	20 grams up to 6 kilograms
Frequency	Common
Resource Value	High; the various species are important native food crops and valuable sources of medicine. The rafts they form are also important hunting grounds. Recent genetic discoveries have given the species new scientific value as well.
Threat Level	None
Attacks	None
Damage Rating	N/A
Movement	Drifts with the current
Build	N/A
Fitness	N/A
Agility	N/A
Awareness	N/A
Will	N/A
Endurance	N/A
Reflexes	N/A
Strength	N/A
Toughness	N/A
Armor	None

PUMP WEED (unclassified)

YANNER

Pump weed is a useless, nuisance organism that is a constant frustration to marine technicians, mechanics, aquaculturalists, and boat captains alike. The organism has two growth forms. One is a low, velvety, moss-like encrusting form that coats submerged rocks and other solid substrates such as boat hulls, water intakes, and pipe works. The second is a thick, mat-like form that supports densely packed, stringy fronds up to 20 centimeters in length. The encrusting base of the life form contains yellowish photosynthetic pigments that give it a golden hue, but the fronds lack any pigments and are almost transparent.

BEHAVIOR

When growing in the open, under direct sunlight, pump weed takes on its low, encrusting form, spreading quickly over the surrounding substrate. When growing in shadow, however, such as in rock crevasses, on the underside of boat hulls, or inside outflow pipes or pump intakes, the organism takes on the thicker, frond-bearing form. The fronds are feeding appendages, filtering the water passing through them for microorganisms and organic detritus. These are apparently absorbed and metabolized for energy in the absence of sufficient sunlight. Pump weed grows quickly and can clog intakes, impede outflows, and foul hulls in only a matter of days.

Though anyone depending on marine equipment for their livelihood finds pump weed an annoying and often costly vermin, the organism intrigues scientists. The growth is an anomaly, not fitting into any traditional classifications, and defying even the newest Poseidon-based taxonomies.

Range	Tropical waters throughout the Pacifica Archipelago
Habitat	Well-oxygenated waters just below the low tide mark
Length	1.5 to 2.0 centimeters in encrusting form, up to 20 centimeters in frond-bearing form
Weight	4.0 to 6.0 grams per square centimeter
Frequency	Common
Resource Value	None
Threat Level	Minimal; the organism is an annoying and time-consuming nuisance to marine industry
Attacks	None
Damage Rating	N/A
Movement	N/A
Build	N/A
Fitness	N/A
Agility	N/A
Awareness	N/A
Will	N/A
Endurance	N/A
Reflexes	N/A
Strength	N/A
Toughness	N/A
Armor	None

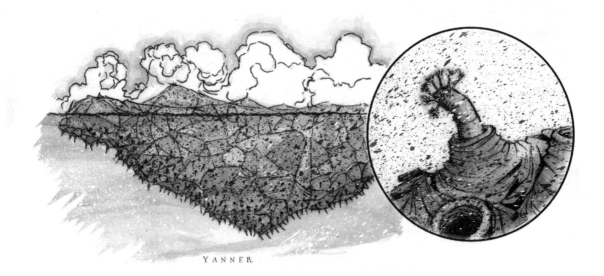

YANNER

REEFER COLONY
(*Insula victus*)

Reefers are unique colonial, worm-like organisms that build one of the most unlikely structures in nature. The animals are large for reef-building organisms, with individual worms growing to a meter in length. The anterior end of each worm is bifurcated into a number of tiny barbed tendrils with which the organism combs the water for planktonic prey. The body of each worm is ringed with hairy ridges that hold it securely within its tube-like shell. The skin and meat of the worm is a dark orange color derived from the shell pigments of the tiny organisms it consumes.

Like other reef builders, these animals secrete interconnected shells that together form the larger structure of the reef. Reefer shell is comprised of an insoluble organic polymer analogous to a natural form of bioplastic (PG 143), and it is typically muddy yellow in color. Though ultimately not as durable as bioplastic, the material is tough and semi-rigid. As the worms secrete the polymer, their waste gases are trapped within the structure of the material, lending the reef shell slight positive buoyancy. This buoyancy is a key aspect of the animal's ecology.

BEHAVIOR
Reefer colonies grow quickly, continuously adding new individuals to the reef through both sexual and asexual reproduction. When the colony reaches a genetically determined size limit, the worms begin secreting catabolic enzymes that degrade the base layers of the reef. The polymer slowly melts away, and after several weeks, the body of the reef breaks free from its foundation. The positive buoyancy of the reef material lifts the colony to the surface where it subsequently drifts along at the whim of the current.

The weight distribution within the reef causes the whole structure to roll over as it rises, so that the worms, which once covered the upper surface of the reef, now protrude from the underside of the floating mass. The buoyancy of a reefer colony is so slight that it floats along like an organic iceberg with only about 10% of its mass above the surface of the water.

Mature reefer colonies can be several hectares in surface area, forming veritable floating islands when they reach the surface. Encrusting marine growths, sea birds, and other transient species quickly colonize the exposed parts of such reefs. Larger reefer islands often support terrestrial vegetation that grows from seeds washed or blown onto the structure. The dangling worms continue to feed as these floating islands drift aimlessly for months, often supporting remarkably complex secondary ecologies. Eventually, stresses caused by wave action work to break the reef into smaller and smaller fragments. These fragments eventually become waterlogged and sink to the seafloor where they establish new reefer colonies, beginning the life cycle anew.

A reefer colony is an obvious navigational hazard for ships and other watercraft and should be given a wide berth, as much of its structure remains submerged. Native fishermen and frontiersmen have been known to use reefer islands as temporary camps and refuges, and more than a few castaways have been saved by dragging themselves aboard passing colonies.

Range	Temperate and tropical waters worldwide
Habitat	Colonies originate at the lowest reaches of the photic zone
Length	Up to 150 meters in diameter
Weight	Up to 25 metric tons
Frequency	Uncommon
Resource Value	Medium; natives and frontiersmen use them as convenient way stations and they have saved the lives of numerous castaways
Threat Level	None
Attacks	None
Damage Rating	N/A
Movement	Drifts with current
Build	N/A
Fitness	N/A
Agility	N/A
Awareness	N/A
Will	N/A
Endurance	N/A
Reflexes	N/A
Strength	N/A
Toughness	N/A
Armor	N/A

SAND ARCHER (*Peloris telum*)

The sand archer is a fairly common mollusk analog that lives in the sands and muds of the intertidal zone. The animal is mustard colored and shell-less with a long, tapered body. The animal can be large for a mollusk, exceeding six kilograms after only a few years of growth. The creature has four long eyestalks that support sensitive photoreceptors, and a tube-shaped mouth tipped with a hard, hollow, spine-like radula. The spine is barbed along its length and can be as large as two centimeters in diameter.

BEHAVIOR

The sand archer lies in ambush just below the surface of the substrate in which it is buried, its eyestalks protruding just above the sand. When a likely animal strays within a few centimeters, the archer attacks. Seawater, drawn from the outside, is forced into the mouth tube by rings of powerful muscle. The spine and mouth tube are hydraulically ejected from the animal's head and into its prey. This harpoon is strong and sharp enough to penetrate the hides of most small sea creatures, and is often enough to kill smaller animals outright.

After spearing its prey, the sand archer quickly draws its body deeper into the mud, pulling its meal after it. If the prey is small enough, it is typically pulled beneath the sand. If it is larger, and still struggling, the archer pulls it tight against the seafloor and allows it to struggle to death. If the prey proves too large or strong the archer's mouth spine may be torn free. If this happens, the mollusk regrows a new radula harpoon in just a few days. The sand archer feeds by sucking body fluids from its prey, drawing them through its hollow spine and mouth tube.

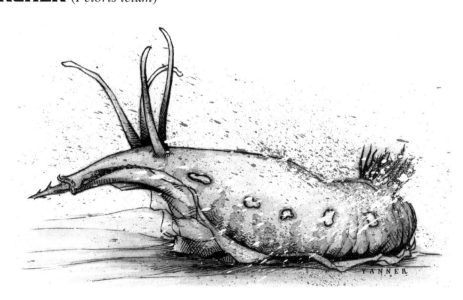

Sand archers generally attack only manageably small targets, but they will harpoon larger creatures in self-defense. If a larger organism attacks a sand archer, or a hapless human steps on one, the mollusk will fire its harpoon in an attempt to fend off the assault. A sand archer spine is ejected with sufficient force to drive the harpoon deep into a human foot, causing tremendous pain and opening the body to a number of potential infections. To avoid sand archer attack, natives are taught from childhood to shuffle their feet instead of stepping from foot-to-foot when wading in a likely archer habitat. Shuffling steps prevent a person from stepping directly on top of a buried sand archer thereby eliciting the defensive harpoon discharge.

Range	Throughout the Pacifica Archipelago
Habitat	Sandy or muddy intertidal zones
Length	Up to 65 centimeters
Weight	Up to 10 kilograms
Frequency	Common
Resource Value	Low; the meat is edible but rather flavorless.
Threat Level	Medium; frequently harpoon unwary beachcombers
Attacks	Harpoon 6
Damage Rating	1
Movement	1
Build	-12
Fitness	0
Agility	-4
Awareness	-4
Will	0
Endurance	0
Reflexes	-4
Strength	-6
Toughness	-3
Armor	None

SEA GHOUL (*Voro inferi*)

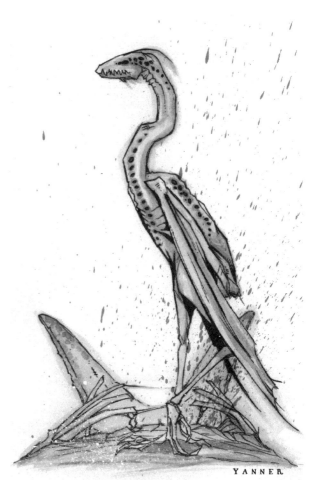

YANNER

This avian analog's name is apparently a play on their seagull-like abundance and their scavenger ecology. In keeping with their name, ghouls are ugly creatures, with mottled gray and white skin. They have long wings supporting flight membranes that are so thin they are almost transparent. The bird's body is lean and provides so little buoyancy that when floating in the water the animal's snake-like head and neck are all that show above the surface. Their small jaws match their small heads, but are tipped with pairs of bony plates somewhere between beaks and conventional cutting teeth.

BEHAVIOR

Ghouls have a number of both dorsal and ventral eyespots, but seem to rely most on their sense of smell to find the carrion they eat. Ghouls forage in small flocks of up to 20 birds, which gather into larger groups if abundant or particularly big carcasses are available. When such feeding congregations occur the grunting calls of the squabbling animals can be deafening, and it seems that individuals spend as much time fighting over the food as eating it. Native Poseidoners have learned to avoid these large feeding groups. They typically indicate the presence of a substantial amount of carrion, implying that either a large predator is nearby, or at the very least, that scavengers more dangerous than the ghouls may soon arrive.

Ghouls are abundant throughout the Pacifica Archipelago. They are edible but have a gamy, unpleasant flavor that keeps them relatively safe from native hunters. Ghouls are regularly eaten in survival situations, but care should be taken even then. Though their meat is edible, their liver organ analogs are rich in various chemicals that are highly toxic to humans. These chemicals are thought to help the species metabolize poisonous bacterial wastes that accumulate in the rotting food they consume. The GEO has lost a number of soldiers and field biologists to ghoul liver poisoning, prompting the inclusion of this otherwise harmless species in this report. Sea ghouls are not otherwise a threat to humans, and have never been documented attacking anything larger than the occasional herring.

Range	Planetwide
Habitat	Most coastal habitats on Poseidon support at least one subspecies of sea ghoul
Length	20 to 50 centimeters
Weight	1.5 to 2.2 kilograms
Frequency	Abundant
Resource Value	Minimal; the species is edible but barely palatable. Natives consider large flocks reliable sign that larger, more dangerous animals might be nearby.
Threat Level	Minimal; the animal's liver is highly toxic
Attacks	Ingested toxin
Damage Rating	N/A
Poison	Respiratory suppressant Onset time 15 minutes Duration 1 hour Damage Rating 6
Movement	Land 1/3, air 5/14
Build	-16
Fitness	2
Agility	0
Awareness	0
Will	0
Endurance	1
Reflexes	0
Strength	-8
Toughness	-3
Armor	None

SALTWATER PSEUDOEEL
(Malalongus periculosus)

The pseudoeel is a close relative of the land lizard (MG 175), actually sharing the same genus. The salty, as local hunters call it, is found exclusively in saltwater, however, and lacks even the rudimentary forelimbs of its cousin. Like the land lizard, salties are actually amphibians, but unlike their rela-

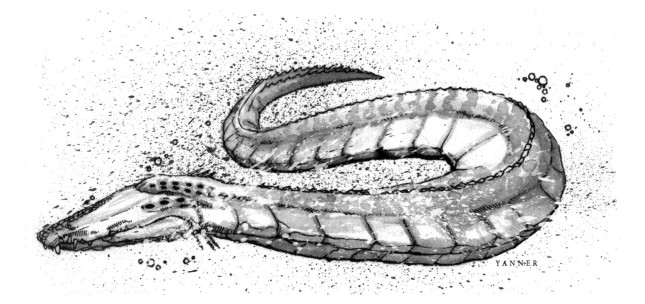

tives, the species is restricted to an entirely aquatic life.

Salties are typically much larger than land lizards, reaching seven or eight meters in length. They have a similar eel-like body form with long, laterally compressed tails. Their primary jaws are elongated and lined with over a hundred sharp, conical teeth. Their lateral jaws are not quite as vestigial as those of land lizards and feature serrated bony ridges that help grip struggling prey. Salties are bicolored, with dark blue-gray hides dorsally and pale gray underbellies. Black vertical stripes lend the species particularly effective camouflage when hunting through the vegetation of the shallows and the shadows of deep water.

BEHAVIOR

Pseudo eels are voracious predators, and kilo-for-kilo one of the most formidable animals on Poseidon. They are fearless and aggressive, and native hunters claim they are also frighteningly cunning. Salties hunt throughout a variety of habitats, from shallow coastal swamps and marshes to sargassum rafts (MG 154) and mangrove stands (MG 153). They are equally effective as ambush predators or high-speed attackers. They slip slowly through vegetation or lie in wait in the muddy bottom. They have been known to rush up with the surf to pull unwary animals from the shore, and there are several documented cases of salties pursuing divers into the locks of underwater habitats.

Salties are typically solitary animals, though they will periodically group together and hunt larger prey in loose packs of eight to ten animals. Biologists suspect that these packs may represent kin or breeding groups, but are unable to differentiate genders in the field and so have yet to verify the theory. Individual salties are extremely dangerous, but these breeding packs are monstrous aggregations that are formidable enough to threaten even greater whites. All possible diligence should be exercised to avoid encountering such packs.

Range	Tropical and subtropical waters worldwide
Habitat	Prey-rich waters to 100 meters in depth.
Length	5.0 to 8.0 meters
Weight	350 to 475 kilograms
Frequency	Uncommon
Resource Value	Low; the species is edible but too challenging to hunt safely

Threat Level	High
Attacks	Bite 8
Damage Rating	9
Movement	4/10
Build	9
Fitness	3
Agility	3
Awareness	1
Will	2
Endurance	5
Reflexes	2
Strength	6
Toughness	3
Armor	2

SINGER-IN-THE-DARK
(unclassified)

GEO biologists have always considered stories about the so-called singer-in-the-dark just tales told to frighten native children - that is until now. Native folklore is full of references to some unknown creature called the singer-in-the-dark, or the night singer. Many old timers swear they have heard the creature's haunting calls or knew someone who was lost to a singer. Until a recent report from a GEO field expedition, these tales were considered exaggerated hearsay or simple fantasy.

The only feature consistently attributed to singers-in-the-dark is a mournful, strangely beautiful song. The descriptions in the native stories vary, but the call is supposed to be low and musical and heard only on night-darkened beaches. Uniformly, however, the tales claim that anyone venturing into the dark to investigate the sound is never seen again.

A current GEO field expedition, collecting data for this very report, recently submitted an emergency addendum to this document. While camping on the beach of a small island in the New Hawaii chain, the team heard a strange musical call apparently originating from somewhere down the surf line. Several party members went to investigate and a short time later the calls ceased. When the investigators subsequently failed to return the rest of the group went looking for them, but found no trace. Several days of searching was no more fruitful, and this office has been forced to acknowledge that the missing biologists are likely dead.

The only evidence of the encounter is a sensory recording (PG 166) made by an implant-equipped team member. The recording (interlinked file

#5816) is of an eerie, strangely compelling sound with complex subsonic harmonics. Researchers at HIST are already trying to determine the purpose of the complex sound, and suspect it may be a sort of natural siren's call used to attract or confuse potential prey.

Based on this recent evidence, this office has no choice but to give new credence to the native lore regarding singers-in-the-dark, and to advise all field personnel and frontiersmen exploring night-time shorelines to consider any unusual animal calls as warning that a lethal predator may be lurking in ambush.

Range	Based on the wide distribution of native stories featuring singers-in-the-dark, the species may be found throughout the Pacifica Archipelago
Habitat	Nocturnally along empty shorelines
Length	Unknown
Weight	Unknown
Frequency	Apparently very rare
Resource Value	Unknown
Threat Level	Extreme
Attacks	Unknown
Damage Rating	Unknown
Movement	Unknown
Attributes	Unknown
Armor	Unknown

SNOW WEASEL
(*Niveus hexipedis*)

Little is known about this south polar species. Several naturally freeze-dried corpses have been studied, but there have been only a few documented sightings of living specimens. The creature's anatomy does reveal some information about its ecology, however. The animal is a mammaloid, with thick white fur and thicker blubber. It is a long bodied hexiped, with splayed feet and completely webbed toes. The animal's thick, otter-like tail is well suited to swimming and its muscles contain abundant myoglobin analogs indicating the creature can hold its breath for some time.

The snow weasel's head is large, and its teeth are those of an opportunist. The animal's eyespots run the length of its body, and though most are covered by long fur, they appear completely functional. The large olfactory lobes of the animal's brain indicate its sense of smell is of primary importance. Tiny mineral-rich, gel-filled pockets in the animal's tympanic apertures also imply that the species is sensitive to magnetic fields, perhaps allowing it to navigate over the featureless ice fields of its range. This may be key to the animal's survival, allowing it to reliably travel from thermal oasis (MG 155) to thermal oasis.

BEHAVIOR
Though biologists speculate about the snow weasel's ecology, little is known for sure. The animal's dentition implies it is an omnivore, taking advantage of whatever food it encounters. The animal is likely a scavenger at times, but its well-muscled body, long canines, and sharp claws indicate it is also an able predator, likely hunting fish, birds,

YANNER

and the various small land animals that make their homes in and around thermal oases.

The animal is a known camp vermin, but a potentially dangerous one considering its size and predatory features. Several GEO and Incorporate research operations on the islands and ice flows of the south polar region have apparently been raided by hungry snow weasels, as indicated by tracks, spore, and a pair of sightings. Though no attacks against humans have been reported or even seem likely, it is relevant to include these animals in this report as a potential threat to personnel working within the creature's range.

Range	South polar region
Habitat	Polar oases and open ice packs
Length	1.4 to 2.3 meters
Weight	35 to 45 kilograms
Frequency	Rare
Resource Value	Unknown
Threat Level	Medium; the animal is likely an able predator
Attacks	Claw (x4) 4, Bite 5
Damage Rating	Claw 3, Bite 6
Movement	3/10
Build	-1
Fitness	2
Agility	1
Awareness	1
Will	2
Endurance	2
Reflexes	2
Strength	0
Toughness	0
Armor	1

STRING WORM
(*Funiculus veneficus*)

YANNER

The string worm (MG 156) is a rare and dangerous animal that has only recently been classified. Though long known to Poseidon's natives, the string worm is, luckily, seldom encountered because of the nature of its intractable habitat. String worms live in the tidal mud reef ecosystems (MG 155) of the planet's temperate regions. They are secretive and appear to be long lived. The creature is actually a fish analog that has undergone some dramatic evolutionary changes that make it almost unrecognizable as a member of that group.

String worms reach up to three meters in length and up to 20 centimeters in diameter. Though they have rudimentary, fin-like structures as part of their skeleton, these are vestigial and buried within the organism's muscle tissues, lending the creature a notably worm-like appearance. String worms are uniformly pasty white in color, and have rudimentary, almost function-less eyespots. Their skin is smooth and loose, and covered with glands that secrete a thick coating of mucus.

The string worm's mouth is lined with small but very sharp cutting teeth, and its jaws are wide for the animal's size. The creature's lips support 10 to 12 tentacle-like palps that can be as long as two meters. Though motile, these palps are poorly muscled, and are not used to capture prey but instead are used to poison it.

BEHAVIOR

String worms live buried in the thick flowing ooze of Poseidon's tidal mud reefs. They spend the vast majority of their time at rest and will often not move for days. When they do finally stir, it is usually only to feed, or to reluctantly move to more productive hunting grounds.

String worms lay coiled in the mud with their head upturned toward the surface. They worm their lip palps through the mud, stretching them outward from their mouths like the spokes of a wheel. The fish listlessly wriggles the tips of the palps where they stick out of the mud, and they appear like the ends of small tasty invertebrates. Unsuspecting predators hunting though the mud are easily duped and readily pounce on the apparent prey.

The palps are easily torn or bitten off so they can be just as easily swallowed. The palps are a Trojan meal, however, containing highly concentrated neurotoxins potent enough to kill even the largest local fauna. The toxin kills in seconds, and the string worm simply swims through the surrounding ooze to collect its prey.

Even if a potential meal is not fooled by the worm's poisoned bait, it can still fall prey to the animal's toxin. String worms are keenly sensitive to vibration, and will typically react if any organism wanders within a meter or two of their outstretched palps. Muscular contraction can be used to flush the lethal toxin into the surrounding mud and water, where it can still overcome some species by passing through their skin or gills.

Unfortunately, humans are susceptible to the waterborne toxin, and if exploring tidal reefs,

should consider a sudden numbness in any exposed skin as a sign of string worm poisoning. They should immediately move to dryer ground as complete paralysis may shortly follow, and the worm will soon be looking for its prey.

Range	Temperate regions supporting mud reef ecosystems
Habitat	The wetter, more fluid channels of the mud reef ecozone
Length	Up to three meters in length
Weight	Up to 120 kilograms
Frequency	Rare
Resource Value	Native healers have discovered that the string worm's neurotoxin, in extremely small doses, serves as an effective local anesthetic. In the days of the Abandonment, this made the species a prized catch for hunters, and it remains such for the more isolated, and isolationist, native groups.
Threat Level	High
Attacks	Ingested or diffused toxin
Damage Rating	N/A
Poison	Paralytic neurotoxin Onset Time 20 seconds Duration 5 hours
Damage Rating	4
Movement	3/5
Build	4
Fitness	2
Agility	1
Awareness	1
Will	0
Endurance	2
Reflexes	1
Strength	3
Toughness	2
Armor	None

SWEET NOODLES (*Dulcis dulcis*)

Sweet noodles' pale white stalks consist of small fleshy capsules stacked one on top of another, and reach lengths of up to two meters. Single organisms consist of clusters of eight to 10 stalks and for some as yet unknown ecological reason seldom grow in proximity to one another. The root-like holdfasts that secure the organisms in the mud are shallow and easily dislodged, and the long fronds are flexible, drifting lazily back and forth in the current.

BEHAVIOR

Sweet noodles are slow-growing marine algae that thrive only in nutrient-rich sediments at the dim limits of the photic zone. Sweet noodles are photosynthetic and manage to acquire sufficient nutrients from the sediments in which they grow, despite their lack of true, functional root systems. The organism is widely distributed, but grows sparsely, with individuals seldom found close together. The mechanism of this alopatry is unclear, and biologists are curious both about how it works, and why the organism demonstrates the behavior in the first place.

Sweet noodles are included in this report for only one reason—they taste good. In fact, they are arguably the best tasting, most popular indigenous food species on the colony world. Poseidon's biochemistry is distinctly lacking in compounds that humans find sweet. The sugars common in the planet's plants can be nutritious, but they are not very flavorful, and refining them does not help. One of the few exceptions to this apparent rule is the sweet noodle. The organism has a fleshy texture and citrus flavor most akin to Terrestrial lychee nuts, and is a favorite treat among natives, old and young alike.

The algae is naturally rare and so difficult to find growing wild, and its alopatric behavior and eccentric habitat make it difficult to cultivate. Oddly, the flavor quickly fades after the organism is harvested, and so it is usually picked just before it is eaten. Consequently, though there is a growing interest in the dish in the finer eateries of the larger settlements, the market is mostly unsupported.

What little sweet noodle a village successfully cultivates is saved for special occasions, picked fresh and served still chilled from the depths. Native children love sweet noodles, and it has become a tradition across the archipelago to serve the algae in place of birthday cake.

Range	Distribution includes but may not be limited to the Pacifica Archipelago
Habitat	Nutrient-rich sediments within the lower photic zone
Length	Up to 2 meters
Weight	2.2 to 4.5 kilograms
Frequency	Rare
Resource Value	High; the algae is a valued native treat, and just about the only indigenous sweet on Poseidon
Threat Level	None
Attacks	None
Damage Rating	N/A
Movement	N/A
Build	N/A
Fitness	N/A
Agility	N/A
Awareness	N/A
Will	N/A
Endurance	N/A
Reflexes	N/A
Strength	N/A
Toughness	N/A
Armor	None

THORNROW (*Vepres vepres*)

YANNER

Thornrow is a hardy, fast-growing shrub that bristles with long, formidable thorns. The stem of the plant is dark red, and the stringy, compound leaves are yellowish green. The stems and branches grow in densely packed tangles, protecting the leaves and small flowers from hungry herbivores. The plant grows in large patches that become impenetrable thickets for all but the smallest animals.

BEHAVIOR

Thornrow grows best in the arid coastal regions of Westcape, though some farmers have tried establishing the plant on New Jamaica and Prime Meridian. The shrub requires bright sunlight and its roots are susceptible to fast fungus (MG 168) infection when growing in excessively damp soil. The species' extensive root system evolved for dry, sandy substrates and grows deep to tap desert water tables. In fact, Westcape ranchers find the plant a reliable means of locating productive well sites. When growing wild, the plant can make terrain impassable, and it is virtually impossible to clear without using fire or low-grade explosives.

Despite its troublesome natural form, thornrow has become a valuable sort of living construction material useful in making livestock fences and barriers. If properly pruned the plant can be coaxed to form corrals and hedgerows that are proof against any indigenous life larger than a chub (see page 71). Collecting and then replanting the shrub is difficult work and a thornrow fence takes several years to grow to functional size, but in Westcape at least, the result is worth the effort. The fence is durable, self-repairing, and a uniquely effective deterrent to predators. In Perdition (MG 116), some thornrow fences have been in use for more than 65 years.

Reports have filtered out of Westcape claiming that the local native resistance is using thornrow thickets to its tactical advantage. By cutting well-camouflaged tunnels into the hearts of these tangled bushes, many wild thornrow groves have supposedly been turned into secret weapon caches and hideouts.

Range	Westcape region of the Pacifica Archipelago
Habitat	Arid sandy soils
Length	Up to four meters tall and in thickets over 50 meters in diameter
Weight	Up to 80 kilograms per plant
Frequency	Common
Resource Value	Native ranchers have long been using the plant as a natural form of fencing to protect livestock from indigenous predators
Threat Level	Low
Attacks	Accidental impact
Damage Rating	1
Movement	N/A
Build	N/A
Fitness	N/A
Agility	N/A
Awareness	N/A
Will	N/A
Endurance	N/A
Reflexes	N/A
Strength	N/A
Toughness	N/A
Armor	N/A

WEEDEATER (*Aqua bovis*)

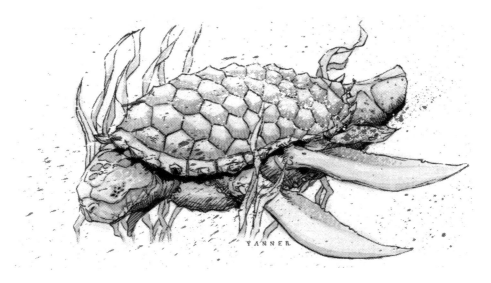

A weedeater is a large, lethargic mammaloid that is best described as a cross between a Terrestrial manatee and a sea turtle. They are robust creatures with thick layers of insulating blubber under a tough, lumpy, brown hide. Their vital regions are covered with hard bony plates and spiny ridges that are proof against smaller predators, and their dense skeletons feature unique, pointed, subdermal protrusions that make them painful mouthfuls for larger predators. The weedeaters ancestors were hexipeds but their fore and mid-limbs have evolved into stiff, paddle-like fins, and their hind limbs have become small, stumpy vestiges.

BEHAVIOR

Weedeaters are slow swimmers that paddle along the water's surface moving from kelp (MG 181) bed to kelp bed. They eat continuously, presumably because the marine plants on which they graze are so low in calories and nutrients. The animals are docile and lack any means of attack, surviving in Poseidon's hungry ecology only because of their armored hides and sharp bones.

Weedeaters live in small herds of four to eight animals and only form larger groups during the calving season. In early summer, weedeaters converge on certain remote islands. These nursery islands are perennial rookeries, and have apparently been serving as such for thousands of years. Soon after dragging their considerable bulks ashore, the females give birth and lay about for several months nursing their hungry pups. The young's dermal plates do not harden until the third month and so the calves are particularly vulnerable during this time.

At the end of the nursery season, just prior to the colony breaking into smaller herds and returning to the feeding grounds, there is a mating frenzy with males and females from different herds interbreeding in a weeklong free-for-all. Gestation lasts until the next season when the animals return to their ancestral rookeries and the cycle begins again.

Weedeaters are an important native food stock in New Hawaii, where the large kelp forests support wild populations. In other parts of the archipelago, where kelp is not abundant enough to support the species, villages often raise domesticated weedeaters, rearing them on diets of kelp, sargassum (see page 89), terrestrial vegetation, and compost. The flesh is dark red and flavorful, coming closest to beef of any of Poseidon's indigenous meats.

Special note to Justice Commission personnel—native insurgents in the Sierra Nueva Cluster have apparently been utilizing the unusually dense, sharp-pointed bones of this species as symbolic and effective hand-to-hand weapons. The mid-limb femur of the animal is perfectly shaped to serve as a sort of war hatchet or tomahawk. It has reputedly become a badge of honor among these war-like groups to kill a "Despoiler" using one of these skeletal hammers. As a consequence of this information, the Marshal Service has issued standing orders that anyone found in possession of such a weapon should be immediately arrested on charges if terrorism.

Range	Temperate and tropical regions supporting forests of Poseidon kelp
Habitat	Kelp forests
Length	2.5 to 3 meters
Weight	Up to 420 kilograms
Frequency	Common
Resource Value	High
Threat Level	None
Attacks	None
Damage	N/A
Movement	1/2
Build	6
Fitness	2
Agility	-2
Awareness	0
Will	0
Endurance	3
Reflexes	-1
Strength	4
Toughness	2
Armor	7

WRAPAROUND (*Ambulo infitialis*)

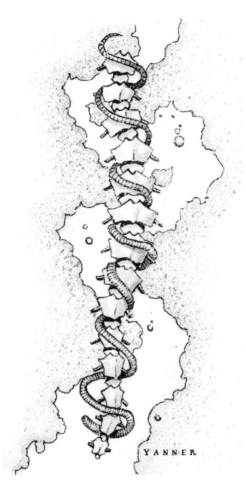

YANNER

The wraparound is a nasty parasite that is occasionally found in various species of Poseidon fish. Unlike many of the parasites adapted to fish hosts, however, this one can cross species and infect warmblooded animals, including humans.

Wraparounds are nematode worm analogs, pale green in color with long, tapered, bodies. The surface of each worm supports three evenly spaced, body-length rows of tiny hair-like bristles that allow it to securely grip its host's tissues. There is no apparent mouth, though the anterior end of unimplanted worms has a deeply recessed indention lined with more of the bristle hairs. This aperture is misleading, however, as it deadends and serves no purpose in the acquisition of nutrients.

BEHAVIOR

The vector for wraparounds has not been conclusively identified, but it is assumed that the parasite is passed from one host to another via the ingestion of tissues infected with egg or larval-stage worms.

As the parasite grows in length, it coils repeatedly around its host's spinal column, drawing nutrients from the animal's body fluid by osmosis. When it reaches sexual maturity the worm embeds its posterior end into its anterior aperture, and the two ends of the coil quickly grow together, fusing the creature into a seamless helix. The worm then asexually produces thousands of tiny eggs that fill its own body structure, eventually killing it. Enzymes released at its death cause long protein chains in the worm's tissue structure to contract. Complete contraction can take several days, but as it occurs, the pressure the coil applies to the host's spinal column first causes severe pain, then nerve dysfunction, and eventually paralysis. It does not take long for Poseidon's hungry ecology to recycle an infected host that has reached the paralytic stage, presumably passing on the dead worm's eggs to any number of predators or scavengers.

Wraparound infection in humans was much more common in the days of the Abandonment, but it still occasionally occurs today. Before the worm reaches sexual maturity, most anti-parasite drug treatments will kill the animal. After the worm has coiled, however, killing it will initiate contraction. At this point, only skilled surgery will prevent paralysis. Colonial records from the time of the Abandonment verify that wraparound paralysis, if left untreated for more than a few days, runs an increasing risk of becoming permanent.

Range	Temperate waters planetwide.
Habitat	Parasitic infestation of pelagic fishes
Length	35 to 40 centimeters
Weight	22 to 27 grams
Frequency	Rare
Resource Value	None
Threat Level	Low
Attacks	None
Damage Rating	N/A
Movement	N/A
Build	-30
Fitness	0
Agility	-4
Awareness	-8
Will	0
Endurance	0
Reflexes	-6
Strength	-15
Toughness	-8
Armor	None

XENOSILICABENTHOID
(*Peloris vergrandis*)

Xenosilicabenthoids, or X-clams, are innocuous benthic invertebrates that, except for a single biochemical anomaly, are otherwise unremarkable. These small animals are best described as a cross between a gastropod and a bivalve. The organism has a two-part spherical shell hinged at the dorsal edge. Its body consists of a visceral mass and a snail-like muscular foot, the entirety of which can be sealed within the ball-shaped shell. The shell is whitish and the animal's body is brown with irregular black spots.

BEHAVIOR

X-clams live in some of the deepest parts of Poseidon's oceans where they drag themselves slowly though the mud feeding on the vast bacterial mats that grow between the sediment layers. The animal's ecology is simple and uninteresting, and the species would not have been included in this report if not for one biochemical oddity.

A graduate student at HISTOS (MG 114) recently discovered that the shell of the invertebrate contains trace amounts of xenosilicate. At first the finding was suspect, but further study has verified that the species' shell invariably contains minute but measurable levels of Long John. This information has set off a frantic race in the mining sector to determine the relationship between the animal and the ore. Some suspect that the distribution of the clam may be indicative of productive Long John fields. Others are convinced that the animal may provide the key to manufacturing synthetic xenosilicate lattices. Regardless, all agree the animal represents a curious and potentially valuable biochemical mystery.

Range	To date only known from the deeper reaches of the Pacifica Archipelago

Habitat	Bacteria-rich, deep-ocean sediments
Length	2.0 to 3.0 centimeters
Weight	3.5 to 6.5 grams
Frequency	Rare
Resource Value	Unknown; the species may represent a key to more efficient xenosilicate prospecting or even synthetic manufacture
Threat Level	None
Attacks	None
Damage Rating	N/A
Movement	Negligible
Build	-40
Fitness	0
Agility	-4
Awareness	-8
Will	0
Endurance	0
Reflexes	-6
Strength	-20
Toughness	-10
Armor	N/A

ZIPPER
(*Venenum corroboro*)

Zippers are small wasp-like insect analogs. They are dull colored, long winged and rather unremarkable in appearance. They have a pair of long stingers on their forelimbs, and use these to inject potent venom. Zippers are found across the Zion Islands, as well as in the southern reaches of the Northwest Territories.

BEHAVIOR

The insects live in wooded areas, in colonies of less than 100 individuals. They chew hive-like structures into the rotting wood of dead or dying trees, and raise their larvae on the bodies of other insectoids they chase down and envenom. Zippers are fast and agile fliers and their prey is hard pressed to escape.

Zippers are not typically a threat to humans, but they will attack if their hive is disturbed. Their stings are uniquely painful, but it is the effect of their toxin on human physiology that is truly remarkable. A single sting is sufficient to trigger a powerful endorphin rush in most humans. The venom from several stings acts like the designer drugs used by military personnel, giving the target a rush of energy and strength beyond their normal levels. Eight to 10 stings, on the other hand, are

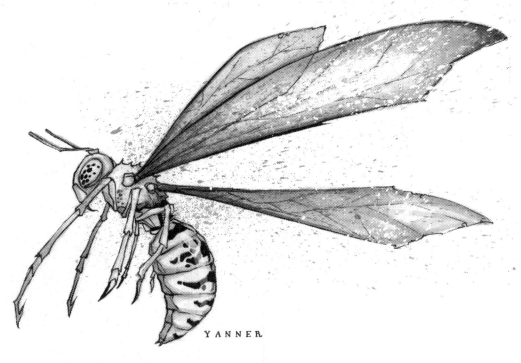

YANNER

typically sufficient to cause convulsions, cardiac arrest, and death.

The natives of these regions have been using zipper venom as a recreational drug since just after the Abandonment. Until recently, such utilization was considered an odd custom but innocent enough. Over the past year, the insect has become a popular draw at some nightclubs in Kingston, where the "natural high" of its sting is used to enhance the sensations of partying customers. Acute allergic reactions are suspected of causing a number of deaths, however, and even Kingston's notoriously lax law enforcement authorities are beginning to take notice of the problem.

Alternatively, reports have reached the GEO Office of Colonial Affairs that claim the Sierra Nueva insurgents have begun manufacturing effective combat drugs from the insect's venom. These reports remain mostly speculative, but suggest that extracts from the venom offer users the same benefits, and risks, as drugs such as reflex serum (PG 135). Law enforcement and military personnel operating in the Sierra Nueva region are advised to keep this possibility in mind.

Range	Apparently restricted to the Zion Islands and the Northwest Territories
Habitat	Mature woodlands
Length	2.5 centimeters
Weight	1.5 grams
Frequency	Uncommon
Resource Value	Valued as a source of recreational drugs and possibly utilized in the manufacture of native combat drugs
Threat Level	Low
Attacks	Sting 2
Damage Rating	N/A
Poison	Neurotransmitter analog Onset time 10 seconds Duration 15 minutes per sting Damage Rating 2 for up to five stings, 8 for more than five stings
Movement	Land 1/2, Air 4/12
Build	-30
Fitness	0
Agility	2
Awareness	-2
Will	0
Endurance	0
Reflexes	0
Strength	-15
Toughness	-8
Armor	None

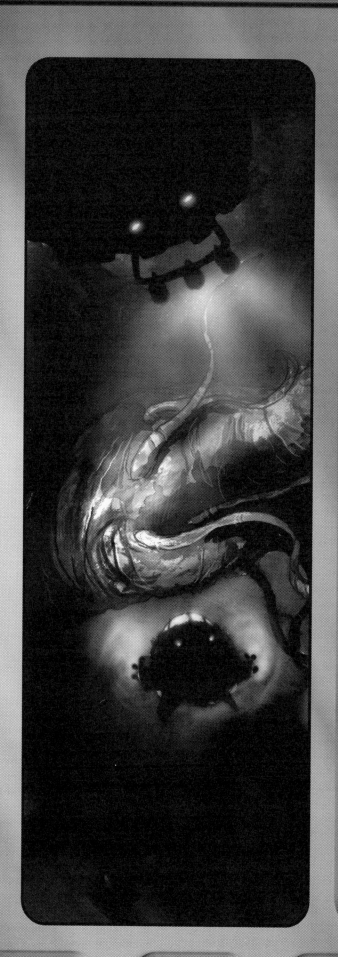

DISTANT DEEPS

CHAPTER 04

Tyger! Tyger! burning bright
In the forests of the night,
What immortal hand or eye,
Dare frame thy fearful symmetry?

— William Blake

INTRODUCTION

Since the dawn of the Stone Age, humanity has depended more and more on technology for survival. For most of this history, the species ceased adapting to new environments—it used technology to adapt new environments to it. With the development of advanced biotechnology, humanity is once again learning to adapt—but this time, the species manipulates the very building blocks of evolution to its own ends. However, biotechnology simply allows humans to alter their bodies' capabilities, to improve their usefulness as tools. Humanity, as always, is defined by its use of tools.

Take the tools away, and all that is left is a slow, weak ape.

Distant Deeps is designed to force the players to question—and test—their characters' reliance on technology. The scenario takes away many of the shields and safety nets that technology offers, and shows the player characters that on Poseidon, the divide between civilization and the wilderness is far more narrow than it is anywhere else.

The scenario is nominally set in New Hawaii, in the Coronado reefs region (MG 45). It can be moved to another location, but this should be a remote area that is volcanically active - fortunately, lots of places on Poseidon meet these criteria. The Nippon Industrial State plays an important role in the background of the scenario, but the moderator can replace the NIS with another Incorporate state if the scenario is repositioned closer to another company town or Incorporate holding. Much of the action takes place underwater, so characters must have access to diving gear or biomods.

The scenario's events center on a group of unusual colonists who call themselves "neo-tribalists." One of them is an escapee from the NIS arcology at Simishir. Her name is Konomiko, and she is a cog-nitive synergist, a genie designed for enhanced intelligence (FM 79). She is a certified genius and a master of computers and electronics. Sadly, she is also insane and will probably get a lot of people killed, perhaps even the player characters.

HOOKING THE CHARACTERS

Ideally, the characters should be drawn in using one of these plot hooks. The characters could be...

• hired to locate a runaway called Konomiko from Simishir.

• investigating the disappearance of an NIS cargo blimp.

• tracking down wanted criminals who were last seen heading for the Coronado reefs.

• researchers from Coronado Station

If none of these suit, and you need to force the characters to get involved, their transport can fall victim to Konomiko's computer virus (see page 111).

THE TIGER ROCKS REGION

The Coronado Reef is a 250 kilometer-wide maze of corals and kelp forests, a vast and often beautiful wilderness. One of the most beautiful sections is called the Tiger Rocks. A 300-meter-deep fault in the ocean floor delves dangerously close to a small magma pocket. Hot springs and plumes of sulphurous, smoky water rise out of the rift. The reef-making polyps in the area have adapted to tolerate these conditions, and feed off the carbon and sulfur in the water. The corals they make are tinged with black carbon and bright yellow sulfur, and from the air, the region is a spectacular sight.

Looking at the Tiger Rocks region from the air is certainly the wisest approach. The hot currents make navigation tricky, and underwater visibility is greatly reduced by the volcanic dust and silt. Dangerous predators, from polypods to the occasional ghoster, lurk in the reefs.

The fault at the heart of the Tiger Rocks is two kilometers long, and varies between 50 and 500 meters in width. The ocean floor was cracked open by rising magma about 10,000 years ago, and there is still a reservoir of molten rock beneath the surface. This is the tail end of the volcanic material, and it has almost broken through again. There have

families, began to reassert themselves. Even when the GEO and Incorporate states managed to restore some level of law and order, not all the tribes chose to reintegrate into 22nd Century civilization. The neo-tribalist philosophy is that technology has advanced enough to support a high quality of life outside the traditional structures of modern civilization. Most neo-tribal groups on Earth live in Free Zones. Some are farmers or pastorals, others are semi-nomadic hunter-gatherers with a spear in one hand and a bodycomp in the other.

The revelation in 2165 that the Athena Colony had not only survived but prospered by adopting a similar approach was seen as a validation of the neo-tribalist philosophy, but there are great differences between neo-tribalism and native culture. The natives were forced to abandon their advanced technology—neo-tribalist groups rely on technology for their autonomy and quality of life. The natives were forced by circumstances to change, but neo-tribalists have chosen their way of life.

In 2199, however, the neo-tribalist movement has largely vanished. A few scattered groups remain in the wilds of the Free Zones, while many others have been reabsorbed into urban civilization. There is a small subculture of "weekend tribalists" who live in cities and work regular jobs, then slip out for weekend excursions into the wild, but by and large, neo-tribalism as a way of life is seen as the preserve of cranks and knife-fetishists outside the Free Zones.

Diana Farr believes that CommCore, the global computer network, is largely to blame for the demise of neo-tribalism. Ubiquitous computer access means that civilization is everywhere, that there is no divide between tribe and not-tribe. It is impossible to build a new way of life when the old one is no more than a voice command away. CommCore's satellites reach every point on Earth, and the infrastructure of the net is woven into the very fabric of life on Luna and Mars. Poseidon is the only truly free world, and even its information networks are growing rapidly.

The neo-tribalist community on Poseidon is completely isolated from CommCore, as well as private and government networks. There has been no trace of them since they left the spaceport in Haven. They have built a hidden community in the lava tunnels around the Tiger Rocks, fishing and hunting to sustain themselves. They have a maincomp,

been many small tremors and lava flows in the region lately, and the signs point to there being a small eruption within a few hundred years.

There are numerous lava tunnels beneath the reefs. These tunnels, formed when the outer shell of a lava flow cools and solidifies while the inner core keeps flowing along, can mainly be found to the east and north of the rift, where the continental shelf slopes down towards the deeps of Poseidon's Reach. Most of the lava tunnels are flooded, although a few of the ones on high ground are partially drained at low tide.

Biogene owns the only really good maps of the region. Most characters will have to rely on GEO records, which are of poor quality. Any Piloting or Navigation rolls made in the Tiger Rocks region will suffer a -1 penalty, -3 in the deeper reefs.

THE NEO-TRIBALIST MOVEMENT

The rise of neo-tribalism began during the Blight Years. As governments and societies crumbled, the old forms of the tribe, of small groups of extended a well-equipped infirmary, and a bioplastics press. They generate their own electricity from the geothermal springs.

Diana Farr's original following consisted of a dozen Earth-born people looking for a new life on Poseidon. Since she established the tribe in 2195, it has grown to 39 people. A third of these are refugees from Simushir, the Nippon Industrial State's company town. Conditions in Simushir are harsh, and these former indentured workers chose to take their chances in the wild rather than continue to suffer in the shantytowns. There are also several escaped criminals from Atlantis. Both the ex-cons and the ex-NIS refugees were drawn to the neo-tribalists for the same reason—an escape from the pervasive information networks. It is almost impossible for a fugitive in a major settlement not to leave some kind of electronic footprint or digital trail. An escapee can be literally caught in the net.

Diana is the acknowledged head of the tribe, although she merely considers herself the first-among-equals. She had the original idea of starting a neo-tribalist commune on Poseidon, and it is her drive and fervent belief that keeps the tribe together. She has managed to integrate starry-eyed idealists, downtrodden indentured workers, and hardened criminals into the same tribe. She has a powerful personal charisma and enthusiasm. She believes that the Incorporate states—and, for that matter, the notion of the nation-state—is as outdated as feudalism. The future of humanity lies in small tribal groups. She points to the asteroid colonies and the Families on Mars as evidence of this trend.

Her staunchest supporter is a silva hybrid named Aldo, a former GEO Peacekeeper. He accepted the offer of relocation, but found that the old myths and stereotypes about hybrids were still prevalent in civilian life, even on Poseidon. He met Farr before she left Haven. He was caught up in her visions of a new way of life, one in which the lies and stories propagated by CommCore and the media industry would be forgotten. In the tribe, Aldo accepted the role of protector and has managed to acquire a few black-market weapons for self-defense. Aldo strenuously opposed Diana's decision to allow the escaped convicts to join the tribe, and he has been very moody and irritable for the last three months.

Rumors of a newcomer settlement hidden from the GEO have been circulating amid the criminal underground for some time. Four prisoners in a Justice Commission holding cell in Atlantis bribed a guard to let them escape, and sailed out into the Coronado Reefs looking for this safe haven. Iko Yoshitama (pharium dealing), Ronald Gray (armed robbery), Carl Hoffman (pharium possession, smuggling) and Nia Temi (illegal mining) encountered the neo-tribalists and were allowed to join the group. Hoffman and Yoshitama have adapted well to their new lives, but both Gray and Temi are looking for a way out. Gray privately holds the opinion that Diana and her little neo-tribalist cult are lunatics, and would have run out weeks ago if he could. However, he is well aware that this is one of the safest places on Poseidon for an escaped criminal to hide. He is also terrified of Aldo.

Temi wants to leave the Tiger Rocks region, not because she dislikes this new, simpler life with the neo-tribalists, but because she is a trained geologist and is worried about the volcanic activity in the rift. A medium-intensity seaquake could cause an eruption or outflow. She has been trying to convince Diana to move the settlement to another location for some time now, but the tribe will not migrate until they can work out a method of transporting their heavy equipment without being detected.

THE SIMUSHIR REFUGEES

There are worse places than prison. The coffin-hotel residential stacks of Simushir, for example, make most prisons look clean and comfortable. Rotting bioplastic buildings infested with fast fungus choke the narrow streets. Chain-link fences and roaming camera drones keep the workers in line and under surveillance 30 hours a day. The Tower looms over the whole city like a watchful giant.

Escape is virtually impossible. A microchip is implanted in the wrist of every NIS worker, and these chips track their every move. If any worker gets past the security perimeter, the chips begin to broadcast a low-power homing signal that NIS security can trace from up to 10 kilometers away. Even if one escapes from Simushir, there are no other major settlements on Ina Island.

While the low-ranking workers suffer, the NIS elite live in luxury in the shining corporate arcology. At the heart of this vast complex are research labora-

tories, staffed by the best minds the NIS can acquire—or create. Cognitive synergists, or "brain-children," are expensive to genetically engineer, but their incredible intellect is worth the investment for the Incorporate states. Six engineered children were born in the NIS Advanced Medical Institute on Earth in 2182, and two were sent to Poseidon.

By the time she was 16, Konomiko had graduate degrees in computer science, electronic engineering, and mathematics, as well as severe paranoia and schizophrenia and an addiction to numerous mood-stabilizing and anti-depressant drugs. The move to Poseidon seemed to have a positive affect on her mental condition, and her psychologists recommended her drug dosages be decreased. For six months, Konomiko excelled in the lab. Then she vanished.

She has become consumed by her paranoia about being watched. To Konomiko, Simushir was full of staring eyes. The stars in the sky were surveillance satellites tracking her. The sound of the surf was feedback from hidden microphones or the fans of unseen surveillance remotes. Over six months, she carefully laid a plan of escape. She wrote computer viruses to disable the security systems. She tracked down the likely location of the rumored "netfree tribe." She hacked into the Simushir personnel database, identified 12 workers tagged as "malcontents," and anonymously arranged for them to find out about the neo-tribalists. Finally, she altered inventory and shipping records and had a maincomp and other gear loaded onto a cargo blimp—which was then hijacked by the escapees.

During their escape, the former indentured workers found a teenaged girl dressed in native clothing. She claimed to have been abducted from her village by an NIS security officer. The escapees took her with them. Some suspect the girl of being more than she appears, but the Simushir refugees have adopted her as a good luck charm. When the cargo blimp grounded on the Coronado Reefs, the fugitives protected Konomiko until they were all rescued by the neo-tribalists.

Konomiko has moved the computer equipment from the crashed drone to a nearby sea cave, and has continued her work on cryptography and anti-surveillance technology. Her paranoia drives her onwards, and she dreams of a future where the skies are clear of hateful eyes. The natural, harmonious lifestyle of the neo-tribalists makes far more sense to her, to be free from government and authority and law.

What she has not realized is that the true law on Poseidon is enforced not by computers and drones, but by the old common law of the jungle and the deeps.

WHAT DREAD HAND?

The player characters enter the Tiger Rocks region in pursuit of whatever goal drew them here. The scenario assumes they are in a powered vehicle of some sort, such as a jumpcraft. If they have onboard sensors capable of analyzing ocean variables, scans will detect signs of geothermal activity, principally elevated temperature readings. If the characters are actively looking for another craft (a crashed jumpcraft or the missing cargo blimp), a Challenging Intellect + Electronics roll will allow them to pick up some metallic debris on radar about three kilometers to the northeast of the central rift.

The characters are passing over an extensive section of the yellow-black mottled reef when they are unlucky enough to be spotted by Konomiko. As far as the neo-tribalists know, she is out hunting rubber shrimp. In actuality, she came out onto the reef so she could do some work on her implanted microcomputer in privacy. She assumes the characters are an NIS retrieval team and panics.

Konomiko uses her microcomputer and uplink jack to connect to the stolen NIS maincomp, which in turn contacts the computer on the characters' vehicle. The maincomp broadcasts a digital signal disguised as an electronic distress call. If the characters answer the call and try to lock in the source of the signal, the maincomp unleashes a specialized virus on the vehicle's computer system.

It then hits their onboard computer with a specialized virus. As the virus spreads through the computers, the vessel begins to crash. The surface of the water rushes up to engulf the characters' vessel.

The moderator should allow the pilot to make an Average Dexterity + Piloting roll to put the jumpcraft down more-or-less safely. The waters around Tiger Rocks are shallow, and the vessel will smash off various reefs and outcroppings before coming to rest amid the patterned rocks. The water is deep enough that the jumpcraft will completely submerge if it is not equipped with a marine conversion package, but the characters should have time to get out before it sinks.

Even as the aircraft crashes, Konomiko's viruses will spread to and shut down any computer systems networked to the vehicle's onboard computer. Depending on the severity of the crash, the characters may be injured, and if the jumpcraft sank, much of their equipment and supplies may be damaged or lost. Their craft will be disabled and possibly irreparable. The basic goal of this encounter is to strip away the technological advantages of the characters, plunging them into a hostile and dangerous wilderness.

THE WILDERNESS

Once the characters have recovered from the crash, and retrieved whatever equipment survived, they can start traveling. Swimming with any sort of heavy equipment is difficult, so the characters will have to abandon much of their gear or rig some sort of floating raft. The nearest outpost is Coronado Station to the east; the native village of Delta is about 300 kilometers to the south.

If the characters' plot hook requires them to travel deeper into the Tiger Rocks, they should head north. They may also have detected metallic debris a short distance to the northeast (see The Cargo Blimp, below). The crash will have been disorienting at the very least, so the characters will first have to work out which way they are facing.

Once they start moving, the characters will discover that the Tiger Rocks region is a labyrinth of reefs and volcanic ejecta. Maintaining a steady course is next to impossible. The characters will have to clamber in and out of the water, over reefs and rocks, to proceed in a straight line. If they try to keep to a course while staying in the ocean, they have to navigate a maze of orange-and-black-patterned rock walls and lava tunnels. Emphasize the confusing terrain, and call for regular Navigation or Orienteering rolls, as appropriate. Ask the players what route they take at every possible junction. Describe the maze-like reefs, the currents of hot water, and the clouds of fish and shrimp that swarm around.

KONOMIKO'S VIRUSES

Before she escaped from the NIS Arcology, Konomiko was working on the development of military-grade viruses designed to infect and disrupt C3 (Command, Control and Communication) networks. The viruses had to be able to penetrate security measures and shut down as many different computer systems as possible. Her solution was to create a set of "beachhead" programs. These mimic normal data packets, and can be inserted into a datastream. When the packet reaches the target computer, its only function is to command the target to contact the attacking computer and upload a virus tailored to that machine.

While Konomiko's system is effective, it can be easily defeated simply by isolating computers from the network. Of course, on a battlefield, such a defense would be suicidal—if every defending unit cuts itself off from the network to hide from the virus, the attack has essentially succeeded in disrupting the lines of command and communication. Out in the wild, losing CommCore, MetWatch, and GPS data is not as much of a disaster.

Since leaving Simushir, Konomiko has developed many new second-generation viruses, allowing her to disable civilian craft, drones, and even bodycomps.

Terrain features the characters might encounter include:

• A tall, steep reef, exposed at low tide, which the characters must climb over or spend some time swimming around.

• A hot water vent, which is mobbed by thousands of small sea-horse-like creatures that enjoy the current. A blimp was feeding on these creatures, but has become tangled in the rocks. The water is heating the blimp's internal gases, and it is dangerously close to exploding violently.

• A soft spurt, hidden beneath a thin layer of silt. Unwary characters may step on it and risk being poisoned.

• Hungry bloodhunters may be attracted to any food the characters are carrying.

• Black smokers—rock chimneys belching out soot and carbon-heavy water from deep underground— are the chief cause of the strange colors of the Tiger Rocks, and can be found throughout the area.

Don't let the players relax. Keep describing the terrain and asking them questions about what they are doing. Interrogate each player individually—if they split up, so much the better. Eventually, one or more players will probably get frustrated with the slow progress and stop paying attention to the moderator's descriptions of the terrain and questions about their route. Anybody who stops paying attention out in the wild is being foolish.

If one or more characters split off from the main group, or forge ahead without due care, they are in trouble. Polypods—the great tentacled hunters of Poseidon's deeps—are not especially common around Coronado, but they are not unheard of. This particular female specimen has taken up residence in a hole next to a deep-water channel in the reefs. Larger creatures like sunbursts swim down the channel to the rich feeding grounds of the hot, inner reefs. Without warning, the polypod explodes out of the hole, wrapping its powerful tentacles around the body of its prey, crushing and devouring it. The deep-water channel crosses the route the characters are taking, so the lead character is the first one scented by the polypod. The only warning sign is a single sniffer tendril—one of the polypod's sensory organs—resting on the lip of the hole. The lead character should be allowed an Awareness roll to notice the tendril. If the character fails, their first sight of the polypod comes as it bursts out of the hole and grabs at them.

Characters injured in the fight will attract the attention of smaller predators and scavengers, drawn by the scent of the blood in the water. Wounds may also become infected in the warm, silted water. If the characters have no supplies with them, they will have to forage or hunt for food. The most advanced firearms are not as good as a simple fishing spear when hunting small game, and any larger creatures on the reefs are dangerous predators. Reefworms are the easiest source of food, but if the characters can rig a net, they can scoop up all sorts of small fish and shrimp.

This sojourn in the wilderness can last from a few hours to several days, depending on where the characters are heading. When they are in danger of wandering out of the Tiger Rocks and out of the scenario, or if they're in trouble, then move on to the next encounter.

IN THE MIDST OF CHAOS

The neo-tribalists go on six-person hunting expeditions, lasting three to six days depending on how far they range. One of the expeditions, led by Petyr Rachmanov, is returning to the neo-tribalist base at the heart of the Tiger Rocks when they meet the characters. The hunters look like natives at first glance, but while they wear native-style clothing, their hunting gear is of modern design, and they carry high-quality medical and survival equipment.

Rachmanov was born on Earth, in the Hanover city-state, where he was trained as an engineer. He applied for a transfer to Poseidon after a disastrous divorce and spent three years working in the xenosilicate refinery at Lebensraum. The sight of all the refined Long John, and the thought of all the longevity treatments it represented, overwhelmed him. If xenosilicate meant that he would live thousands of years, then he was damned if he was going to spend any more time at a job that bored him and trivialized his life. He took his hydrofoil and sailed off into the ocean.

As long as the characters are not acting in an obviously threatening manner, Rachmanov will make contact with them, offering them food and medical treatment if they need it. He will explain that he is part of a community of people trying to forge a new life out here, away from GEO or Incorporate supervision. He will suggest that the characters come back to the neo-tribalist base with him. He will try to avoid getting into a long discussion of who the neo-tribalists are: The community depends on being a secret from the rest of Poseidon, and he doesn't want to let the location of the tribe slip until the characters are heavily outnumbered and can be subdued if necessary.

If the characters do attack, or attempt to flee, Rachmanov and his hunters will not try to stop them. Instead, they will swim back to the neo-tribalist's lava tunnels, and send Aldo, Ronald Gray, and a few other, better-armed tribesmen out hunting.

THE CARGO BLIMP

If the characters were looking for a downed flyer, or if they picked up a magnetic anomaly before Konomiko forced them to crash, they may encounter the wreckage of the NIS Cargo Blimp used in the escape from Simushir. Most of the balloon material was salvaged by the neo-tribalists, so only the skeletal framework of the cargo gondola remains, wedged between two reef walls. Examining the wreckage reveals that the blimp was made in Simushir. The empty cargo crates once contained bioplastic molds, although one crate is marked "electronic equipment."

THE LAVA TUNNELS

Rachmanov leads the characters into the heart of the Tiger Rocks, to the lava tunnels where the neo-tribalists make their home. Entering the tunnels is a strange experience. Primitive wooden structures hold stacks of crated supplies and salvage; a hand-crafted hunting spear rests against a brand-new autodoc (FM 28). Throughout the tunnels, people wearing native clothing and carrying high-tech equipment go about their business.

About a kilometer of tunnel has been completely drained and sealed off with airlocks. There are two entrances, both of which are carefully concealed behind foamed bioplastic sculpted to look like stone, and infused with stone chips to give a more realistic sonar and thermal profile. One of the exits is currently under repair, but can be used in an emergency. Inside, the tunnels are well lit and very warm due to the geothermal power plant in the lowest tunnel. Hanging metallic curtains (made of material from the blimp) divide the side corridors up into small rooms, while the central corridor con-

tains the few pieces of machinery the tribe uses, the medical robot, and the meeting hall.

A staircase has been carved out of the rock, following the path of a lava tunnel down the wall of the rift, to a chamber where geothermal steam runs a small electrical generator. The steam is then vented out into the ocean. There is also a small cache of seismic equipment. Anyone examining the data they produce and making a Routine Intellect + Geology check will see that the rift is highly unstable, and that a small eruption could occur at any time.

The characters will be introduced to Diana, the leader of the tribe. Aldo will lurk in the background, trying to size up the characters and determine how much of a threat they are. Diana will invite the characters to stay and rest for a day or so, as guests of the tribe. She will willingly answer any questions the characters have, and will talk about her philosophy at length. Diana should be played as a pleasant, enthusiastic person. She firmly believes that she is right and the rest of society is wrong, but she is not a crazed fanatic.

While speaking with the characters, Diana will be called away by Nia Temi (an ex-con and geologist) to examine the power plant. Temi has been urging Diana to move the tribe away from the volcanic region for some time now. The characters are free to wander the lava tunnels, but they will not be allowed out without an escort—Aldo will inform them of this. If the characters protest, he will growl that the reefs are dangerous for the unwary. Aldo has been in a bad mood ever since the ex-cons were allowed to join—he really dislikes Ronald Gray— and he does not like the characters much either.

The rest of the tribe will keep out of the characters' way. They will not ignore the characters completely, but they will exclude the outsiders from the day-to-day life of the tribe. Observant characters will note that there are three distinct groups in the tribe —the original tribalists, the Simushir refugees, and the ex-cons. The tribalists come from a range of backgrounds on Earth, but here they are all working towards a common dream. They defer to Diana when it comes to dealing with people outside the tribe.

The Simushir refugees may have exchanged their NIS-issue jumpsuits for the native garb of the tribe, but they still have not shed their corporate mentality and habits. They huddle around the edges of the tunnels when not working, and act in six-person work teams. When talking to the characters, they stare at the floor and act as quiet and respectful as possible. If the characters are looking for the missing cargo blimp, the refugees will be quite helpful, describing how they escaped and where they ditched the blimp. They will not mention Konomiko at all, and will not let the characters leave without Aldo acting as an escort.

If the characters ask the refugees about Konomiko, they will be met with blank stares and shrugs. The refugees are very protective of her, and hide her origins from everyone. If the characters press the issue or ask other members of the tribe, the refugees will attempt to remove the characters, either by framing them, convincing Aldo or Diana that the characters are dangerous, or arranging an accident for them. They feel they have nothing to lose, and if backed into a corner, will go to any lengths to protect one of their own.

Of the escaped convicts, Ronald Gray will immediately try to ingratiate himself with the characters. He will try to get one or more of them to talk to him away from the tribesmen, and then launch into a long diatribe about how insane Diana Farr is and what Aldo is going to do to them. Gray will insist that the characters will not be allowed to leave the lava tunnels. After all, the tribe is based around secrecy—no one gets back to civilization to inform on them. He will offer to help the characters if they help him escape. He will say anything to get them to help him: For example, if a character mentions something about their vehicle crashing, Gray will claim he overheard Aldo and Farr discussing electromagnetic pulse weapons.

If any characters go down to the lower tunnel to the geothermal plant, they will meet Nia Temi. She is convinced that the settlement's current location is too unstable, and that the tribe should move. The major problems will be transporting the heavy equipment and machinery and constructing a new home without being noticed. While Diana and Aldo plan to send scouts to deal with the latter problem, Temi's task is to work out a solution to the transport issue. The tribe has a single minisub and a pair of catamarans hidden in the reefs. When the lava tunnel settlement was originally being constructed, the parts for the various machines were brought in the sub over several weeks. Temi wants to move more quickly than that.

Finally, Konomiko will follow and observe the characters, trying to decide if they are a danger to her. Most of the tribalists believe the story that she was a native runaway picked up by the Simushir refugees. Certainly, Konomiko dresses and acts like a genuine native, but her disguise is far from flawless. All she knows about native culture is culled from NIS reports and CommCore, and if anyone with a good Native Culture skill questions her, she will not be able to give the right answers. Of course, the most serious problem with Konomiko's disguise, and one she tries desperately to conceal, is that she lacks aquaform biomods.

Konomiko is skilled at deflecting questions. If she has heard the characters asking about "Konomiko" before they talk to her, she will adopt the name "Jessica". One reason she pretends to be a native is that many people assume natives know nothing about technology or current affairs, and therefore do not question them. Among newcomers, they tend to fade into the background, becoming almost irrelevant. If someone does ask her questions, she will try to turn the conversation back on them, getting them to reveal details about themselves. When that doesn't work, she has a whole range of personalities to use, ranging from an irritatingly perky and sarcastic kid to a sullen teen to a near-catatonic abuse victim. She'll adopt whichever persona and mode of behavior she thinks is most likely to stop the questions.

When roleplaying Konomiko, the moderator should remember that she is a manipulative genius, and possibly a sociopath. She will play into any expectations the characters have, and will identify any characters likely to be protective of her. Any emotion she shows, no matter how genuine, is just her logical solution to a problem. When Konomiko loses her emotional control, which can happen at almost any time, she is prone to fits of severe depression, crying, and screaming, and has the disturbing tendency to claw the skin around eyes (hers or others') with her fingernails.

None of the people in the tribe (other than Konomiko) know anything about what caused the characters' vehicle to crash, although they are aware that at least one other jumpcraft has crashed in the reefs within the last few weeks. The Tiger Rocks are a fairly out-of-the-way place, so two crashes means that most of the recent traffic has fallen out of the sky. Most blame it on a Styx-like effect, although a few are beginning to wonder if Aldo has not acquired a missile launcher or some other anti-aircraft weapon.

Let the characters wander around talking to people for a while. Aldo will keep shadowing them: If the characters want to speak to anyone alone, some of the characters will have to somehow occupy or distract the huge GEO-trained hybrid. Once things begin to drag, Diana Farr will find the characters and invite them to dine with her. One section of the tunnels is furnished with simple bioplastic chairs and tables. The meal is, unsurprisingly, fish and seaweed-derived food. About 20 people eat at the same time as the characters.

Diana will begin by asking if the characters have any questions about the tribe or the settlement. She will enthusiastically explain the philosophies and origins of neo-tribalism, as well as her opinions of the current political situation on Poseidon. If asked, she will relate where the various members of the tribe came from. She will openly admit that four members of the tribe are wanted criminals, and that the Simushir refugees left the NIS illegally. If asked about the native girl, Diana will be more reticent. Privately, she suspects the girl's family abused Konomiko, and that the best place for her is with the tribe, surrounded by people who care for her.

The conversation will also touch upon topics such as the relationship between humans and the wilderness in the current era. Diana's belief is that technology and biomodification have made cities and governments obsolete, that humanity can go back to older forms of social organization without sacrificing any quality of life. The characters should be encouraged to argue and consider their own opinions. The tribalists may also give the characters survival tips about any problems encountered on the trek through the reefs.

Diana will ask the characters about what brought them to the Tiger Rocks, and will ask them to describe their crash in detail. Her next action will largely depend on who the characters are, why they are here, and what they have done since meeting the tribe. The location of the tribe must be kept secret. She must decide if she can let the characters return to civilization knowing where the settlement is. Due to Temi's urgings, Diana has decided to move to a more stable area, but moving the tribe will take weeks. Diana must decide whether or not to keep the characters in custody until the move is finished, so the tribe can slip away to an unknown home.

If the characters are GEO Marshals, Native Patrol, or any other sort of law-enforcement agents, or the sort of people who would report the tribe to such authorities, then Diana will regretfully tell them they cannot be allowed leave. She trusts Incorporates even less than she trusts the GEO, so any characters who openly declare they work for an Incorporate state will be imprisoned. Diana is well disposed towards natives, independents, and anyone who seems to be genuinely interested in her neo-tribalist philosophy.

Obviously, the manner in which Diana presents this news will depend on the characters. If the group consists of heavily armed Peacekeepers or Incorporate operatives, then Aldo and a half-dozen other armed tribesmen will be lurking in the shadows, and will rush out to cover the characters. It should be made clear to the players that fighting back will result in one or more of them getting killed. Of course, if the characters are elite combat machines, it is entirely possible that they could

take on the entire tribe and win. Try to guide the scene towards a non-violent ending, but if the players want to go on a killing spree, let them, and skip onto the Konomiko Runs section.

If the characters argue, Diana will listen. Her goal is to protect the secrecy of the tribe - she doesn't want to imprison anyone if she can avoid it. If the characters come up with a plan to protect the tribe's secrecy and it sounds plausible, Diana will agree... but Aldo will not. He will insist that the characters remain with the tribe for at least five days, while preparations for moving are begun. That way, even if the characters do betray the tribe, there will be enough lead-time to get most of the equipment to a safe location.

Assuming a firefight has not erupted, the characters are shown to a private section of the tunnels and left alone. Aldo stands guard, watching them unobtrusively.

FORESTS OF THE NIGHT

The next section of the scenario can go in several different directions, depending on what the characters do. The following events wills occur:

• A jumpcraft from the NIS flies over the rift. It is carrying a Human Resources Retrieval Team. The neo-tribalists hide.

• Konomiko panics, convinced that the HRRT are there to recapture her (they are) and that the characters led them here (they didn't). She sneaks out of the tunnels and heads for her hidden maincomp.

• If the characters try to catch Konomiko, the NIS spot them, and the tunnels are attacked.

• If Konomiko isn't stopped, she forces the NIS to crash in the same way she attacked the characters. The NIS jumpcraft sinks into the rift and explodes.

• The explosion ruptures the rock encapsulating the magma chamber, and the eruption Temi feared begins.

HUMAN RESOURCES

To the Nippon Industrial State, Konomiko is a significant investment, one that must be recovered. When she first escaped, the best agents in Simushir were sent out to find her. Now, months later, the NIS have been forced to bring in cheap labor to cover more ground. The group known as "NIS

HRR Team #4" is a hired band of low-grade thugs from Nomad. They have a decommissioned military jumpcraft, which they have rearmed with twin racks of missiles and a chaingun. NIS satellite scans finally noticed the wreckage of the cargo blimp, and Team #4 was sent to search the region.

When they approach the blimp, they will launch a constellation of scout drones, which will examine the wreckage. The drones will then spread out looking for any signs of settlement. Anyone outside the neo-tribalists' lava tunnels has a chance of being spotted by the drones.

If the drones do spot something interesting, the jumpcraft flies in for a closer look. The team operates on a strict "shoot first, ask questions later" policy. They know they are looking for an Asian girl in her teens, so anyone else is a valid target. The thugs will use their sonic stunners if collateral damage to Konomiko is an issue, but otherwise they have no qualms about hurting people.

KONOMIKO RUNS

Believing that the jumpcraft is full of NIS bogeymen come to take her back to the lab, Konomiko decides the only thing to do is use her computer viruses. Her uplink jack does not have the range to contact the maincomp, so she will have to swim closer to it. She puts on her gill pack and attempts to sneak out of the tunnels. If the characters try to stop her, the Simushir refugees will try to restrain or slow them—anybody who threatens Konomiko is an enemy in their eyes.

Once she is in the airlock, she will wait until it is flooded and the outer door is open, then shoot the locking mechanism, jamming the door open. The airlock cannot be used without flooding the tunnels. There is a second exit, but it is being repaired. A Routine Strength + Mechanics roll is sufficient to open the inner door.

Konomiko will swim to her maincomp, which is hidden in a cave about four kilometers from the rift. The characters can try to catch her, but she is terrifyingly intelligent and dangerous. She is probably weaker and slower than most characters, but the moderator should give her every advantage. If followed, she will attack from ambush at the right time, in the right place. Despite her tactical genius, she is unsuited to any sort of combat, and will employ hit-and-run tactics if she fears the characters are trying to capture or delay her.

The HRRT's drones may spot the characters or Konomiko while they are swimming in the region. The moderator should call for Routine Awareness + Hiding rolls at irregular intervals. Characters who fail have been spotted by the drones, and the jumpcraft will home in on their location.

Ideally, if the characters are chasing her, they should catch Konomiko before she reaches uplink range. The jumpcraft should then arrive. The best way to defeat the HRRT is to let Konomiko hit them with her virus programs.

If the characters stay in the tunnels and ignore Konomiko, the moderator should play up the claustrophobia and paranoia of the tribe trapped in a confined space. Aldo has a small surveillance drone in the waters outside the airlock and can track the HRRT drones and jumpcraft. Eventually, one of the HRRT drones will notice the jammed airlock, and the jumpcraft will fly over the rift to investigate. Aldo will decide to fight back and lead a contingent of armed natives out the other airlock to try to shoot down the jumpcraft in a surprise attack. This short firefight will end when Konomiko reaches her maincomp.

BURNING BRIGHT

The area at the heart of the Tiger Rocks region is volcanically unstable. Beneath a thin sheath of stone is a rising bubble of magma, the last dregs of an old eruption. Any significant impact or explosion could rupture the capsule around the magma chamber.

A torpedo or a crashing jumpcraft certainly qualify.

If the characters have managed to defeat the HRRT before Konomiko activates her viruses, or if they lured the jumpcraft away from the rift, the eruption will be avoided. Otherwise, the characters see either a torpedo exploding on the floor of the rift, or an out-of-control jumpcraft power-diving into the seabed.

The initial impact shakes the reefs, and can be felt up to kilometer away. As the magma begins to shift and flow, water rushes into the cracks in the sea floor. The resulting clouds of steam and boiling water flood the rift area. Lava begins to ooze out, following the channels in the reefs. Inside the tunnels, the hot-water spring powering the generator becomes choked with rising molten rock. The generator shuts down, and the tunnels are plunged into darkness. Many of the tribe members panic and stampede for the second airlock. Characters still in the tunnels are likely to be trampled or crushed if they get in the way. Diana will try to restore order, but as the air temperature in the tunnels rises, her attempts will become increasingly half-hearted. As molten rock floods the lower tunnel, she will agree that the settlement must be abandoned. Evacuating the tunnels will take some time using only one airlock. A maximum of four people can fit in the airlock, and it takes nearly three minutes to run through an exit cycle.

If the characters were imprisoned, they can seize the opportunity caused by the combat and explosions to escape.

Outside, in the water, the local wildlife panics. Thousands of fish rush away from the central rift, swimming desperately for cooler, safer waters. The reefs are normally full of activity, but this migration is far more impressive. Clouds of fleeing marine animals will blot out the light from the surface. This is extremely disorientating and confusing to those attempting to orient themselves underwater. The combination of the billowing steam and panicked fish makes any action or combat more uncertain. Visibility is reduced to a fraction of normal, and the sea is turbulent with frantic motion.

Predators will take advantage of the situation, chasing after the retreating schools. The moderator may wish to introduce a school of bloodhunters or even a lesser white or two to make the characters' situation even more precarious.

As the eruption progresses and more lava reaches the surface, the water temperature rises considerably. The moderator can use the burning rules (PG 119) to resolve exposure to the water, but the damage rating should begin at 2. The damage rating will rise depending on how long the characters remain exposed, how well protected they are, and how close they get to the eruption.

Depending on their goals and situation, the characters may be trying to:

• Get as many people out of the lava tunnels as possible
• Escape from the lava tunnels themselves
• Capture Konomiko

• Capture any of the escaped criminals

Confusion and chaos should dominate this section of the game. To emphasize this, hit the players with quick-fire questions about what each character is doing. Describe everything in short, choppy bursts, and remember that visibility is at a fraction of normal range.

ON WHAT WINGS?

The eruption will make the central area of the Tiger Rocks a hostile environment. To survive, the characters will have to move out into the reefs. They may be injured, and may have some or all of the non-player characters in tow. The nearest settlement is Coronado Station—however, the NIS were tracing the HRRT Jumpcraft until Konomiko's virus hit it, and they will send out a rescue team. Any character who passes a Routine Intellect + GEO Culture roll will also remember that the Haven Institute of Science and Technology usually dispatches an observation drone or science team to the site of an interesting eruption. The characters can choose to wait for one of these to rescue them.

None of the characters should have a functional communications device, thanks to Konomiko's viruses. An Average Intellect + Electronics roll allows a character to jury-rig a simple radio transmitter, which might be able to reach Coronado Station or Delta. If the characters have retrieved Konomiko's maincomp, it has a satellite uplink and radio transmitter than can easily reach civilization. It will take between two and five days for a rescue craft to arrive.

After the eruption, the inner reefs will be nearly empty of fish. Hunting will be considerably more difficult than normal. Any supplies that were in the lava tunnels will have been destroyed, so the characters will have to survive on the bounty of the sea. The best shelter is probably in the small sea cave where Konomiko hid her computer.

Of the 39 neo-tribalists, at least 10 will have died in the confusion unless the characters somehow intervened. The survivors will be in shock, but Diana will be able to rally them to action. They intend to travel to the native village at Delta. If the characters are friendly with the neo-tribalists, they can help this exodus. Delta is over 300 kilometers from the Tiger Rocks, too far for the entire tribe to swim. Diana will send a small, experienced group to the village. This group is to make contact with the natives and arrange for fishing boats and rescue vessels to pick the tribe up.

If the characters ended up opposing the neo-tribalists, or if they are blamed for the attack on the settlement, Aldo will decide that it would be for the best if the characters do not make it back to civilization. The Silva has a small weapons cache that survived the eruption, which contains a sniper rifle and a few handguns. He will recruit a few loyal and angry tribesmen, and go hunting.

This final firefight will take place amid the shallow channels and reefs. While Aldo is a trained soldier, the rest of the tribesmen are not, and will simply rush in, guns blazing. Aldo will try to track the characters and shoot at them from a high ridge. The best approach for the characters is to bring the fight underwater, where the guns will be less effective.

If the characters survive the wilderness and the attack, a GEO or NIS jumpcraft will eventually arrive to pick them up. The first thing they will see when they get back on CommCore is a news report mentioning the underwater eruption and their rescue.

WRAPPING UP

If the characters were sent out to retrieve Konomiko, and succeeded, the NIS will pay them. The fee is likely to depend on how valuable the characters think Konomiko is. If they know she is an engineered brainchild, they can extort considerably more money from the NIS. She is worth at least 2,000,000 scrip to the NIS, but they are more likely to have the characters killed and Konomiko captured by another team than pay that much.

Konomiko's computer contains her notes and copies of her viruses. The notes are written in an extremely eccentric code, and are nearly useless to anyone else. The viruses are capable of shutting down a variety of systems, but after a few attacks, computer programmers will develop countermeasure programs. Still, the software will be extremely valuable on the black market.

Both the Simushir refugees and the ex-cons are wanted by the authorities. The characters can help hide the neo-tribalists, or give their location to the NIS or the Marshal Service.

If the tribe manages to reach Delta intact, they will spend two months there resting and rebuilding.

Diana's vision of a new social order will be informed by her contact with a real native tribe. Eventually, she and Aldo will decide to form a new settlement in the Sierra Nueva, and will join Bataku's insurrection. Many of the neo-tribalists, led by Nia Temi, will object to joining a terrorist organization and will found a second settlement in Shangri-La, north of the Pacifica Archipelago. If the characters helped the tribalists, they now have one or two hidden refuges they can go to if they need help.

NPC STATS

KONOMIKO

Species: Modified Human
Origin: Colonial (Urban)
Backgrounds: University, Incorporate.
Profile:
Goal Survival
Motivation Paranoia
Attitude Varies.

Primary Attributes: Build -2, Fitness 1, Agility 1, Dexterity 2, Awareness 1, Intellect 3, Presence 0, Will 1

Derived Attributes: Endurance 2, Reflexes 2, Strength -1, Toughness 0

Aptitudes: (Superior) Tech, Communication (Strong) Life Sciences, Physical Sciences, Subterfuge, Survival

Primary Skills: Computers 6, Remote Operations 6, Electronics 5, Incorporate Culture 5, Mechanics 4, Negotiation 4, Damage Control 4, Physics 3, Meteorology 3, Geology 3, Chemistry 3, Astronomy 3, Biochemistry 3, Genetics 3, Demolitions 2, Native Culture 2

Biomods: Uplink Neural Jack, Improved Blood Oxygenation, Salt Tolerance, Immunological Symbiote

NIS THUGS

Species: Modified Human
Origin: Colonial (Urban)
Backgrounds: Street, Colonial
Profile:
Goal Survival

Motivation Pride
Attitude: Arrogant

Primary Attributes: Build 2, Fitness 1, Agility 1, Dexterity 0, Awareness 0, Intellect 0, Presence 0, Will 0

Derived Attributes: Endurance 2, Reflexes 1, Strength 1, Toughness 1

Aptitudes: (Superior) Close Combat (Strong) Firearms, Athletics, Culture

Primary Skills: Armed Combat 4, Unarmed Combat 4, Street Culture 4, Aquatics 3, Shadowing 3, Persuasion 3, Handguns 2, Mechanics 2, Law 2, Native Culture 2, Psychology 2

Biomods: Improved Blood Oxygenation, Salt Tolerance

Weapons: Large-Caliber Handgun, Handheld Stunner

Armor: Light Vest

ALDO THE HYBRID
Species: Silva Hybrid
Origin: Earth Reservation
Backgrounds: GEO, Rural
Goal: Survival
Motivation: Professionalism
Attitude: Confident

Primary Attributes: Build 3, Fitness 4, Agility 0, Dexterity 0, Awareness 2, Intellect 0, Presence -2, Will 1

Derived Attributes: Endurance 3, Reflexes 1, Strength 3, Toughness 2

Aptitudes: (Superior) Firearms, Stealth (Strong) Close Combat, Communication, Culture, Subterfuge

Primary Skills: Handguns 4, Longarms 5, Unarmed Combat 5, Mountaineering 4, Hiding 4, Shadowing 4, Sneaking 4, Driving 4, First Aid 4, Persuasion 4, Throwing 4, Aquatics 4, Tracking 4, Tactics 4, Military Culture 4, Foraging 3, Strategy 3, Armed Combat 3, Street Culture 2, Native Culture 2, Colonial Culture 2, Navigation 2, Demolitions 2, Computers 1

Biomods: Neural Jack, Multiglands, Night Vision
Weapons: Hanover Arms MP9 Submachine Gun, P400-A Revolver, Diamond Knife
Armor: Light Vest

NEOTRIBALISTS
Species: Modified Human
Origin: Colonial (Urban)
Backgrounds: Street, Colonial
Goal: Survival
Motivation: Discontent
Attitude: Rebellion

Primary Attributes: Build 0, Fitness 2, Agility 1, Dexterity 1, Awareness 0, Intellect 0, Presence 0, Will 0

Derived Attributes: Endurance 1, Reflexes 1, Strength 1, Toughness 0

Aptitudes: (Superior) Close Combat (Strong) Stealth, Athletics, Survival

Primary Skills: Armed Combat 4, Unarmed Combat 4, Street Culture 4, Aquatics 3, Shadowing 3, Sneaking 3, Hiding 2, Handguns 2, Mountaineering 2, Foraging 2, Native Culture 2, Native Culture 2

Biomods: Salt Tolerance
Weapons: Small-Caliber Pistol
Armor: None

INDEX

INDEX

BLUE PLANET v2
PLAYER'S GUIDE

Whether you are a newcomer or native, this guide contains everything a **Blue Planet** player needs to survive on the new frontier.

Hardcover   **256 Pages**   **$27.95**

BLUE PLANET v2
MODERATOR'S GUIDE

Whether you are new to the Blue Planet universe or a veteran moderator, this book contains information vital to running exciting and effective adventures on the new frontier.

Hardcover   **256 Pages**   **$27.95**

UPCOMING RELEASES

ANCIENT ECHOES
May 2001

BLACK CRUSADE
July 2001

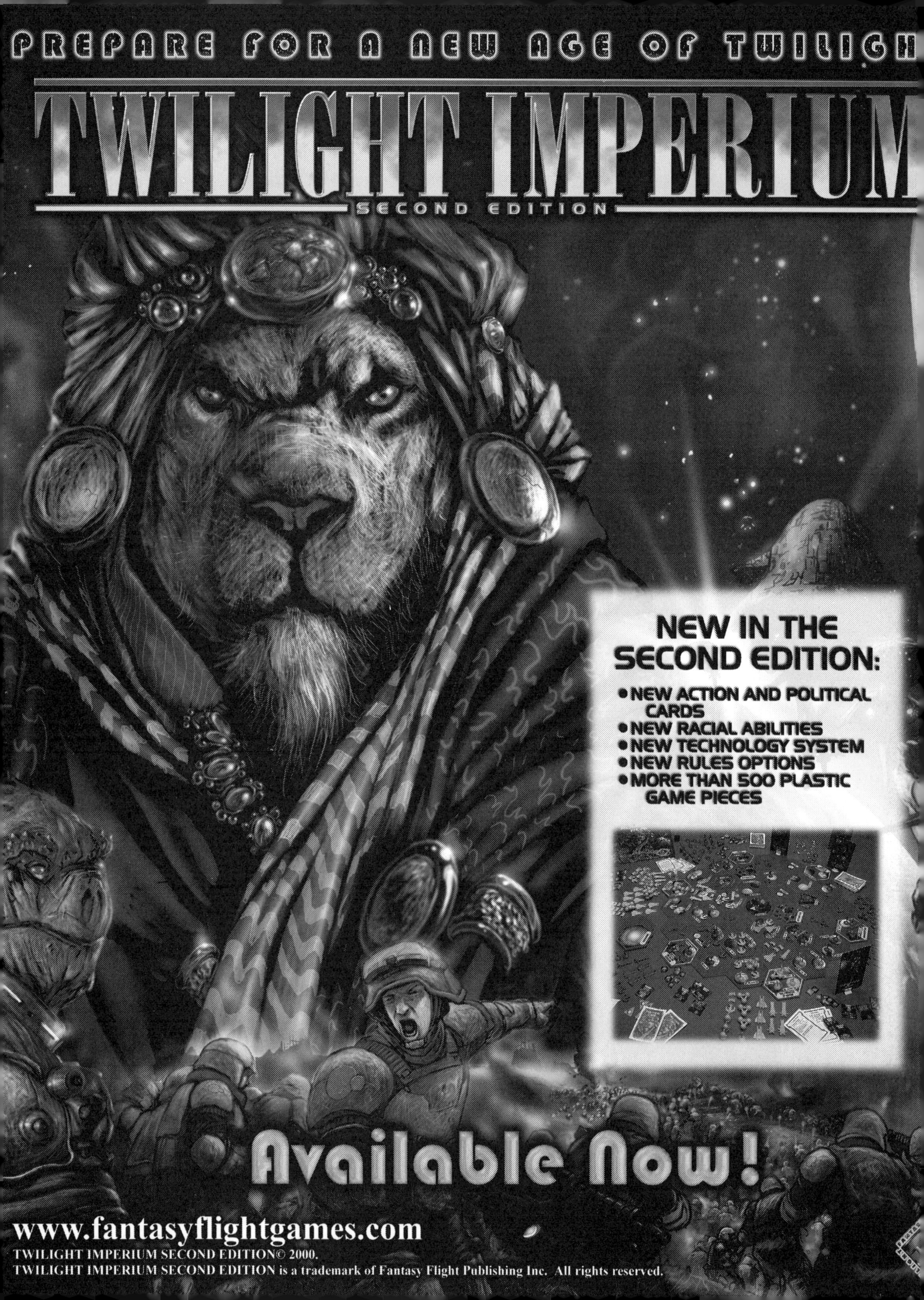
PREPARE FOR A NEW AGE OF TWILIGH
TWILIGHT IMPERIUM
SECOND EDITION
NEW IN THE SECOND EDITION:
• NEW ACTION AND POLITICAL CARDS
• NEW RACIAL ABILITIES
• NEW TECHNOLOGY SYSTEM
• NEW RULES OPTIONS
• MORE THAN 500 PLASTIC GAME PIECES
Available Now!
www.fantasyflightgames.com
TWILIGHT IMPERIUM SECOND EDITION© 2000.
TWILIGHT IMPERIUM SECOND EDITION is a trademark of Fantasy Flight Publishing Inc. All rights reserved.

LEGENDS & LAIRS

TRAPS & TREACHERY

CORE RULEBOOK

COMING IN JUNE 2001

Other Products From

FANTASY FLIGHT GAMES

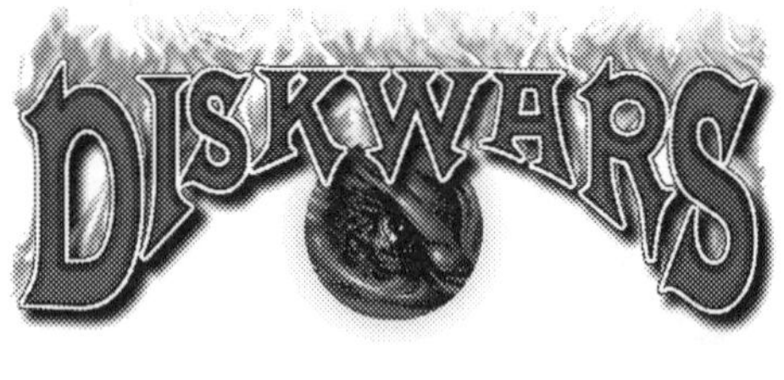
DISKWARS

DISKWARS (DW01-37)

Suggested Retail Price $9.95

Eight mighty armies have gathered to do battle with magic, steel and cunning. Does your army have what it takes to triumph? Diskwars is like nothing you've ever seen before. Build your own custom fantasy army out of beautifully-illustrated battle disks and wage war on your opponents. Each army pack comes with monsters, magic spells, unique personalities and more! Diskwars is playable by any number of players on any flat surface.

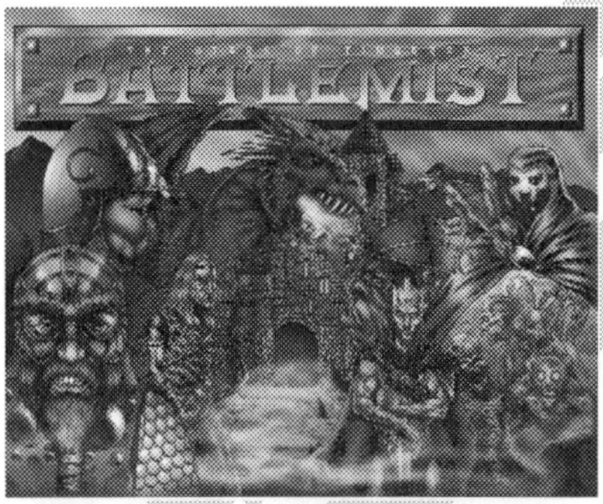
BATTLEMIST

BATTLEMIST (BM01)

Suggested Retail Price $49.95

Second in the HexPlay series, Battlemist is a fantasy boardgame of brave heroes, mighty battles and terrible magic. Up to six players battle for possession of the mystical Stars of Timmoran through warfare, quests and cunning. Whoever controls the Stars control the fate of Menarra.

Battlemist Expansion Sets:
BM02 The Sails of War $24.95

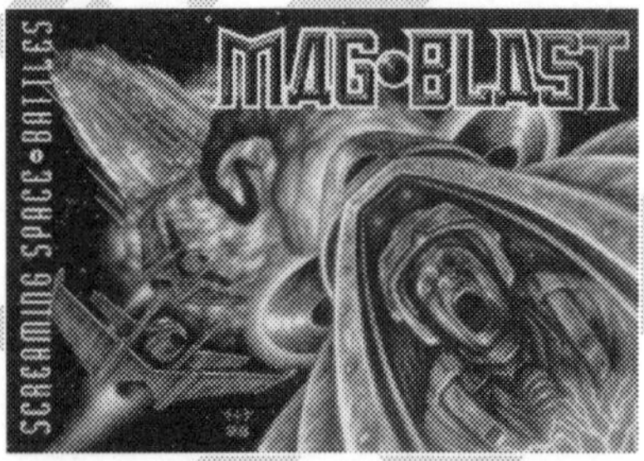
MAG•BLAST
SCREAMING SPACE•BATTLES

MAG•BLAST (VA01)

Suggested Retail Price $16.95

Set in the Twilight Imperium universe, Mag•Blast is a fast-paced, non-collectible card game of furious space combat. Up to six players build their fleets and try to protect their flagships while mercilessly turning their opponents' flagships to spacejunk. Mag•Blast is easy to learn and fast to play. Interstellar war has never been so much fun!

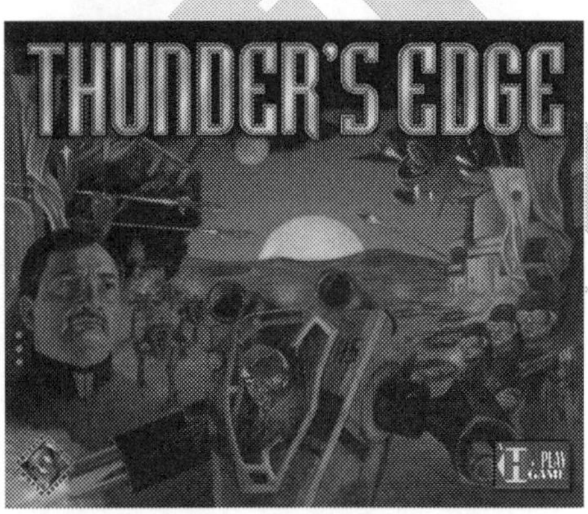
THUNDER'S EDGE

THUNDER'S EDGE (TE01)

Suggested Retail Price $49.95

Once nothing more than another backwater mining colony, the planet Thunder's Edge is now a hot-bed of politics and mechanized warfare. The factions of Earth government are on the brink of civil war, for whoever controls Thunder's Edge will control the future of space travel. Thunder's Edge is a HexPlay boardgame of political influence and military tactics in a near-future science fiction setting.

Thunder's Edge Expansion Sets:
TE02 Demon Canyon $24.95

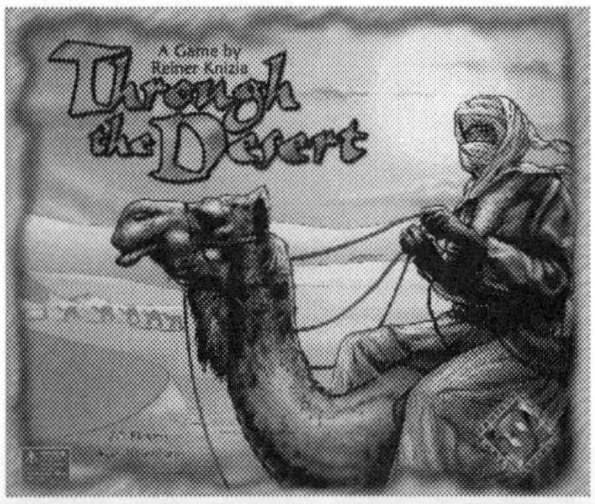
A Game by
Reiner Knizia
Through the Desert

THROUGH THE DESERT BOARDGAME (KN01)

Suggested Retail Price $37.95

Nominated for German Game of the Year 1998. From the award-winning game designer Reiner Knizia comes a game of strategy, patience, and cool plastic camels! In THROUGH THE DESERT, two to five players each control a tribe of nomads vying for control of the desert. By establishing caravans and taking over oases, the players gain points as their tribes increase in power.

To order via credit card, or for more information, visit http://www.rpg.net/ffg